Superplonk 1998

Malcolm Gluck

CORONET BOOKS
Hodder and Stoughton

Copyright © 1997 by Malcolm Gluck

First published in Great Britain as
a Coronet paperback original in 1997

The right of Malcolm Gluck to be identified as the Author of
this Work has been asserted by him in accordance with the
Copyright, Designs and Patents Act 1988.

10 9 8 7 6 5 4 3 2 1

British Library Cataloguing in Publication Data

Gluck, Malcolm
Superplonk 1998
1. Wine and wine making – Great Britain – Guidebooks
I. Title
641.2′2′0296′41

ISBN 0 340 66624 2

Typeset by Palimpsest Book Production Limited,
Polmont, Stirlingshire
Printed and bound in Great Britain by
Mackays of Chatham PLC, Chatham, Kent

Hodder and Stoughton
A division of Hodder Headline PLC
338 Euston Road
London NW1 3BH

'Incidentally, I treated myself pre-Christmas to a copy of the High Street guide, which I find equally enthralling! I fear that this will also become another annual "must have"'

Mrs B.F., Beckenham

'The moment you give a wine the magic score of 16 or above, it disappears entirely from the shelves'

Mr N.W., Cambridge

'May I sincerely thank you for a number of things: *Superplonk 1997*, *Streetplonk 1997* and *Gluck, Gluck, Gluck* . . . For the working man on a limited income as well as a person who appreciates value for money, your book has provided me with a genuine improvement of the quality of my life'

Mr R.J., Stoke Gifford

About the Author

Malcolm Gluck is the wine correspondent of the *Guardian*, mitigating the effects of tasting several thousand bottles of wine a year by cycling in all weathers all over London. He writes a weekly Saturday column, *Superplonk*. Last year he presented his own BBC-2 television series – *Gluck, Gluck, Gluck*. When he is not raising a glass, he helps raise a family.

To Owen Marshall, for never a dull moment

'These pieces of moral prose have been written, dear Reader, by a large Carnivorous Mammal, belonging to that sub-order of the Animal Kingdom which includes the Orang-outang, the tusked Gorilla, the Baboon with his bright and scarlet bottom, and the gentle Chimpanzee.'

Logan Pearsall Smith

CONTENTS

INTRODUCTION

This book has always been priced the same as a bargain bottle of wine. It will only go higher over my dead or seriously incapacitated body. However, there is a problem in maintaining so modest a price: every year, the book gets fatter because more and more eligible bottles tickle its author's palate. More pages mean higher production costs. I have been faced, therefore, with the stark reality that something had to go. Should I restrict myself to shorter entries? I was loath. Would it be an idea to drop or drastically curtail the length of the introduction? I was reluctant. What about removing altogether the usual generous introductions to each individual retailer? *This* sacrifice of my many children seemed the most acceptable. After all, what is there new or newsworthy to say every year about Budgens or even Waitrose, to the extent that several thousand words must be expended. So – my customary introductory exercise in soul-exposure has survived the chop but I have found a way satisfactorily to shorten the retailer's long introductions.

None of the above will surprise regular readers of this book, I dare say. Equally, you might imagine – being the generous soul that you are – that come its publication I would be ensconced somewhere warm swinging breezily in a hammock to the neighbourly thwack of sea on sand, sleeping off the months of wine tasting, with all those thousands of bottles, upon which this guide is based. But no. Not a bit of it. Early November, I throw myself at the mercy of British Rail, or Railtrack, or whatever its blessed name is nowadays, and travel the length and breadth of Britain's bookshops, local and national TV and radio stations, ready to append my signature to any freshly bought copy of the book and to extol its myriad virtues over the airwaves. I keep a diary during this seven-week tour. I try not to take myself too seriously as I trek (alone, I might add – I do not, as I have discovered other authors do, insist on being accompanied everywhere by a publisher's minder). I stick pictures of myself in my children's bedrooms so they will not fail to recognise me when I return. I get through a fistful of Pilot Hi-Tecpoint V5 extra fine ballpoint pens made in Tokyo and a pile of Muji recycled paper notebooks also made in that locality. I was unaware, until I considered the matter, of the crucial part Japan plays in my scribbling life.

Day 1
8.50am
The BBC's Broadcasting House at the top of Regent Street in London's West End is a labyrinth designed by an intoxicated anti-social architect. Having got past the commissionaires and the receptionist, I eventually find the small bit I want, a studio to which admission is only granted upon interrogation by robotic voices. This studio, not unlike *Tardis* in its modest exterior yet interior wealth, is designated IU and I have agreed to be locked up in one cell of it for the morning and give seven consecutive interviews to various local BBC radio stations. Why did the BBC publicist who arranged it all cackle hysterically and remark, 'Are you sure? Really sure you want to do this?' when I said yes? I soon find out. I sit, alone, in Studio IU – pale blue/green walls with blue chairs and green, turquoise, and red mikes. Has this large cupboard of a pastel-blend studio been designed specifically to be cool on the eyes? I sit and wait for something technological to occur. I am reading *Aunt Margaret's Lover* by Mavis Cheek, earphones neatly encapsulating each shell-like. After ten minutes of blissful silence, arboreal noises are heard: the sound of leaves crackling and twigs sighing (snapped off before reaching their prime as branches). It fills my ears and renders further Cheek study impossible. 'Is that Michael?' a sharp voice interjects over the twigs cracking. Oh dear. Not a

promising start. But then it's Radio Devon, county of clotted cream. I forgive this lapse. The second interview proceeds nicely until I am cut off in mid-question (the interviewer's fault, I am told by an engineer who rushes to the rescue) but the third, Radio Cornwall, is perfect. I am beginning to feel frazzled – and there are four interviews to go! And lo! The sound of manic vacuum cleaning fills the earphones. 'Malcolm? This is Nick from Radio Nottingham.' And so it goes. Oh rats! Radio Cornwall has cut back in. Now I know why the BBC publicist cackled so hysterically. By the time interview seven is over my ears droop as despondently as a hound-dog's dewlaps, my hands quiver, Cheek's prose seems Sanskrit on the page.

Day 2
Waterstone's – Reading, Berkshire
6.45pm

Taxi driver outside Reading station says waste of time hiring him, so I walk. In Broad Street a beggar is deeply engrossed in sifting through a mountain of plastic coat hangers outside Dorothy Perkins. I hope he has the gumption to sell them at tuppence each tomorrow. The hangers look modern and clean. Worth tuppence out of anyone's pocket.

The Waterstone's at 89 Broad Street is a beautiful construction, a converted eighteenth-century chapel. Opposite the table where I am invited to prattle on wine and in front of which customers will ask me to sign copies of their books there is a stone tomb in a glass case. It commemorates a citizen who died in seventeen something. This is a surprise. But so is the very lively young man who greets me when, signing over, I throw myself aboard the 9.05pm to Paddington with seconds to spare. 'Cup of tea, sir? Something to drink? A sandwich?' Could this be the 'new golden age of rail travel' we've been hearing about?

Days 3 and 4
Preston/Longridge/Leeds/London/Crow Sound
3.10pm Royal Oak to Euston Square

Two refugees with children in new clothes alight at Paddington. The woman cannot thank me (no English) for the seat I give her. Her smile is thank-you enough for me. Can it be her first Hammersmith & City tube line journey? The baby she holds and its elder sibling look well resigned to travelling. How long will they survive? Where are they from? She looks, to me, a mixture of Romanian gypsy and southern Italian (with that brilliant falcon-focussed brown of eye). Even the older kid, tiny waif, has this ocular specificity. The woman's husband rattles around in second-hand trousers and a jacket several sizes too large for him (hugely inadequate protection against the raw November weather which will buffet them when they surface). He picks up from the filthy carriage floor a dislodged baby's milk bottle and jams the teat back in the mouth of the silent child – she is all gaze, wide- and wild-eyed. Staring at her future?

3.40pm to Preston

V. S. Pritchett is my companion on this journey. He has often elected to come in the past but always ended up getting brutally shoved aside by some trendy poet or American parvenu author; he has, however, displayed patience and stolidity in the face of these rejections, his spine unbending; it balefully stares at me on the shelf as only Sir Victor's books can. It has been so regarding me for some years. The book was published in 1953. It is a collection of essays. The first of these concerns itself with tourism. How appropriate for a Londoner on his way to Lancashire, and I am quickly engrossed in the book, only to lift my head at the Pavlovian aroma of coffee suddenly close by.

The passenger opposite is served a full cafetière smelling rich and exotic, sufficient to obscure the burnt rubber aroma the locomotive is disposed to give off. A fresh cafetière?!! More evidence of the 'new golden age of rail travel'? Another thing that has changed in my five years of doing autumnal nationwide book signings travelling by rail is the introduction and spread of the mobile phone. Ten years ago it was an exotic luxury. Five years ago it was uncommon. Today I am the only passenger without one and the air is thick with the conversations of men and women talking into the ends of their bent arms. Did Nostradamus foresee this development (*and man shall talk unto man, fist shalt communicate with fist*)? The constant tinkle and trilling of each incoming call is like being in a car park where a vandal is selectively roaming and setting off alarms; when several coincide, one feels shut up with a group of competing campanologists.

I find time to look at a pile of readers' letters recently received. I offer replies by speaking in to my little battery-powered Philips Voice Tracer Pocket Memo 191. When Linda comes to transcribe my voice into solid typescript will she find only the ghost of a voice? A ghost muttering incomprehensibly in a belltower?

4.55pm

On the left side of the train the evening is spread out across the sky not like 'a patient etherised upon a table' as imagined by the affected symbolism of T. S. Eliot. It is spread out like a hot tomato soup, red and ripe and scorched orange at the rim. The sun is slipping away and it is only minutes from 5.00pm. And then . . . the patient dies. By six minutes past five, and several miles further north by InterCity, the glow has gone from the sky and it is night.

Waterstone's, Preston 7pm

Tesco provides one of the best events ever. Five corked bottles, a record for a booking signing, present themselves in various stages of stinkitude. The assembled drinkers and book buyers are delighted to be able to compare a good bottle with a duff one and they go home empowered and knowledgeable. (When I later inform Tesco of this unique event, they are not entirely amused to have achieved fame in this way. But I point out that had they not been so incredibly generous with the number of bottles they contributed, there might have been fewer corked specimens.)

Heathcote's, Longridge
9.30pm
Here at this restaurant (so highly regarded by my *Guardian* food and drink editor, Mr Matthew Fort, that he is writing a book about its chef/proprietor Paul Heathcote) I enjoy a meal which is unusually well textured. It is indulgent hedonism from first lick to last wipe of the bread on the plate. I drink an auslese with pheasant, potatoes interleaved with asparagus. Suspect the wine waiter thinks a man who drinks sweet German wine with game is dangerously mad. Gives my table a wide berth.

Preston/Leeds
No Earl Grey tea in the hotel. Never heard of it. But *Guardian* freshly served on carpet outside room some compensation. (*The Times* is offered free to inmates of this Forte Post House. Since the only aspect of this once regal newspaper which has not changed for the tattier is the crossword – its haughty crypticity as uncompromising as ever – giving it away is presumably the only way to pile on readers.) The hotel seems full of spivs toting weaponry. This explains itself when I depart and see a notice, strung across two sides of the street, advertising a national snooker tournament. Was not the bristly desperado, now I come to think of it, at the table next to mine at breakfast the ex-world champion? Name of White? I have several colours to choose from. He could be a Green, a Brown, a Blue, even Pink and he might well be a Black. But not, I fancy, a Mr Yellow.

The street market is bustling now, the farm animals have long gone and the detritus of a million families lie for us vultures to pick over. I commence negotiations to acquire a miniature electric iron, circa 1940, with a splendid imitation-pearl handle, but can't agree on the price.

10.12am is not 10.10am! This two-minute difference allows

me to catch the train in time. A trawl through various divisions of the football league is my reward as the so-called Transpennine Express takes me from Preston to Leeds, via Blackburn, Accrington, Burnley (Manchester Road), Hebden Bridge, Halifax, Bradford (Interchange), Pudsey (New) & Leeds (thence on to Scarborough via Garforth, York, Malton, Seamer, and Scarborough). Seamer, eh? Is that where the cricket ball delivery of that name was first bowled? Or was the place named in honour of it? They take cricket seriously in Yorkshire, I believe – or used to at any rate.

The old lady opposite my seat cleans her glasses on her newspaper. It is the *Daily Mail.* Must be the first time since this newspaper was published that it has ever enabled a reader to see things more clearly. A discussion concerning hot chocolate breaks out between the passenger in the next row and the man pushing the refreshment trolley.

Foolishly I have abandoned Pritchett in favour of J. G. Ballard's *Cocaine Nights.* I read it through, forcing myself onwards, but think it massively stylistically inferior to *Empire of the Sun* and no improvement imaginatively on *The Drowned World* which I read during my science fiction phase very many years ago.

Leeds – midday

Prior to my evening signing, I must buy four bottles of wine at Safeway in the City centre, in order that Mr Peter Levi, who is interviewing me for the local BBC radio station, can provide his listeners with authentic slurping on the air. I oblige, spending a little over £12. I spend the rest of the day investigating the Leeds University Bookshop, the Dry Dock Bar (a river barge hauled into the City and catering for the very young), the Craft and Design Gallery (where I purchase several Christmas presents), the Leeds Museum, the Victoria Family and Commercial Hotel in Great George Street (built in 1865 with twenty-five bedrooms but now a Tetley pub frowning on workers' overalls), and a coffee bar opposite the hospital which claims to serve espresso but merely presents a feeble abomination of it. At the signing itself, David is his usual charming and effusive self, Alison is industrious, and the whole shop is a credit to book retailing. The audience is also especially charming. A really beautiful young woman with eyes like *marrons* gives me a roast chestnut. For dinner, I take myself off to the Sous Le Nez en Ville in Quebec Street where I find a bottle of mature Washington State merlot (1985 Columbia Crest, a snip at £12) and I eat scallops with parma ham and then, specially to go with that merlot, ham hock with mushy peas. I am pleased, in this tumultuous and very carcinogenic eatery, to find myself stuck away in a blessedly non-smoking corner. The wine list here is interesting. I very much want to try the Maximin Grunhaus '89, made by an aristocratic gentleman on the Moselle who has a delightful and loquacious young daughter, but there is no appropriate food. The Alsatian wines are also interesting. Would they have gone with the scallops? Yes. But not with the ham. Must have that old merlot with the ham. But should I not stick to fish and white wine at night? More digestible than a whole bottle of red and you do attract a better class of hangover. Pritchett is a charming companion again. I particularly like his observation that 'Snobbery is often a form of romanticism; it is the chastity of the perfectionist.' So true of certain wine snobs of my acquaintance.

Days 5 and 6
Manchester/York

Taking the tube to King's Cross, I observe a curious advertisement, paid for by the Institute of Electrical Engineers. 'Dinner is served . . . thanks to engineers' it proclaims and if I telephone 0171 344 5447 I can find out more. What more is there to discover about engineers? Are the cartoon characters depicted in the advertisement engineers? They wear very bright clothes. They drink white wine with their turkey I note. However, what were they doing from 7.55pm to 9.05pm, according to the cartoon clock, before they sat at table and ate?

Discussing engineering? *Doing* engineering? I can't wait for my next dinner party. When the hostess says, 'Dinner is served' I can add, 'Thanks to engineers, thanks to engineers.' And what a witty fellow she will think me!

'Love is the law' is a graffito on a railway siding wall near Kensal Green as the InterCity express shuffles past. Up to as far as Willesden there is a stretch of graffiti of impressive length, colour, design and flair. Are the scrawled designs the work of kids expelled from the educational conveyor-belt for being intractably creative? What a waste of talent – it's a sin. They should be sent to work designing tube cards for the likes of the Institute of Electrical Engineers.

I am reading some wine statistics. Australian wines at certain price levels are outselling French wines, it would appear. Is the Frog traditionally in our throat being shoved aside by the Kangaroo in our gullet?

I turn to my book (Pritchett on Italo Svevo) and unearth: 'It has been their curious fate to learn the lessons of life backward, becoming younger and more apt for life as they grow older.' I know acutely the truth of this observation.

I run across various difficult concepts: Bovaryisme – is it like Hazlittary? Must I read Perez Faldo's *The Spendthrifts*? What is the precise definition of *ultramontane*?

I am sometimes lost for words. I am not Henry James. Words ran in Henry James's veins rather than blood, thought Pritchett. Wine, if anything out of the ordinary, runs in mine I suppose.

We pass Stoke-on-Trent. This is Arnold Bennett country. I must get off the train at Stoke one day and investigate. Three of Bennett's books are masterpieces. There is surely a Bennett museum in the town. Wasn't Stanley Matthews also born here? I saw his last match when Blackpool visited Tottenham in the sixties. Didn't I also once play one of his sons in a tennis tournament? I barely scraped a point if I recall. A young Indian woman across the aisle raises her head and stares at me. Perhaps it is because she and I are the only passengers reading books – the rest of the carriage chewing on mobile telephones as usual – and so she feels the normal barriers don't exist.

'Excuse me,' she says, 'I wonder if you can tell me something? What does post-romantic mean?'

I am seized by a mad moment. 'It means,' I say solemnly, 'when someone loves you enough to lick your stamps.'

She nods and looks serious. My explanation appears to make sense and she returns to her book but I feel immediately desperately guilty. I apologise and provide her with the real meaning, as far as I am able. Hopefully, I do not make a complete Kant of myself.

The Manchester signing is a riotous affair (as usual with this branch). It is Waterstone's biggest shop and thus able to cram in more book buyers in a single evening than the gate of an average third division football match in a single afternoon. My hotel the next morning, the Ramada, serves me kippers. I somehow have the feeling I am the only person to have asked for them in decades. I examine the fish when it arrives for signs of staleness.

Now it's on to the York signing and thus another crossing of the Pennines. This time it's accomplished in a snowstorm. I arrive at York with a sense of having been part of a brave battle with the elements. I lunch with Adam Phillips (propped up on the cruet in front of me) and the Beatles. The blizzard has compelled me to nip inside the Royal York Hotel – it's barely thirty seconds' striding time from York Station – and it is, after all, 1.30pm. I sit out the snowstorm in the Victorian dining room with a second half-bottle of Oxford Landing Cabernet/Shiraz '95 (the first was stinkily corked but a fresh one was brought me, very pleasantly, by the assistant manager), a bowl of soup of the day, grilled steak and 'Ribblesdale' cheese and biscuits. Mr Phillips's book is called *Monogamy*. The muzak, alas, is not so faithful; synthetic derivations from 'Revolver', 'A Hard Day's Night' and 'Sergeant Pepper'. It's the aural equivalent of ready-grated parmesan. By the end of lunch, York

Minster – a blur through the billowing snow blanket – is now revealed as a misshapen, iron-clad perversion. Scaffolding is the fashion with almost every significant monument nowadays. I visit an early-thirteenth-century chapter house and marvel at the architect's ingenuity but feel only disgust at the miniature stonework sculpture (so small you almost miss it as you pass by the entrance) of the flaying of St Bartholomew. The saint is upside down, to keep blood flowing to the brain I guess. Ingenuity of a different and more horrific kind! I also sit in Ann Clitherowe's house. A recusant squeezed to death under a weighted door (in 1760 I think), she was canonised in 1970.

The York Waterstone's is one of the most congenial places in which to sign books and I enjoy myself thoroughly. Much good-humoured ribbing of author as he strives not to get pissed. Respond to many questions, but the most emphatically lengthy is to do with decanting wine. I explain that I always pour wine into a jug at home, and when entertaining I employ two generous three-bottle-sized ones. This not only permits the wine to breathe for a good hour before consumption but also removes all evidence of the origin of the wine, thus men (and it is always men) are prevented from expending valuable gossiping and conversational time examining the label and pontificating but instead get on and just enjoy the wine as liquid. The inside of people's minds is far more rewarding of study than the outside of wine bottles.

Day 7
1.22am
Arrive back from the blizzard-riven hillsides of Yorkshire, the train reluctantly departing from what was once the world's biggest railway station (York) to get me to King's Cross. I left behind me many infuriated passengers confronting the station master and his snow-wrecked schedules. This official handled himself well in the face of unanswerable, hotly delivered criticism. He offered to escort one older woman all the way home – once her train pulled in. She was worried that her

husband, not in a fit state she revealed, would distress himself further if she did not put in an appearance until the early hours. A second rail employee, clutching a huge portable telephone in her gloved hand, then arrived and offered saccharine succour. She was not received kindly. Her red uniform and brassy adornments suggested a hammy couturier whose design brief called for something between a Russian flight attendant and a lion tamer.

5.45am

Awake and prepare myself for children. They recognise me ('You're the man who sometimes sleeps next to Mummy, aren't you?') and dive-bomb the bed.

7.30am

Rather luxurious Jaguar, upholstery smelling of merlot, takes me to Heathrow. This is my publisher's attempt to make me feel like a real bestselling author would feel. I try to imagine I am such – John Grisham, say, or le Carré – but only feel like a wine guide compiler.

9.15am

Bryon Airways whisks me to Plymouth. Now I see their name on the side of the plane I realise it is not called Byron Airways, as I had thought. I feel disappointed. I cannot now write Byron transported me etcetera.

10.20am

Hodder sales rep, the efficient Sue Lear, gives me a whistle-stop tour of the shops, the Barbican area, and the bits of the docks accessible to motor transport.

12.30pm

Plymouth's most literary citizens gather for a literary lunch.

1.45pm

I speak. Waterstone's, who organised the lunch, sell many copies of both my wine guides which I sign with pleasure. Sea air lives up to its aphrodisiac repute: a reader, born in 1913 so she says, flirts heavily with author.

3.15-5.45pm

Driven to Bristol and the Avon Gorge Hotel. From the window of my room, I am afforded a view of the hotel's eponym, the gorge itself. I do not investigate further, being more taken with the edifice opposite the hotel's front door which is St Vincent's Priory – a building with some cheeky ornamental plasterwork.

7.00pm

Book signing at Blackwells, née George's. Thresher provides much wine as well as several members of their staff who cope delightfully with the vast thirst which being among bookshelves engenders. Is it the dust?

9.15pm

Eat a vast and complex Thai dinner with a bottle of Church Road Sauvignon Blanc from New Zealand. Now that this country is properly seen as a Pacific Rim state, not a piece of Dorset towed out to the antipodes, it is fitting that this kind of food and wine should go so naturally, so brilliantly, so sublimely well together.

Day 8
Thursday
8.45am

Give interview over the telephone, lying in bed puzzling over *Guardian* crossword with cup of tea, to Talk Radio. I cannot believe people still make a fuss over Beaujolais Nouveau day, which is . . . yawn yawn . . . today, and I am roused to offer my views on the subject, since I have been telephoned specifically by the radio station for them. I explain that Beaujolais Nouveau was once an ordinary-looking Frog, then it became a handsome Prince, but its fame went to its head and it became a real *ugly* Frog. (No drinker should bother about the wretched concoction. Pinotage from South Africa, as long as it is young, is a much more thrilling beverage.)

Day 9

10.20am

Strolling through Soho after an early morning meeting at the Groucho Club I see a large man dressed in a skirt go down the stairs to the public lavatory in Broadwick Street. Sticking out of his sock is a knife. I decide it is none of my business. Twenty minutes later, at the junction of Great Marlborough Street and Carnaby Street I see the same man enter a second public lavatory. What would you do? Could he be, bearing in mind the reputation of the local lavs, a serial homosexual killer? Should I grab the nearest policeman? I know exactly what to say: 'Excuse me, officer, there's an incontinent Scotsman in full Highland dress wandering about the West End. I think he might be lost.'

Day 10

7-something am

1. No alarm call. What happened to BT? I run about like a demented goose as my wife wakes me and tell me the time. I shower, shave, dress, thump children and marvel at *Guardian Weekend* in less time than it takes to poach an egg.

2. Taxi arrives to take me to Euston as it is too late to trust the Hammersmith & City line. Half-way down Marylebone Road discover I have left my wallet at home. Taxi executes incredible U-turn. I find wallet and resume my seat in taxi.

3. Get to Euston with four minutes to spare. Sprint like maniac to platform seven.

4. Train delayed thirty mins due to absence of interested employees. A body called North London Railways has, so I am informed, caused the problem as the result of an industrial dispute over 'safety notices'. Passengers wander about cursing and muttering about missed connections. No remedy is offered. Then comes the final announcement: 'This train will terminate at Birmingham International.' Since this is where I am supposed to get off, I am not greatly upset. But what of the passengers who expected to go on to Birmingham New Street to catch a further

train? When the train finally gets going and reaches Watford Junction to pick up passengers a voice over the PA systems says, 'This is the *slightly delayed* 10.15 train to Birmingham blah blah blah.' The italics, needless to say, are mine. There was no trace of italic irony in the voice.

5. Just past Bletchley a RAINBOW appears in all its elemental glory. Decide to forgive rail company, telephone company, my memory, and various other guilty parties.

6. Spend several hours at the BBC's *Food and Drink* show. Resist various attempts to get me to talk about wine other than the stuff I consider decent value. Run into the odd mountebank of my slight acquaintance; the sort of person who professes to know about food and wine but in reality is merely in possession of a large appetite for bullshit. Oz Clarke, the heroic Oz, kisses me on both cheeks and congratulates me on my TV series. Various lager louts punch me good-humouredly, making the assumption that because they have seen me on television they are permitted this licence as if some kind of proprietorship had been granted them thereby. Glad when the late afternoon comes round and I can look forward to finishing reading my book on the train.

7. Sneak into waiting room, thumb already in book ready to commence journey into literary paradise . . . but there is someone greeting me. It is an extremely chic and nattily dressed middle-aged mum, wearing very sexy earrings, with two young teenage football supporters in tow. It is Jancis Robinson. We proceed quickly to having a discussion, which does not get heated, about the merits and demerits of the £1.99 bottle of wine. She is firmly opposed to such horrors.

8. I fail to complete reading the novel I have been longing to re-enjoy. I spend the journey discussing all manner of things with Miss Robinson. She is a very smart woman. The Americans would employ the term *cookie* – as in smart, that is, not in mildly mad (which Jancis is most emphatically not). Trying to nail her down to any view which might be considered controversial, or even slightly discomfiting to any section of the wine trade, is like

attempting to bottle fog. I fear she finds me a bore. I wonder if she would be in sympathy with a character in the novel I'm dying to finish? *'Embrace anything too tightly and there is nothing to squeeze.'*

Day 11
6.45pm, taxi rank Paddington station

I find I have reached an interesting speculative idea regarding racial types in Britain. It is based solely on taxi drivers. Since I take taxis all over Britain, and have done so with increasing regularity over the last seven years, I feel I have some basis for remarking that, attitudinally based on racial origin, the drivers fall into two broad categories. First, there are those who are wholly native or at least have had several generations behind them (and are thus, like me, wholly English in outlook even if, like me, they are second-generation immigrant stock). They have been born and raised in, say, a busy metropolis like London or Bristol or Newcastle or Coventry. Then there is the group, somewhat smaller, of born-abroad and first-generation immigrant drivers, mainly it seems to me of Indian subcontinental extraction but also containing a few of African and Caribbean background but not, in my experience thus far, Far Eastern. The difference between these two groups is marked, for the taxi passenger, by the degree of hope and expectation each places on its ability to reach the destination requested by the passenger, when that destination is unfamiliar. The first group, asked by a fare to be taken to, let us say, the back door of the Languages Resources Department of Elgin University, will shake their heads and say, 'Don't know that' and then question the passenger until it is clear that a way can be found. The second group, asked for the out-of-the-way destination, responds brightly with 'We'll find it' and off they set, often get lost, have to ask the way, but get there in the end. The difference between these two groups is simply that which separates pessimism from optimism. Ergo: *The more English you are the more gloomy you turn out to be.*

Day 12

1.30pm

Why do we think nature is beautiful? Is it possible to be human and not think this? Rousseau, old Jean-Jacques, was prepared to grant an atheist his viewpoint if he lived in a city with its noise and thievery. But in the countryside Rousseau felt it was impossible not to believe in a divine creator. I pass a field full of sheep on the train, clouds writhing above, and I find it beautiful to look at. I doubt the sheep have any such feeling, except the one of appetite-satisfaction provided from chewing the grass. Rousseau was a soppy old sod at the best of times.

I tear myself away from these reveries to tackle a sheaf of readers' letters. One in particular, from Mr John Yule of Oxted, asks an interesting question and in response I feel obliged to compose a letter addressed to five supermarket wine-buying department heads. Mr Yule's question concerns the pasteurisation of supermarket wines. Is he right, he wonders, to suppose that around 80 per cent of wines are so treated? I confess I haven't given the matter a thought for some years, in the belief that it was no longer carried out since the introduction, over the past decade, of new and more sympathetic technology which made the practice unnecessary. Certainly the practice was widespread – even amongst so-called 'fine' burgundy producers. Pasteurisation (named after Louis Pasteur) is simply the application of heat to any food, liquid or solid, to kill bacteria and any live yeast cells which in a wine might cause the bottled product to re-ferment. This latter consideration is, of course, especially relevant where there is residual sugar in the wine which any living yeast, given half a chance, will turn into alcohol by restarting the fermentation process. I inform my correspondent that I will investigate the matter and report back.

Arrive in Newcastle, one of my favourite places in Britain, in the early afternoon. I wander past one of the earliest stretches of Hadrian's Wall, now incorporated into the Miners Hall where

Stephenson first demonstrated his miner's safety lamp. Frost is everywhere, icing on an inedible cake. It is a lovely, lovely sight to see.

One fact of life encountered on a national book-signing tour is the discovery of exotic, incomprehensible tongues. These secret languages are short on vowels and employ a vocabulary no longer spoken – if spoken can be said to be how they are uttered – in London. Not since the *Evening News* went out of business and the *Standard* became Londoners' only paper have we heard these weird tongues. I refer to evening newspaper salesmen, who in Newcastle stand on street corners in the City centre bawling utter gibberish. Why do these men shout *STANDARD!?* The paper they offer is called the *Chronicle*. I am lost and do not feel that any attempt by me to enquire of these vendors as to the reason why would be sympathetically met.

The central Arcade, built for a Victorian middle class, offers ceramic walls, a mosaic floor, great acoustics, and a decent busking violinist. I slip him a quid. Well, it's almost Christmas.

Grainger Market – worth the trip alone – is in Nelson Street. It boasts Corks Wine Bar and the Old Cordwainer Hall dated MDCCCXXXVIII (though the two lapidarily inscribed Wardens, Thomas Gilroy and John Walker, sound like characters out of Coronation Street). Fenwicks' Christmas window is a riot of animated dummies.

In Market Street there is a plaque on what is now a Lloyds Bank. It reads:

> *On this site formerly stood Anderson Place in which King Charles I was prisoner from 13 May 1646 to 3 February 1647 during the Scottish occupation of the City.*

After the signing, a merry affair as always with much ribbing of author, I take myself off to the 21 Queen Street Restaurant for a potage of fish followed by grilled seabass with a 1996 sauvignon blanc.

Nice way to finish my book tour. On a bass note.

On another note altogether, you may be interested to learn

of the reaction of some of our leading supermarkets to the query posed by the aforementioned Mr Yule regarding wine pasteurisation. I was pleased at the response from the five supermarkets I wrote to on Yule's behalf. Nick Dymoke-Marr of Asda replied:

'As a rule we do not seek for our wines to be pasteurised, be that using the methods of flash, tunnel or hot bottled pasteurisation. There are, however, some exceptions, particularly relating to the filling of lower-strength products which are high in sugar content and are either fully or semi-sparkling.' A list of Lambrusco and spumante products between 3 per cent and 8 per cent in alcoholic strength followed. Mr Dymoke-Marr continued: 'All other wines we stock are cold-filtered to remove proteins, yeasts or particles which may affect the wines' stability. We generally recommend to our suppliers that red wines are less filtered than whites ... we have also experimented with zero filtration on ... more robust reds.'

Mrs Angela Mount of Somerfield also confirmed 'that none of the wines which we sell, with the exception of Lambrusco, are pasteurised.'

Julian Brind who heads Waitrose's wine-buying operation said much the same thing and that 'micro-filtration' was now-adays the preferred method.

At Safeway, Mrs Elizabeth Robertson concurred with this approach saying, 'Off-hand I cannot think of any of our wines that are pasteurised ... ah yes, except of course Lambrusco which HAS to be pasteurised and suffers as a consequence.' She then went on to comment: 'I believe that USA and Canadian [trade] buyers are also still rather keen on pasteurisation, when it is sold to them as the ultimate fail-safe ... It's not unusual to learn of routine triple-filtration, including carbon, in Italy – thus all those white odourless wines. Standard Burgundy may also still get the treatment if buyers are not vigilant, because young unripe Pinot Noir is so unpleasantly harsh and the heat treatment mollifies it somewhat.'

And then there was Sainsbury's double response. Allan

Cheesman, director of off-licence buying, told me, '. . . as a process it [pasteurisation] is far less common in the 1990s than in my early days of the Trade in the early seventies when hot/warm bottling was *de rigueur* . . . with all levels of quality wines.' He went on to add that 'cellar hygiene and modern wine making and handling practice make the process [of pasteurisation] today redundant . . .'

Mr Peter Holland, a technical manager at Sainsbury, also wrote to me. He confirmed that 'Generally the practice of pasteurisation of wine is reducing and being replaced by the use of sterile membrane filtration coupled with bottle rinsing using sterile water. The use of membrane filtration has reduced the risk of yeast or bacteria contamination in bottled wine and is now a commercially acceptable practice, especially for dry wines because any accidental microbial contamination is unlikely to cause a problem. However the practice is not an absolute guarantee against microbial infection. Therefore pasteurisation can still be carried out on wines of a higher risk to secondary fermentation, i.e. high residual sugar and reduced alcohol . . . Pasteurisation may also be carried out on other wines where the wine maker believes in additional security and the heat treatment is deemed not to be . . . detrimental to the product.' A list of pasteurised Sainsbury wines followed, including the usual Lambrusco and low-alcohol and sweet stuff. Surprisingly, however, own-label wines from Sicily, Valencia, and reds from the huge Val D'Orbieu winery in southern France were also on the list. Back to Mr Cheesman at this point who confessed surprise at the inclusion of these wines as candidates for pasteurisation and he revealed that 'I am asking for a review of their operation and why?' Some weeks later he was able to tell me that Sicily has been instructed to drop pasteurisation immediately and adopt sterile filtration, that Valencia would follow suit within three months, and that the French producer would be carrying out a side-by-side test for Sainsbury's quality evaluation. This would involve comparing sterile filtered reds with reds coarse-filtered and flash-pasteurised as normal, testing both reds for any residues, and tasting both to see if any difference in flavour was discernible. Mr Yule did not, I am sure, imagine for one moment the hive of activity his question would occasion. All credit to him for asking it. And all credit to the supermarkets who are dynamically devoted to their customers' interests in a way which makes them as unlike the old-fashioned wine merchant as a mobile phone is unlike a smoke signal.

Now what all this adds up to as far as we wine drinkers are concerned is this: we are drinking much tastier and fresher wines today than were available years ago and supermarkets are deeply concerned to maintain high standards of fruit in their wines without technical processes – however well-meaning – spoiling it. The cheaper wines I used to drink in the toddling stage of my boozing career simply could not compare with their equivalents today. There is no doubt in my mind that the antique-method, crude heating of wine did more than destroy bacteria. It muddied the style, bruised the fruit, and blunted the individuality of every bottle. The wines we drink today, those attached to the least intimidating price tags, are more exciting and more complex, healthier and, in the final analysis, cheaper than anything the consumers of yesteryear poured down their throats.

Yes, cheaper. Subsequent to the biochemical innovations of Monsieur Pasteur has been the financial ingenuities of the British wine retailer. When I paid eleven bob for a bottle of Costieres du Gard in 1965 I was faced with a red wine of mere tolerable drinkability and of a somewhat coarse rustic mannerism which consumed a significantly higher percentage of the then average British weekly income than the equivalent wine would today. In 1997, for example, I can stroll into Tesco and hand over £2.99 for a bottle of Cabernet Sauvignon Vin de Pays de la Haute Vallee de l'Aude, from the same Languedoc–Roussilllon area, and not only be vastly better served by a richer, more invigorating wine but be much less out of pocket. These are the twin fruits of the wine revolution and I see no reason to doubt that British supermarkets will keep up their good work on our behalf for as long as there are vines in sunny climes to harvest to slake our thirsts.

Health Warning!

This section, which first appeared in *Summerplonk* earlier this year, may, I hope, save you from working yourself up into a state. Let me explain.

I get a few letters a week from readers (both column and book) telling me that a wine which I have said is on sale in a certain supermarket is not there and that the wine has either sold out or the branch claims to have no knowledge of it; I get letters telling me that a wine is a bit dearer than I said it was; and I get the odd note revealing that the vintage of the 16-point wine I have enthused about and which my correspondent desperately wants to buy is different from the one listed.

First of all, let me say that no wine guide in the short and inglorious history of the genre is more exhaustively researched, checked, and double-checked than this one. I do not list a wine if I do not have assurances from its retailer that it will be widely on sale when the guide is published. Where a wine is on restricted distribution, or stocks are short and vulnerable to the assault of determined readers (i.e. virtually all high-rating, very cheap bottles), I will always clearly say so. However, large retailers use computer systems which cannot anticipate uncommon demand and which often miss the odd branch off the anticipated stocking list. I cannot check every branch myself (though I do nose around them when I can) and so a wine in this book may well, infuriatingly, be missing at the odd branch of its retailer and may not even be heard of by the branch simply because of inhuman error. Conversely, the same technology often tells a retailer's head office that a wine is out of stock when it has merely been completely cleared out of the warehouse. It may still be on sale in certain branches. Then there is the fact that not every wine I write about is stocked by every single branch of its listed supermarket. Every store has what are called retail plans and there may be half-a-dozen of these and every wine is subject to a different stocking policy according to the dictates of these cold-hearted plans.

I accept a wine as being in healthy distribution if several hundred branches, all over the country, not just in selected parts of it, stock the wine. Do not assume, however, that this means every single branch has the wine.

I cannot, equally, guarantee that every wine in this book will still be in the same price band as printed (these bands follow this introduction). The vast majority will be. But there will always be the odd bottle from a country suddenly subject to a vicious swing in currency rates, or subject to an unprecedented rise in production costs which the supermarket cannot or is not prepared to swallow, and so a few pennies will get added to the price. If it is pounds, then you have cause for legitimate grievance. Please write to me. But don't lose a night's sleep if a wine is 20 pence more than I said it is. If you must, write to the appropriate supermarket. The department and the address to write to is provided with each supermarket's entry.

Now the puzzle of differing vintages. When I list and rate a wine, I do so only for the vintage stated. Any other vintage is a different wine requiring a new rating. Where vintages do have little difference in fruit quality, and more than a single vintage is on sale, then I say this clearly. If two vintages are on sale, and vary in quality and/or style, then they will be separately rated. However, be aware of one thing.

Superplonk is the biggest-selling wine guide to such an extent that all the other wine guides' sales put together do not reach even a fraction of it. I say this not to brag but, importantly, to acquaint you with a reality which may cause you some irritation. When *Superplonk* appears on sale there will be lots of eager drinkers aiming straight for the highest-rating wines as soon as possible after the book is published. Thus the supermarket wine buyer who assures me that she has masses of stock of Domaine

Piddlewhatsit and the wine will withstand the most virulent of sieges may find her shelves emptying in a tenth of the time she banked on – not knowing, of course, how well I rate the wine until the book goes on sale. It is entirely possible, therefore, that the vintage of a highly rated wine may sell out so quickly that new stocks of the follow-on vintage may be urgently brought on to shelf before I have tasted them. This can happen in some instances. I offer a bunch of perishable pansies, not a wreath of immortelles. I can do nothing about this fact of wine-writing life, except to give up writing about wine.

Lastly, one thing more. And let me steal from myself yet again:

'Wine is a hostage to several fortunes (weather being even more uncertain and unpredictable than exchange rates) but the wine writer is hostage to just one: he cannot pour for his readers precisely the same wine as he poured for himself.'

I wrote this last year and it holds true for every wine in this book and every wine I will write about in the years to come (for as long as my liver holds out). I am sent wines to taste regularly and I attend wine tastings all the time. If a wine is corked on these occasions, that is to say not in good condition because it has been tainted by the tree bark which is its seal, then it is not a problem for a bottle in good condition to be quickly supplied for me to taste. This is not, alas, a luxury which can be extended to my readers.

So if you find a wine not to your taste because it seems pretty foul or 'off' in some way, then do not assume that my rating system is up the creek; you may take it that the wine is faulty and must be returned as soon as possible to its retailer. Every retailer in this book is pledged to provide an instant refund for any faulty wine returned – no questions asked. I am not asking readers to share all my tastes in wine, or to agree completely with every rating for every wine. But where a wine I have well rated is obviously and patently foul then it is a duff bottle and you should be compensated by getting a fresh bottle free or by being given a refund.

How I Rate a Wine

Value for money is my single unwavering focus. I drink with my readers' pockets in my mouth. I do not see the necessity of paying a lot for a bottle of everyday drinking wine and only rarely do I consider it worth paying a high price for, say, a wine for a special occasion or because you want to experience what a so-called 'grand' wine may be like. There is more codswallop talked and written about wine, especially the so-called 'grand' stuff, than any subject except sex. The stench of this gobbledegook regularly perfumes wine merchants' catalogues, spices the backs of bottles, and rancidises the writings of those infatuated by or in the pay of producers of a particular wine region. I do taste expensive wines regularly. I do not, regularly, find them worth the money. That said, there are some pricey bottles in these pages. They are here either because I wish to provide an accurate, but low, rating of its worth so that readers will be given pause for thought or because the wine is genuinely worth every penny. A wine of magnificent complexity, thrilling fruit, superb aroma, great depth and finesse is worth drinking. I would not expect it to be an inexpensivce bottle. I will rate it highly. I wish all wines which commanded such high prices were so well deserving of an equally high rating. The thing is, of course, that many bottles of wine I taste do have finesse and depth but do not come attached to an absurdly high price tag. These are the bottles I prize most. As, I hope, you will.

20 Is outstanding and faultless in all departments: smell, taste and finish in the throat. Worth the price, even if you have to take out a second mortgage.

19 A superb wine. Almost perfect and well worth the expense (if it is an expensive bottle).

18 An excellent wine but lacking that ineffable sublimity of richness and complexity to achieve the very highest rating. But extraordinary drinking and thundering good value.

17 An exciting, well-made wine at an affordable price which offers real glimpses of outstanding, multi-layered richness.

16 Very good wine indeed. Good enough for any dinner party. Not expensive but terrifically drinkable, satisfying and properly balanced.

15 For the money, a good mouthful with real style. Good flavour and fruit without costing a packet.

14 The top end of the everyday drinking wine. Well-made and to be seriously recommended at the price.

13 Good wine, true to its grape(s). Not great, but very drinkable.

12 Everyday drinking wine at a sensible price. Not exciting, but worthy.

11 Drinkable, but not a wine to dwell on. You don't wed a wine like this, though you might take it behind the bike shed with a bag of fish and chips.

10 Dead average wine (at a low price), yet still just about a passable mouthful. Also, wines which are terribly expensive and, though drinkable, cannot remotely justify their high price.

9 Fit for parties for failed Conservative candidates.

8 On the rough side here.

7 Good for pickling onions or cleaning false teeth.

6 Hardly drinkable except on an icy night by a raging bonfire.

5 Wine with more defects than delights.

4 Not good at any price.

3 Barely drinkable.

2   Seriously – did this wine come from grapes?

1   The utter pits. The producer should be slung in prison and the key buried.

The rating system above can be broken down into six broad sections.

Zero to 10: Avoid – unless entertaining a stuffy wine writer.

10, 11:   Nothing poisonous but, though drinkable, rather dull.

12, 13:   Above average, interestingly made. Solid rather than sensational.

14,15,16:   This is the exceptional, hugely drinkable stuff, from the very good to the brilliant.

17, 18:   Really wonderful wine worth anyone's money: complex, rich, exciting.

19,20:   A toweringly brilliant world-class wine of self-evident style and individuality.

Prices

It is impossible to guarantee the price of any wine in this guide. That is why instead of printing the shop price, each wine is given a price band. This attempts to eliminate the problem of printing the wrong price for a wine. This can occur for all the usual boring but understandable reasons: inflation, economic conditions overseas, the narrow margins on some supermarket wines making it difficult to maintain consistent prices, and, of course, the existence of those freebooters at the Exchequer who are liable to inflate taxes which the supermarkets cannot help but pass on. But even price banding is not foolproof. A wine listed in the book at, say, a B band price might be on sale at a C band price. How? Because a wine close to but under, say, £3.50 in summer when I tasted it might sneak across the border in winter. It happens, rarely enough not to concern me overmuch, but wine is an agricultural import, a sophisticated liquid food, and that makes it volatile where price is concerned. The price banding code assigned to each wine works as follows:

Price Band

A Under £2.50   B £2.50 to £3.50   C £3.50 to £5

D £5 to £7   E £7 to £10   F £10 to £13

G £13 to £20   H Over £20

All wines costing under £5 (i.e. A–C) have their price band set against a black background.

ACKNOWLEDGEMENTS

I could not put this little volume together were it not for my assistant, an indulgent editor (and marvellously accommodating printer), a superb copy editor, and lots of dedicated people backing up my efforts at Hodder & Stoughton. I owe thanks, therefore, to Linda Peskin, Kate Lyall Grant, Craig Morrison, Helen Dore, Martin Neild, Kerr MacRae, Jamie Hodder-Williams, Karen Geary, and Katie Gunning. As ever, I am also grateful to Felicity Rubinstein and Sarah Lutyens. I would also like to thank all the young women who fill shelves and stomachs at Books for Cooks, that extraordinary retailer, and who put up with my vinous behaviour in the cause of research. I owe a debt to Gerry, my postman, and all the other stalwart men and women of letters at Paddington sorting office. I'd also like to say thanks for being around to the Reverend Tom Gillum of St Stephen's – his church is a constant inspiration to this agnostic.

ASDA

Asda Stores Limited
Asda House
Great Wilson Street
Leeds
LS11 5AD
Tel 0113 243 5435
Fax 0113 241 8146

What's wonderful.

The eccentric bursts of chutzpah by Nick Dymoke-Marr and Alistair Morrell, the two senior buyers here, give Asda, which is a mighty big retailer, the occasional cosy glitz of the corner wineshop run by the nutter who loves wine to the extent of discussing riesling with his German Shepherd when there aren't any customers in. These oddities include certain wines, like the own-label Greek stuff, some terrific regular price cutters sticking out of tubs on the shop floor, some mould-breaking designs in wine labels, and the appointment of PR consultants whose affairs never cease to entertain.

What's maddening.

They always send me their list of post-Christmas bargains, some of which are mind-bogglingly brilliant value, too late for me to include in my *Guardian* column. Also, some of the labels are so outrageous as to baffle even the barmiest buff.

ARGENTINIAN WINE   RED

Argentinian Red 1996, Asda   15   B

Good rich texture and fruit which is nicely balanced between
a rousing ripeness and a velvety textured finish in the back of
the mouth.

La Rural Mendoza Malbec 1996   14.5   C

Vivacity, style, richness, flavour and oodles of pizzazz. This is
soft, big and exceedingly drinkable.

ARGENTINIAN WINE   WHITE

Argentinian White 1996, Asda   15   B

Solid thwack of flavour, soft and very full. Delicious cheek to
both texture and fruit.

La Rural Mendoza Pinot Blanc/Chardonnay
1996   15   C

AUSTRALIAN WINE   RED

Chateau Reynella Basket Press Shiraz
1994   14.5   E

Juicy edge to the soft fruit which is the civilized side of full.

Chateau Reynella Basket-Pressed
Cabernet/Merlot 1994   16   E

Ripe cabernet and soft leathery merlot deliciously combine both aromatically and fruit-wise in layers of unflagging flavours. A very convincing wine. Sheer satiny class.

Hardys Bankside Shiraz 1995 `14` `D`

Wins on its approach, rather than its quiet departure.

Hardys Nottage Hill Cabernet Sauvignon/ Shiraz 1994 `15` `C`

Penfolds Bin 28 Kalimna Shiraz 1994 `14` `E`

Expensive but very impressively fruity and fine. Dry and flavourful.

Penfolds Rawson's Retreat Bin 35 Cabernet/Shiraz 1995 `13.5` `C`

Peter Lehmann Vine Vale Grenache 1996 `14` `C`

Soft, aromatic, ripe, tasty. Perhaps too accommodating to instant likeability to handle robust food.

Rosemount Estate Cabernet/Shiraz 1996 `13.5` `D`

Juicy, ripe, soft, very Aussie. It really swarms all over the tastebuds.

Rosemount Estate Shiraz 1994 `14` `D`

Rosemount Shiraz/Cabernet 1995 `15` `C`

South Australia Cabernet Sauvignon 1995, Asda `15` `C`

Begins warm and savoury, ends freshly and cherry-bright. Lovely stuff for a cold winter's day.

South Australian Cabernet Sauvignon 1994 `13.5` `C`

**South Eastern Australia Shiraz/Cabernet
1996, Asda** `13` `B`

Curiously light-minded and unadventurous.

AUSTRALIAN WINE · WHITE

Chateau Reynella Chardonnay 1995 `16.5` `E`

Superb texture, fruit, flavour, balance and lush yet sophisticated style. It is one of the best vintages of one of Australia's tastiest chardonnays.

Cranswick Oak Aged Marsanne 1996 `14` `C`

Lemony excellence. Has zest and richness which, deliciously, hint at cloyingness but stay in balance in spite of wobbling. Great with fish dishes.

Geoff Merrill Sauvignon/Semillon 1996 `14` `C`

Layers of lemony fruit tickle the palate and engage brilliantly with fish dishes.

Hardys Nottage Hill Chardonnay 1996 `15` `C`

Lovely vintage here: controlled, slightly musky, deep, yet well balanced and full of flavour. A terrific chardonnay of clout, class and value for money.

**Hardys Stamp of Australia Grenache/
Shiraz Rose 1996** `11.5` `C`

**Hardys Stamp of Australia Riesling/
Traminer 1996** `13` `C`

Odd gawkiness, but some style – probably best with light Chinese dim sum dishes.

Jackdaw Ridge Australian White   `11` `B`

Kingston Chenin Verdelho 1996   `15` `C`

Good with Thai food and grilled prawns. Has a waxy apricot edge to its citric fruit (subtle). Good glugging.

Kingston Semillon/Verdelho 1996   `14` `C`

Great shellfish wine. Has a lovely cleanness of crisp fruit.

Mount Hurtle Sauvignon Blanc/Semillon 1996   `16.5` `C`

Utterly delicious in the most wicked New World wine way. It reeks of clean stainless steel fruit, pebble fresh acidity and underripe melon and lime with a hint of green apple.

Penfolds Barossa Valley Semillon/ Chardonnay 1995   `15` `D`

Classy stuff: achingly toothsome fruit, shrouded in smoky melon and pear.

Penfolds Barossa Valley Semillon/ Chardonnay 1996   `16` `D`

Utterly delicious wine with a ripe, open approach to the fluidity of its fruit which is gently oily and subtly opulent, with a melony, lemony and pineappley edge.

Penfolds Bin 202 Rhine Riesling 1996   `14.5` `C`

Interesting softish fruit with a crisp pineapple tang. Will develop well in bottle over the next year.

Penfolds Rawsons Retreat Bin 21 Semillon/Chardonnay/Colombard 1996   `15` `C`

Richly textured, warmly fruity (some complexity on the finish where the acidity is most pertinent), this is an excellent vintage for this wine.

Peter Lehmann The Barossa Semillon, 1996
`15.5` `C`

Gorgeous creamy fruit of a richness which will go well with all manner of gently spiced oriental dishes as well as straightforward grilled mackerel. It is, for all this, an elegant sipping wine of considerable style.

Rosemount Estate Chardonnay 1995
`16` `D`

Beautiful controlled fruit with vivacity and restraint. This paradox is Rosemount's hallmark.

Rosemount Estate Semillon/Chardonnay 1996
`14` `D`

Elegance personified.

South Australian Chardonnay 1996, Asda
`16` `C`

Ooh, I could drink it out of a bucket! The flood of flavour is immense yet calming. It is impossible to feel ill-disposed to humanity after a glug of this rich, deep, yet fresh wine – melon and red grapes to taste – with its lingering finish.

South East Australian Semillon/Chardonnay 1996, Asda
`14` `B`

A lighter style of Aussie – but a refreshing one. Good balance and personality – not abrasive.

BULGARIAN WINE RED

Bulgarian Vintage Premium Merlot 1994
`13` `B`

Liubimetz Merlot Premiere 1994
`16` `B`

Stunning value. Lovely ripe fruit, soft as crumpled satin, with good tannins and acidity. Has depth, style and flavour – and an astounding price.

CHILEAN WINE RED

Alto Plano Chilean Red · 14.5 · B

Great value here. The texture and the fruit are rich and warm but the finish, hinting at dryness, provides balance, style and a delicious farewell.

Chilean Cabernet/Merlot 1995, Asda · 16.5 · C

Has oodles of flavour, balanced and rich, with brilliant tannins, fruit and acidity in single-minded delivery of pure pleasure to the senses. Gorgeous stuff!!

Cono Sur Cabernet Sauvignon 1994 · 15 · C

Rowan Brook Cabernet Sauvignon Reserve 1994 · 14 · C

Rowan Brook Cabernet Sauvignon/ Malbec 1996 · 16 · B

Great value here. The blend provides the palate with a soft leathery aromatic incisiveness with a hint of peppery vegetality, real texture, true richness, genuine style.

Rowan Brook Zinfandel 1996 · 13.5 · C

Soft, zippy, amusing.

Terra Noble Merlot 1995 · 15 · C

Lost a little of its power to stun but it's still a full-throated merlot in perfect contralto voice. Has texture, fruit, and maintains its richness from aroma to the back of the throat.

Valdivieso Malbec 1996 `17.5` `C`

Wonderful wine! Quite wonderful! The texture is the softest velvet, the fruit is exquisite plum and blackberry, the balance is poised.

CHILEAN WINE WHITE

Alto Plano Chilean White `14` `B`

Has an interesting sticky-toffee edge to the fruit. Delicious to sip or to slurp or to enjoy with a tuna sandwich.

Chilean Sauvignon Blanc 1996, Asda `16` `B`

Staggering good fruit here of such high class you look twice at the price. The wine in the glass may be examined with greater sensory scrutiny and be more rewarding. This would be a lovely wine at twice the price.

Cono Sur Chilean Chardonnay 1995 `14` `C`

**Rowan Brook Chardonnay Oak Aged
Reserve, Casablanca 1996** `16` `C`

Rich, woody, elegant, stylish, balanced, flavoursome, drinkable, good with food – what more can one say?

**Rowan Brook Sauvignon Blanc Reserve
1996** `14.5` `C`

Lots of flavour relieved, deftly, by a rich, acidic vein. Classy feel.

Valdivieso Chardonnay 1996 `16.5` `C`

Wonderful richness of complexity and length of flavour. Balanced, elegant, vivid (yet soft and ripe), hugely stylish and totally captivating.

Vina Porta Chardonnay Reserve 1995 | 14 | D

Softness yet pointed and fine on the finish. Not as complex as many other Chilean chardonnays at this price, though.

FRENCH WINE   RED

Beaujolais, Asda | 12 | C

Beaujolais Villages Domaine des Ronzes 1995 | 13.5 | C

Buzet Cuvee 44 1996 | 13.5 | C

Dry and a touch austere. Will soften over two years but I'm not sure how the cherry/plum fruit will ripen.

Cabernet Sauvignon VdP d'Oc, Asda | 15 | B

Cahors, Asda | 13.5 | B

Chateau de Parenchere Bordeaux Superieure 1995 | 15 | D

Ripe, unusually so for such a claret, yet dry and well textured. A wonderfully rich Bordeaux for the money. Has real class here. Uniquely Bordeaux yet with real flavour and F.R.U.I.T. (formative richness undercutting insistent typicity).

Chateau Fonfroide Bordeaux 1996 | 14 | C

Dry, brisk, charcoal-edged fruit of classic Bordeaux go-to-hell stylishness. Great with lamb chops (well-burned ones).

Chateau Haut Plantey Grand Cru St Emilion 1993 | 16 | D

Dry, yes, very dry and with tannin to keep it going for years. But the finish, soft, beautifully textured and fine, is lovely: licorice and blackcurrants with a hint of cedar wood.

Chateau la Domeque, Corbieres 1993 `15` `C`

Chateau l'Eglise Vieille, Haut Medoc 1995 `16` `C`

Very classy stuff: dry, chocolatey, full of itself, yet very rich and satisfying. An elegant, very gripping claret at a down-to-earth price.

Chateau Peybonnehomme Les Tours
Cotes de Blaye 1994 `16` `D`

Dark cherries, ripe blackcurrants and dry, rich plums, tannically well knitted together, make this a stunning wine for the money. A serious claret lover's treat and a terrific merlot-dominated blend.

Chateauneuf-du-Pape 1996 `12` `E`

Not convinced by this. It's a mucked-about-with Chateauneuf. Like seeing racing stripes on a Fiat 500.

Claret, Asda `14` `B`

Amazing price for a true, dry, blackcurranty claret of edgy style and food compatibility.

Cotes du Rhone Villages Domaine de
Belugue 1994 `16.5` `C`

Brilliant, New World sweetness and lushness with big Old World tannins. Lovely wine. Emphatic concentration of flavour here.

Domaine de Grangeneuve, Coteaux du
Tricastin 1995 `15` `C`

Dry, earthy, blackcurranty, well-balanced and priced – this is a solid, soft, vital Rhone.

Domaine de La Baume Merlot VdP 1993

Quite brilliant balance of fruit and acidity and tannin. A bustling, handsome brute with couth manners and massive richness. For the money, one of France's finest merlots.

Domaine de la Baume Merlot VdP d'Oc 1994

One of the tastiest merlots on sale. World-class. Almost perfect precision.

Fitou, Asda

Plastic-corked and proud of it. A brilliant, fruity sausage and mash wine.

James Herrick 'Cuvee Simone' VdP 1996

More acidic and tannic than previous (glorious) vintages. I'd be inclined to drink this in spring '98 when it should be a 16+-pointer.

La Baume Philippe de Baudin Cabernet Sauvignon VdP d'Oc 1994

The tannins are fast running delicious riot with this wine and the fruit has got drier, angrier, less lush and the result is a concentrated cabernet of some class and style.

La Domeq Syrah Vieilles Vignes 'Tete de Cuvee' 1995

Delicious through-put of flavour here: dry yet ripe, rich, multi-layered fruit of substance, flavour and charm.

Mas Segala Cotes du Roussillon Villages 1996

Not as richly fruity or textured as previous vintages. It may be the wine is young, but I wonder if it will improve dramatically.

Merlot, Vin de Pays d'Oc, Asda `15` `B`

Montagne Noire Rouge VdP de l'Aude 1996 `14` `B`
Rich, earthy, dry, convincing. Well-priced and packed with flavour.

Montagne Noire Syrah/Merlot 1996 `15.5` `B`
A rich wine which has hints of dry herbiness cloaked by a blanket of warm fruit. Brilliant value.

Morgon Jambon 1996 `13` `D`
Some substance here – some.

Oak Aged Cotes du Rhone 1996, Asda `13` `C`
Light with earthy overtones. Not bad, but it seems to be straining for effect.

Red Burgundy 1995, Asda `11` `C`

St Chinian, Asda `14` `B`

Tramontane Grenache VdP d'Oc 1996 `15.5` `B`
Cigar smoke and trucker's tyres – warmly baking in the Midi sun. A great, sustaining, savoury glug which is tasty enough to be served as soup.

Tramontane Syrah VdP d'Oc 1996 `14` `B`
Cherry-ripe yet dry, a hint of tobacco. Mouth-watering tippling.

FRENCH WINE   WHITE

Bin 050 Sauvignon Blanc/Carignan 1996 `14` `B`
An organic wine with an earthy edge to its tingling, fruity freshness. Good with food and fellowship.

Chablis 1995, Asda `13` `E`

Expensive, but hints of class give it some merit.

Chablis Premier Cru Les Fourchaumes, 1995 `14` `F`

Expensive, yes, very expensive, but it is on form: delicately fruity with a clean finish, and nicely balanced.

Chardonnay, Vin de Pays d'Oc, Asda `14.5` `C`

Chateau la Blanquerie Entre Deux Mers 1995 `14` `C`

Cotes de Bergerac 'Confit de la Colline' 1995 (half bottle) `15` `D`

Cotes du Rhone Blanc Chateau du Trignon 1995 `15.5` `D`

Cuckoo Hill Chardonnay/Vermentino, VdP d'Oc 1996 `12.5` `B`

Revealing name, for a wine in which it seems to me the vermentino lays an egg for the chardonnay to hatch.

Cuckoo Hill Viognier VdP d'Oc 1996 `14.5` `C`

Crisp with an apricot edge which though an echo of a full-blooded viognier is nevertheless charming. A terrific aperitif.

Domaine Baud Chardonnay Jardin de la France 1996 `14.5` `B`

Astonishing value when you think what gets ripped off the £2.99 by the Exchequer and Customs & Excise. A rich, demure wine of some style and class, recognisably chardonnay in profile, and real balanced flavour.

Domaine de Trignon Cotes du Rhone 1996 `14.5` `D`

I love the quaint thatched roof on this solid modern edifice. It's a crisp modern piece of architecture, in other words, with a characterful finish.

Domaine des Deux Roches St Veran 1996 `16` `D`

Astonishing! A terrific white burgundy under seven quid. It has a deliciously vegetal aroma, opulently textured, almost buttery fruit and a clean rapier-thrust finish. This is an elegant wine of finesse and flavour.

James Herrick Chardonnay VdP d'Oc 1996 `14.5` `C`

New World restrained by Old World coyness. A chardonnay of subtlety and crisp fruit which is always nicely understated.

La Domeq 'Tete de Cuvee' Blanc 1996 `15.5` `C`

Old French style in a hippy treatment of newfangled wine-making. It's faintly luscious, quite elegant and very crisp to finish.

Macon-Vinzelles Les Cailloux 1996 `14.5` `D`

Creamy, mildly lemonic with a nutty smoke undertone, this is a very tasty Macon blanc of very pretty fruit.

Montagne Noire Chardonnay, VdP d'Oc 1996 `15` `C`

Excellent value for such ripe fruit on excellent form. It's well textured yet never too full or rich.

Montagne Noire Sauvignon Blanc 1996 `15`

Fantastic price and fantastic fruit for less than £3.50! This is not only an elegant sauvignon of wit and style, crisp and fresh, but has flavour and a hint of richness – it'll go brilliantly with fish cakes, etc.

Muscadet de Sevre et Maine Sur Lie, Domaine Gautron 1995

Rather numbed – as if in bereavement for long-dead fruit.

Pouilly Fume, Domaine Coulbois 1995

I like it but not so much that I'd enthusiastically pay £7.75 for it.

Premieres Cotes de Bordeaux Blanc, Asda

A sweet wine at an accommodating price which has enough depth and richness to serve as an after-dinner glass with a goat's cheese and a bunch of grapes.

Sancerre Domaine de Sarry 1996

Far from indecent if not especially exciting value.

Sauvignon de Bordeaux, Asda

Spring Vale Blanc VdP 1995

Vin de Pays des Cotes de Gascogne, Asda

Citric pineapple gives it a slightly exotic edge. Makes a super aperitif.

Vouvray Denis Marchais Hand Picked 1996

Yes, it's off-dry, even a touch honeyed. But it's a wonderful aperitif: individual, rich, enticing, ripe, invigorating, floral.

Yves Grassa Oak Fermented Chardonnay 1996

Woody yet full of fruity litheness and flavour. Briary aroma, rich fruit in the middle, lemony to finish. Can you ask any more from a five-quid chardonnay?

GERMAN WINE WHITE

Hochheimer Holle Riesling Kabinett Aschrott 1995 `12` `D`

Give it two to three years to show itself more vividly.

Northern Star Dry White 1996 `13` `B`

Faintly floral, attempts at crispness, almost succeeds.

Northern Star Medium Dry White 1996 `12` `B`

Sweet, but good for Lieb lovers looking for a way out.

Ruppertsberger Nussbein Riesling Auslese 1993 (50cl) `13.5` `C`

St Ursula Deidesheimer Hofstuck Kabinett 1994 `13.5` `B`

Villa Eden Vineyards Riesling Kabinett QMP 1996 `12` `C`

Nice try (in its blue bottle) but it needs more real personality, at a fiver, to be successful. It's a £2.99 wine at best. Will work with fish and salads where the dull honeyed edge is at its most attractive but it's not fully formed.

Wild Boar Vineyards Riesling 1996 `14` `C`

If this is the way new-style, dry, crisp but faintly floral German rieslings can go, then all power to their elbow and full glasses to ours!

GREEK WINE RED

Marble Mountain Cabernet/St George 1996 `15.5`

A wonderful surprise to anyone who thought the Greeks had lost the art of growing rich, characterful wine grapes about the time Aristotle died.

Temple Ruins Greek Red 1996 `14` `B`

Brilliant chilled with food, or merely with the Sunday papers.

GREEK WINE WHITE

Marble Mountain Roditis/Chardonnay 1996 `13.5`

A somewhat muddy edge to the fruit fails to mark it higher.

Temple Ruins Greek White 1996 `14.5` `B`

Greek wine like you've never tasted it before! Full of flavour, nutty and fruity, with a balancing freshness and elegance – and a surprising persistence of flavour. Great stuff!

HUNGARIAN WINE RED

Hungarian Merlot 1996, Asda `14`

A simple, dry, everyday drinking wine, The fruit is not bold, but then neither is the price, and, chilled, it is extra-drinkable.

HUNGARIAN WINE   WHITE

Deer Ridge Oak Aged Chardonnay 1996   `15.5` `C`

Utterly delicious richness, texture and flavour – creamy yet ripe, smoky yet fresh.

**Deer Ridge Sauvignon Blanc/Traminer
1996**   `13.5` `B`

A very pleasant tipple – if not exciting.

Hungarian Muscat, Asda   `14.5` `B`

Tastes of grapes. How rare! A simply delightful wine to watch Coronation Street with (i.e. spicy, fresh yet established, and easy to swallow).

Hungarian Pinot Blanc 1996, Asda   `14` `B`

Delicious price, delicious apricot-edged fruit. Great with a Chinese take-away!

Mecsekalji Chardonnay Reserve 1996   `14` `B`

Attractive simplicity and directness. A soft engaging wine.

Sopron Sauvignon Blanc Reserve 1996   `15` `B`

A grassy sauvignon of nettle-edged bite and bustle. Brilliant crispness and clear-headed fruit make it superb with oyster, crab, poached cod and even mild Thai dishes. Fantastic value.

ITALIAN WINE   RED

**Amarone della Valpolicella Sanroseda
1993 (50cl)**   `15` `D`

A real treat for the solo hedonist with a book in an armchair.

A ripe, off-dryish, figgy (yet dry to finish) wine of quaintness and rich insistence of flavour.

Barolo Bricco Fontanile, Veglio Angelo 1993 `14` `E`

Light but teeth-grippingly pruney and dry. Interesting with roast chicken and tarragon.

Chianti 1996, Asda `11` `B`

Chianti Classico 1995, Asda `11` `C`

Very light, very. The earthiness only clocks in well after the fruit has disappeared down the gullet.

Chianti Colli Senesi Salvanza 1995 `13` `C`

Coltiva Il Rosso 1996 `14` `B`

Cherry-ripe and slips down the throat easily. Light but lissom.

Due Rossi Merlot/Refosco 1996 `13` `C`

La Vis Pinot Nero 1995 `13` `C`

Light! Touch too light!

Lambrusco Rosso, Asda `12` `A`

Montepulciano d'Abruzzo, Cantina Tollo 1996 `13.5` `B`

Pleasant, light, drinkable.

Montepulciano d'Abruzzo La Luna Argenta 1995 `15.5` `B`

Gorgeous zip, personality and dry, rich fruit of huge food-friendliness. Classy but fun, serious but never solemn, hugely drinkable yet not simply a great gush of fruit.

Rozzano Villa Pigna 1996 `15.5` `C`

Rich, finely sculpted fruit of finesse and style. Lovely texture.
A terrific wine.

Sicilian Rosso, Asda `16.5` `B`

New blend of an old favourite, which hit a low sweet note last
year, but it's back to form with oodles of soft, rich fruit, a
tannic touch on the finish and a very good grip. Terrific value.
Fun slurping.

Valpolicella Classico 'Sanroseda' 1996 `13` `C`

Light and somewhat expensive.

Valpolicella N V, Asda `11` `B`

ITALIAN WINE WHITE

Cantina Rosata `12` `B`

Coltiva Il Bianco 1996 `14.5` `B`

Honey and ripe melon finish it off. An excellent glug for
light lunches.

Due Bianchi Sauvignon/Pinot Bianco 1996 `14` `C`

Complex nuttiness and a grassy freshness make this clean-cut
specimen an unusual Italian. Interesting specimen.

Frascati Superiore 'Colli di Catone' 1996 `11` `C`

La Vis Trentino Chardonnay 1996 — 14 — B

Starts like a sauvignon but musters enough melony chardonnay-ness on the finish to be an all-round attractive tipple. Good with shellfish.

La Vis Valdadige Pinot Grigio 1996 — 14 — C

Delicious, clean and crisp. Like a sushi chef's knife edge (sans fish).

Lambrusco Bianco, Asda — 12.5 — A

Lambrusco Rosato, Asda — 12 — A

Lambrusco Secco, Asda — 11 — A

Recioto di Soave Castelcerino 1993 (half bottle) — 14 — C

Sicilian Bianco, Asda — 13.5 — B

Soave, Asda — 13.5 — B

Good basic fish-and-chip soave. Very clean and fresh and not one whit taut or undernourished.

Soave Classico 'Sanroseda' 1996 — 13.5 — C

Not bad, but £3.99 is asking for trouble.

MOROCCAN WINE — RED

Domaine Mellil Cabernet/Syrah 1996 — 14 — B

Warm and loving. Delicious fruit, the right side of dry, which is impactfully concentrated and rich.

Domaine Mellil Moroccan Red Wine `15` `B`

PORTUGUESE WINE RED

Bright Brothers 'Old Vines' Estramadura 1995 `13.5` `C`

Soft and ripe.

Bright Brothers Trincadeira 1996 `13` `C`

Very light and puppyish sort of wine.

PORTUGUESE WINE WHITE

Fiuza Barrel Fermented Chardonnay 1995 `16` `C`

Woody undertone gives this wine purpose and style. Good fruit well coated in flavoursomeness which finishes on a very elegant note.

Fiuza Sauvignon Blanc 1996 `16` `C`

Gorgeous, rich, inviting aroma. Big opulent fruit of textured tautness yet suppleness. Soft finish. Lovely glug.

Vinho Verde, Asda `11` `B`

ROMANIAN WINE WHITE

River Route Sauvignon/Muscat 1994

SOUTH AFRICAN WINE   RED

Athlone Pinotage 1996   13.5 C

Juicy, rather than gripping in the usual whizz-bang pinotage fashion.

Blue Ridge Cabernet Sauvignon/Shiraz 1996   15.5 C

Fairly well-concentrated fruit with a lovely, tobacco edge. Softly textured but not overripe or too sloppy. Good with food, good to glug. And its plastic cork means it will never smell like stale mushrooms.

Bouwland Bush Vine Pinotage 1995   15 C

Not as stunning as it once was, but it'll still warm the cockle of any heart if you ladle it down the throat.

Cape Red, Asda   13.5 B

Nicely drinkable – but for me, only a glass. It is much too eager to please but, that said, good with Chinese food.

Fairview Estate Cabernet Sauvignon Reserve 1995   13 D

Oddly jammy and juicy cabernet.

Fairview Estate Dry Red 1996   13 C

Very juicy and ripe. Great for pasta parties.

Fairview Estate Shiraz 1995   16.5 C

Simply superb the way it gets more and more complex from aroma, through the tastebuds, down the throat and still lingers on the teeth for several minutes. Chocolate, spices, rich damsons, figs and a hint of coffee, this is some shiraz. Not remotely like any Aussie you've ever tasted.

Jennsberg Pinot Noir 1996

This is not at all a bad stab at pinot. Makes you wonder what they do to make it taste like it does in Burgundy.

Kanonkop Bouwland Red 1994

Kumala Shiraz/Cabernet Sauvignon 1996

Landskroon Cabernet Franc 1996

Rich, savoury, charcoal-edged fruit of little resemblance to the Loire specimen except in the faint echo of lead pencil on the finish. But it is very subtle. Much more in evidence is the sheer warmth of the stuff.

Landskroon Pinotage 1995

Rich, textured, burnt rubbery, yet delicious.

Savanha Pinotage/Cabernet 1996

Interesting blend of New World cheekiness (pinotage) and Old World crustiness (cabernet).

Savanha Vineyards Western Cape Shiraz 1996

Stellenzicht Block Zinfandel 1995

Lovely depraved stuff!!! Rich and rounded, vigorous and purposeful, this is a terrifically fulfilling wine. It oozes fruit, style and depth. Has a brazen, bawdy edge.

SOUTH AFRICAN WINE   WHITE

Benguela Current Western Cape Chardonnay 1996

Blue Ridge Chenin Blanc/Sauvignon Blanc 1996 `14.5` `C`

With its smart plastic cork this is an untainted, rich but restrained white of deep charm. Has a gentle creamy edge on the palate. A highly civilised, caressing wine.

Cape White, Asda `14.5` `B`

Faintly cosmetic and a little tarty, this is a splendid aperitif wine whose provenance few will guess.

Fairview Estate Dry Rose 1996 `16` `C`

Possibly the best rose around four quid. Loads of flavour, crisply conceived yet full, and a brilliant finish.

Fairview Estate Dry White 1996 `14` `C`

Crisp and fresh, almost springy-dry-like after an early morning shower but with an exotic lemony hint. Good with food.

Fairview Estate Gewurztraminer 1996 `14` `C`

A lightly spicy gewurz – strong on clean, crisp fruit – and it's great with fish.

Kumala Chenin/Chardonnay 1996 `15` `B`

Rich, cool, fresh to finish but never tart, with lots of initial flavour from eager-to-please fruit. An excellent quaffing wine for the money which also enjoys food.

Muscat de Frontignan Danie de Wet 1996 `16.5` `C`

Only Asda has this wine and all credit to them. A magnificently different aperitif: sweet, honeyed, floral, beautifully balanced and finely cut. Dare to be sweet this Christmas!

Savanha Benguela Current Chardonnay 1996 `16` `C`

Nutty, aromatic, rich, ripe, balanced, swimming in fruit but controlled and finely cut and very firm to finish. Very elegant tippling here.

Savanha Sauvignon Blanc 1996

Flavour, texture, style – a touch expensive close to a fiver, perhaps, since these three virtues are subtly conceived. But the quality is there.

Van Loveren Sauvignon Blanc 1996 `13` `C`

SPANISH WINE   RED

Baron de Ley Rioja Reserva 1991

Expensive but a ripely fruity wine with great classiness. Oodles of flavour.

Bodegas Campillo, Rioja Crianza 1993 `14` `C`

Creamy, banana-y, vanilla-edged red of great interest to grilled meat eaters – it'll be terrific.

Don Darias `14` `B`

El Meson Rioja CVC `13.5` `C`

Rama Corta Tempranillo/Cabernet Sauvignon 1996

A heavy soup impression (initially) gives way to cherry lightness and brightness. Good with lighter meat dishes.

Remonte Navarra Tinto 1995 `14` `B`

Terra Alta Cabernet Sauvignon/Garnacha 1996 `13` `B`

Light enough – on palate as well as pocket.

Terra Alta 'Old Bush Vines' Garnacha 1996   14   C

Soft, ripe, very ready. Has a good earthy touch to it and is a solid glugger and food contender.

Valencia Red, Asda   14   B

Vina Albali, Valdepenas Reserva 1989   15   B

SPANISH WINE   WHITE

La Mancha, Asda   12   A

Moscatel de Valencia, Asda   14   B

Remonte Navarra Blanco 1995   11   B

Valdoro Tierra de Barros Spanish Country White 1996   15   B

Clean fruit with a gentle peachy edge. Bargain bottle for all sorts of grilled food.

Valencia Dry, Asda   12   B

Valencia Medium Dry, Asda   11   B

USA WINE   RED

California Red, Asda   14   B

Grant Canyon Select Red (California)   14 C

**Quivira Dry Creek Valley Cabernet
Cuvee 1992**   16 D

Packed with wild herbs and earthy, faintly spicy cassis-edged fruit. Brilliant stuff.

Talus Californian Merlot 1994   14 D

Rather classy this wine – if not highly typical of California or merlot. But who cares? It's ridiculously easy to quaff.

USA WINE   WHITE

Californian White, Asda   13 B

Grant Canyon Californian White   10.5 C

Talus California Chardonnay 1996   15.5 C

Masses of flavour – like a high-class sweetshop (yet a dry one).

FORTIFIED WINE

Amontillado Sherry Medium Dry, Asda   14 C

Perfect Christmas sherry to warm the toes on after a bout of carol-singing. It's rich, never sweet, and very mature-seeming and wrinkled. Lovely!

Fine Ruby Port, Asda   13.5 D

Fino Sherry, Asda `14` `C`

Dry as a bone, saline as a blow in the face from a fresh sardine, this is great stuff – drink it with grilled prawns.

LBV Port 1990, Asda `14` `D`

Almost as good as the vintage, but sweeter and not so profound, but this is good quaffing port and great with cheese.

Stanton & Killeen, Liqueur Muscat, Rutherglen (half bottle) `15.5` `D`

A rich, sweet, hugely all-embracingly ripe wine.

Tawny Port, Asda `14` `D`

Vintage Character Port, Asda `14` `D`

Sweet and rich and generous at Christmas. Yes, this port is everyone's idea of the perfect uncle.

SPARKLING WINE/CHAMPAGNE

Asti Spumante, Asda `12` `C`

Barramundi Australian Brut `15.5` `D`

Blue Ridge Australian Brut `13` `C`

Cava Brut, Asda `16` `C`

One of the nattiest cavas around. Brilliant value.

Cava Rosado, Asda `15` `C`

Delicious. Quite quite delicious.

Champagne Brut, Asda `13.5` `F`

The lighter style, modern and petticoaty, less serious.

Champagne Rose, Asda `12` `F`

Too playful for such a serious price.

Cordoniu Chardonnay Brut (Spain) `16` `D`

Delicious, classy, lively aperitif or to be drunk with smoked fish.

Cordoniu Premiere Cuvee Brut (Spain) `14` `D`

Cranswick Pinot/Chardonnay Brut (Australia) `16.5` `D`

Tremendous bubbly. Has a biscuity old champagne edge but the final flourish is of light fruit, feather-light and delicious.

Nicholas Feuillate Blanc de Blancs NV `15` `G`

One of the most delicately citric and delicious champagnes around. Expensive elegance.

Nicholas Feuillate Demi-sec Champagne `11` `G`

Touch too fruity/sweet for me.

Scharffenberger Brut (USA) `15` `E`

Light yet rich. Tastes like James Stewart spoke.

Seaview Rose Brut `15` `D`

Light, delicate, amusing.

Veuve Clicquot Yellow Label Brut NV `11` `H`

I wouldn't pay twenty-two quid for it – in spite of its dry drinkability.

Vintage Champagne 1990, Asda

You get a free gift tin with this wine. It's hollow.

BOOTHS

E. H. Booth & Co Limited
4-6 Fishergate
Preston
Lancs
PR1 3LJ
Tel 01772 261701
Fax 01772 204316

What's wonderful.

Wine, where all supermarkets are concerned, is important. But with Booths it's in the blood. Occasionally, post-festive season, they have some fabulous mid-price-range bargain bottles.

What's maddening.

There aren't a lot of branches and they're nowhere near where I live.

ARGENTINIAN WINE RED

Libertad Sangiovese Malbec 1996 `13` `C`
Nice plump texture and soft fruit.

Mission Peak Red `13` `B`
Dry, rather austere.

Valle de Vistalba, Barbera 1995 `14.5` `C`
Lovely mixed blessing of sunshine, herbs, textured fruit and depth.

ARGENTINIAN WINE WHITE

Libertad Chenin Blanc 1996 `14` `C`
Unusually delicious, cloying edge of the fruit makes this a mannered wine but one of charm.

AUSTRALIAN WINE RED

Brown Brothers Tarrango 1996 `13.5` `D`
I just wish it were under four quid, this rubbery, aromatic, soft, well-flavoured wine. It is very versatile – meat or fish – and chills uncomplainingly.

Penfolds Bin 2 Shiraz/Mourvedre 1995 `15.5` `D`
Rich, dry, stylish, this has fluidity of fruit yet tannic firmness of tone. Gorgeous screwcap offers instant drinkability.

Penfolds Bin 407 Cabernet Sauvignon 1994   `14`   `E`

Appealingly perfumed antique leather and blackcurrant, rich tannins jewelling the dry fruit, and an impactful, classy finish. Weak with rich food.

Penfolds Rawsons Retreat Bin 35 1995   `13.5`   `C`

Respectable rather than raunchy.

Plantagenet Mount Barker Shiraz 1994   `13`   `F`

Lovely texture and fruit quality as it enters the mouth but it doesn't give the throat much to enjoy.

Riddoch Cabernet Shiraz, Coonawarra 1994   `13.5`   `D`

Falls away at the end a bit – shouldn't at this price.

Rosemount Estate Shiraz/Cabernet 1996   `15.5`   `C`

So soft and slip-downable it may be a crime.

Wakefield Estate Cabernet Sauvignon, Clare Valley 1994   `15`   `D`

One of the old-fashioned rampant styles of Aussie red, loaded with flavour and depth, but not soppy or puppyish (i.e. all-over-you-soft), so it's great with food.

AUSTRALIAN WINE   WHITE

Barramundi Semillon/Colombard/ Chardonnay NV   `15`   `C`

The ultimate jazzy label fronts the ultimate jazzy wine. Drink it out of a bucket. A mere glass is too restricting.

Booth's Estate Semillon 12 B

David Wynn Dry White 1995 14 C

A light quaff with enough of a lilt on the finish to encourage tumultuous encores.

David Wynn Riesling, Eden Valley 1995 D

Not a typical riesling, and rather highly priced, but decent enough.

Deakin Estate Chardonnay, Victoria 1996 15 D

Ooh, it's luscious and scrumptiously put together. This is the sort of gorgeously soupy chardonnay you serve with poached chicken and mushrooms and take to the patient lying ill in bed – and wham! An hour later the patient is jumping round the room with a happy smile on his face.

Grant Burge Chardonnay, Barossa 1995 E

Clods of flavour, not much subtlety or finesse – but simply superb with complex fish dishes.

Grant Burge Old Vine Semillon, Barossa 1995

Muscular and rippling, deeply tanned and smooth, this is a handsome specimen to drink with rich fish and chicken dishes.

Kingston Chenin Verdelho 1995 14 C

Quirky citric fruit with a fat-edged finish. Touch apricoty? Perhaps. Makes a good appetite-whetter.

Penfolds Clare Valley Organic Chardonnay/ Sauvignon Blanc, 1996

One of the classiest organic whites around: thick fruit of richness and flavour.

Penfolds Clare Valley Organic Chardonnay/ Sauvignon Blanc 1996
`15` `E`

Probably the world's most elegant organic chardonnay/sauvignon blanc link-up.

Penfolds Rawsons Retreat Bin 202 Riesling 1996
`14.5` `C`

Words fail me. (I should never have had the second bottle.)

Penfolds Rawsons Retreat Bin 21 Semillon/Chardonnay/Colombard 1996
`15.5` `C`

Loaded with flavour and rich layers of fruit, it is nevertheless difficult to justify paying more for this wine.

Peter Lehmann Clancy's Chardonnay/ Semillon, Barossa 1996
`14` `E`

Interesting lilt the semillon gives the chardonnay – it seems to stretch it, to make the whole wine seem a riper, rich experience.

Riddoch Chardonnay, Coonawarra 1994
`15` `D`

Great oleaginous texture, great with scallops and suchlike rich sea-food.

St Huberts Yarra Valley Chardonnay, 1994
`15` `E`

Oily, ripe, beautifully balanced as it totters on the edge of over-richness, then acrobatically pulls itself back from the brink. Terrific food wine, developing very well in bottle.

CHILEAN WINE
RED

Carmen Reserve Grande Vidure Cabernet, Maipo 1995
`16` `D`

One of Chile's most velvety, most flavour-packed yet elegant red wines. It is immensely classy and drinkable.

Carmen Reserve Merlot 1995
`17` `D`

Magnificence for little money: superb fruit of great elegance, floral and fruit complexity (herbs, violets, plums and raspberries) and caressing texture.

Cono Sur Pinot Noir 1997
`13.5` `C`

There is a rider attached to my liking of this wine (albeit given a modest rating). I have not tasted the wine finished and filtered as it is on the shelf: rather I have encountered a sample from the winery. It was delicate.

Palmeras Oak Aged Cabernet Sauvignon, Santa Emiliana 1995
`16` `C`

Rich, ready, textured, very classy, this is a terrific wine for the money. It is a great tipple with or without food.

Tierra del Rey Chilean Red
`15` `B`

Good evolved tannins, excellent depth of fruit with alert acidity, and a decent finish of no-hurry-to-quit demeanour. It is immensely drinkable, likeable, charming and good with food.

Vina Linderos Cabernet Sauvignon 1996
`15.5` `D`

Brave the label. It's as inviting as an invitation to a low-key funeral, but the fruit is the opposite of dry or dead. It's delicately ripe, smooth, energetic and lingering.

CHILEAN WINE   WHITE

Andes Peak Chardonnay 1996   `15` `C`

Fills the mouth with an opulence of flavour and ripeness which is scandalously stimulating. Be careful if you offer it to the neighbours. They may stay the night.

Isla Negra Chardonnay, Casablanca Valley 1997   `15` `C`

Ripe, rich, raunchy – but beautifully rippling and rounded.

Via Vigna Chardonnay, Rapel Valley 1997   `15` `C`

Rich and riveting – pear/melon bright – but relieved by a hint of pineapple to the citric edge. Really sloshes it to the tastebuds, this wine.

Vina Tocornal, Rapel Valley 1997   `15` `B`

Terrific style for the money here. Has a subdued richness and classy texture but it never overplays its hand. It stays cool and very stylish.

ENGLISH WINE   WHITE

Epoch V Chapel Down 1995   `13.5` `C`

One of the United Kingdom's most drinkable under-a-fiver bottles. Falls away a bit on the finish, though.

Partnership Dry White, English Wine-growers NV   `13` `C`

Can't see it myself. The dryness, I mean. But it's very pleasant to sip with foreign riff-raff as company to demonstrate the truth of the greenhouse effect on southern England.

FRENCH WINE RED

Abbaye St Hilaire, Coteaux Varois 1994 `13` `B`

Bourgogne Pinot Noir, Cave de Lugny 1994 `11` `D`

Cahors, Cotes d'Olt 1994 `13` `B`

Needs a couple of hours of opening to get it into shape.

Chateau de Canterrane 1980 `13.5` `D`

Chateau du Junca, Haut Medoc 1990 `14.5` `E`

**Chateau la Ferme d'Angludet, Margaux
1993** `12` `E`

Chateau Tourt Choilet, Graves 1990 `10` `E`

Claret, Booths `13.5` `B`

Touches of the dry, very dry, charcoal edge of real claret.

Cote Rotie La Garde 1987 `10` `G`

Cotes de St Mont, Roc des Termes 1994 `13` `C`

Dry and gently earthy.

Cotes du Brulhois, Cave de Donzac 1990 `14` `C`

Good dry herby fruit with decently developed tannins. Excellent with grilled meats.

Cotes du Rhone Villages St Maurice 1995 `13.5` `C`

Not the rich earthy style of Rhone it must be admitted –
though the subtly dry touch of herbs on the finish provides
some cragginess.

Cotes du Ventoux La Falaise 1995 `13` `B`

Only a light cliff to ascend here.

Domaine de Belvezet VdP des Coteaux de l'Ardeche 1995 `13` `C`

Good upfront fruit but a rather sissy finish.

Domaine l'Hortus Cuvee Classique 1995 `14` `D`

Curiously indecisive at first as the fruit can't make up its mind
to become herby and compacted or juicy but in the end this
dualism nicely combines.

Domaine l'Hortus Grande Cuvee 1995 `14` `E`

An expensive bottle but gently impressive with its smoothness
and richness. I would·be inclined to lay it down for a couple
more years.

Echezeaux, Domaine de la Romanee Conti 1990 `10` `H`

Faugeres Gilbert Alquier 1994 `14` `D`

You may say that seven quid for a country bumpkin is a bit
rich. And you'd be right. This wine is richer and better than
many a claret.

Gamay Jardin de la France `11` `B`

Julienas Paul Boutinot 1995 `12` `D`

Mature Margaux Chateau Brane-Cantenac 1977 — 12 F

Lovely tobacco aroma, but the fruit isn't so surprising or brilliant.

Moncenay Pinot Noir, VdP de la Cote d'Or 1994 — 10 C

Really! It almost offends the palate, so earthy is it.

Mourvedre Domaine la Condamine l'Eveque, VdP Cotes du Thongues 1995 — 13 C

Light but has an edgy-rich plum finish.

Nicole Rouge — 8 B

Oak-Aged Claret 1995, Booths — 13 C

Dusty young thing. Like William Hague vinified.

Reserve de Reverend Corbieres Rouge 1994 — 14 B

Vin Rouge, Booths — 14 B

One of the best-value, easiest-to-quaff reds around.

Volnay Joseph Drouhin 1989 — 10 G

Vosne Romanee Cacheux 1991 — 10 G

FRENCH WINE — WHITE

Bergerac Blanc, Booths — 12 B

Sweet – good for grans.

Bergerac Rouge, Booths `13` `B`

Dry, touch austere, a little rustic. Needs food.

Bordeaux Blanc, Booths `12` `B`

Touch of a sweet edge to the initially crisp fruit.

Caves de Berticot Sauvignon Blanc 1994 `13.5` `C`

Caves de Berticot Cotes de Duras Sauvignon 1995 `14.5` `C`

Simply superb clean fresh fruit with sufficient flavour to accompany all fish dishes.

Chapelle de Cray Sauvignon Touraine 1994 `13` `C`

Chateau Beringer Picpoul de Pinet, Coteaux du Languedoc 1996 `13.5` `C`

Good with squid and tomato pie (so Mr Chris Dee, Booth's wine buyer, reckons, and I think he's spot on).

Chateau Lamothe Vincent Bordeaux 1996 `15` `C`

A lovely white bordeaux in the classic Graves style: fresh and mineral-edged. Great with shellfish.

Chateau Roumieu Sauternes, 1990 `15.5` `G`

Drink it now, with creme brulee or fresh fruit (strawberries would be superb with it) or put it down for anything up to fifteen to twenty-five years. It will develop gloriously in bottle and become even more complex and richly honeyed.

Cuvee Classique VdP des Cotes de Gascogne 1996 `15.5` `B`

I love the impishness of white Gascons when they present such easy-drinking, delicious, pineapple-edged fruit. A superb aperitif.

Daniel-Etienne Defaix Chablis, Vieilles Vignes 1994 | 12.5 | F

Seems vegetal and reluctant to please to me. Dry and rather hidebound.

Gaillac Blanc Hardys 1995 | 13.5 | C

Gewurztraminer Turckheim 1995 | 15 | D

Okay, spoil your neighbours with this rose-petal fruity wine. It's delicious, exotic, Thai food-friendly.

James Herrick Chardonnay 1995 | 15 | C

Muscadet sur Lie Domaine du Roc 1995 | 11.5 | C

No, no, I'm being mean. Make it 12 points.

Nicole Blanc | 9 | B

Pinot Blanc Caves de Turckheim 1995 | 15.5 | C

Wonderful price for a terrific pinot of richness and style which will develop well for a couple of years.

Reserve de Reverend Corbieres Blanc 1995 | 13.5 | C

Vin Blanc, Booths | 13 | B

Vouvray Lacheteau 1995 | 15 | C

Dry with a very fruity (pear, lemon and peach) fullness which is quite delicious. The perfect weekend wine with the crossword for company.

GERMAN WINE · WHITE

Liebfraumilch, Booths `13` `B`

**Louis Guntrum Niersteiner Bildstock
Kerner Beerenauslese 1985** `13` `G`

Piesporter Michelsberg, Booths `13.5` `B`

GREEK WINE · RED

Vin de Crete Kourtaki 1995 `13` `B`

HUNGARIAN WINE · WHITE

**Chapel Hill Oaked Chardonnay, Balaton
Boglar NV** `15` `B`

Not a trace of wood, it's all lemon. Thus for sardines, grilled and smoky, this is an utterly divine partner.

Chapel Hill Rheinriesling 1995 `13` `B`

A little unconvincing on the finish.

ITALIAN WINE · RED

Amarone Classico, Brigaldara 1991 `13.5` `G`

Quirkily rich, licoricey, and very prettily textured. But very expensive.

Barolo Giordano 1992 `11` `F`

Capello di Prete Salento, Candido `14.5` `D`

Swirling flavours, soft and full but not overripe.

Chianti Classico Querciabella 1994 `13.5` `E`

Very expensive for haughty drinkability of reasonably well-ordered fruit and tannin. I just would think twice before I paid a tenner for it.

Chianti Classico Querciabella 1994 `14` `E`

Deliciously figgy and licoricey, more like a barolo as it first encounters the tastebuds, then it turns classically Tuscan with a rich finish of terracotta (i.e. baked earth).

Ciro Librandi Classico 1994 `14` `D`

Warm, giving, very hot-blooded and Italian, and very, very soft at heart.

Copertino Castiglione 1992 `14` `C`

Ruche di Castagnole del Monferrato 1994 `16` `F`

Highly perfumed, beautifully fruity, gorgeously shaped – this is a haute couture wine of great class. It is worth twelve quid just to wallow in its subtle complexities and to revel in the joys of ruche, an obscure grape at the best of times.

Salice Salento Candido 1992 `14` `D`

Sangiovese delle Marche Collezione Bodio `12` `B`

ITALIAN WINE WHITE

Frascati Sanantonio 1995 13 C

Trebbiano delle Marche Collezione Bodio 12.5 B

MACEDONIAN WINE RED

Papaver NV 10 B

Light isn't the word for it.

MOLDOVAN WINE RED

Kirkwood Cabernet Merlot 1994 15 B

Very fireside-warm yet rich and with a serious message. The wine is dry yet full of itself – and this self is stylish and individual. Food-friendly and textured.

NEW ZEALAND WINE WHITE

Ponder Estate Sauvignon Blanc, Marlborough 1995 13.5 D

Lovely controlled grassy undertones and richness. The finish is, however, spineless.

Villa Maria Private Bin Chardonnay, Gisborne 1995
`13.5` `D`

Highly drinkable but too highly priced.

Villa Maria Private Bin Chardonnay, Marlborough 1996
`13.5` `D`

Falls a little short of what a six-quid-plus chardonnay should be.

PORTUGUESE WINE RED

Alta Mesa Tinto Estremadura 1995
`15.5` `B`

Brilliant quaffing: soft, slightly rich and flavourful and exceedingly friendly.

Espiga Tinto Estremadura 1995
`13` `C`

Light, almost fruity (but I'm being unkind).

Foral, Douro Tinto Reserva 1994
`13.5` `B`

Food-friendly, dry, touch reluctant to reveal its fruit.

Jose Neiva Estremadura 1994
`13` `B`

Light and cherry-bright.

Quinta das Setencostas 1996
`15` `C`

Very elegant to behold on a dinner table and very elegant to behold in the glass – and in the mouth. A rich smooth brew of some class.

Vinha Nova Vinho de Mesa
`13.5` `B`

Light with dry undertones. Very pleasant tipple.

PORTUGUESE WINE — WHITE

Alta Mesa Estremadura 1995 — 14 B

Soft and brilliantly priced glugging. Real flavour to cope with grilled fish.

Espiga Branco Estremadura 1995 — 14 C

Great flavour and richness here. Excellent food and person wine (i.e. not cooked persons but live conversational ones).

Jose Neiva Estremadura 1994 — 15 B

Real flavour and richness here. Great with chicken and fish.

SOUTH AFRICAN WINE — RED

Capelands Ruby Cabernet, Western Cape 1996 — 13 C

Soft and ripe.

Kumala Cinsault Pinotage 1996 — 16.5 B

Resounds with rich fruit just like a baked pudding set to music (brass section). Big and boisterous.

Western Ridge Cabernet/Shiraz 1996 — 14 C

Has some quiet, determined character under its dry shell.

Western Ridge Ruby Cabernet 1995 — 14.5 B

Really perky food wine – it's not as soppy or as soft as ruby cabernet can be. It has some real assertive characterfulness.

SOUTH AFRICAN WINE WHITE

Altus Sauvignon Blanc 1996 `13` `C`
A very rich less-than-fresh sauvignon.

Kumala Colombard/Sauvignon 1996 `13.5` `B`

Welmoed Sauvignon Blanc, Stellenbosch 1996 `15` `C`
Mustn't grumble here (label apart). This is a firmly fruity wine of great interest to grilled food pyrotechnicians.

Western Ridge Chenin Blanc 1996 `13` `B`
Somewhat earthy to finish.

Western Ridge Sauvignon Blanc 1996 `12` `B`

SPANISH WINE RED

Conde de Valdemar Rioja Crianza 1994 `14` `D`
Calm vanilla undertones. Good with chicken dishes.

Guelbenzu Jardin 1995 `15.5` `C`

Juvene Rioja Tinto 1996 `14.5` `C`
I love the food-compatibility of this wine: dry, earthy, rich, yet, as it finally quits the throat, plummy.

Mont Marcal Cabernet Sauvignon, Penedes 1991 `14.5` `D`
Warm, balanced, herby-edged, rich-textured and excellent with anything meaty off a grill.

Orobio Tempranillo Rioja 1995

Very attractive texture, soft, velvety and rolling, and good rich depth of fruit. Lovely glug.

Tapas Red

Vina Alarba, Catalayud 1995

Touch of sweetness on the finish will help with food if not with glugging.

Vinas de Gain Rioja, Artadi 1994

Striking, bold, dry yet comfortably fruity, mellow, softly rich and well-textured, this is a handsome rioja without wrinkles or arthritis.

SPANISH WINE WHITE

Con Class Sauvignon 1996

A superb specimen of grassy but delicious fruity richness yet crispness and satisfyingly balanced feel. Yes – delicious.

Estrella Moscatel de Valencia

Either as a dessert wine or as a sweet, floral aperitif, this wine is brilliant. It is sunshine itself, packed into a bottle.

Rioja Domino de Montalvo Blanco 1994

I find this wine agreeable as it quits the throat but its mode of entry to the mouth is gawky and unconvincing. Okay wine rather than orgasmic for six quid.

Santa Lucia Lightly Oaked Viura, Manchuela 1995
`15.5` `B`

Superb wine for grilled fish or just for glugging. Full of flavour and style.

Santara Chardonnay, Conca de Barbera 1995
`16.5` `C`

This is one of the very few chardonnays under four quid which gives Chile a run for the same money: rich, perfectly developed, complex, utterly delicious. It has plot, character and wit. It's a literary gem.

TASMANIAN WINE   WHITE

Ninth Island Chardonnay 1994
`14` `E`

URUGUAYAN WINE   RED

Castol Pujol Tannat 1994
`14` `C`

Somewhat expensive and not as rampant as previous vintages, but a perfect grilled-food bottle.

FORTIFIED WINE

Amontillado, Booths
`14` `C`

Lovely rich flavour here. Great as a warming aperitif.

Churchill's White Port
`13` `E`

A golden, dry aperitif. Dry yet rich. Curious stuff, really.

Crusted 1989 Bottled Port, Booths   15 E

Terrific value. Real mature vintage port style, rich and hugely enveloping, but without the equally rich price tag. A well-spent tenner here.

Finest Reserve Port, Booths   14 E

Rich and sweet, it's great with blue cheese, fresh fruit, or simply to lift a blue mood.

Fino Sherry, Booths   15 C

Lustau Old East India Sherry   13.5 E

Manzanilla, Booths   14 C

Nutty and saline – good with grilled prawns and grilled almonds.

Niepoort Ruby Port   13 E

Sweet but never soppy.

San Amilio, Pedro Ximenes Sherry   16 F

The colour of boot polish and almost as thick as it coats the tongue with a figgy, molasses-rich sweetness of fruit. Try it with Christmas cake or pudding. It will be a revelation.

SPARKLING WINE/CHAMPAGNE

Barramundi Sparkling (Australia)   15.5 D

Bollinger Grande Annee 1989   9 H

Don't buy this. It's not good enough – and at this price it's obscene. Buy the Deutz from New Zealand (qv) – it knocks Bollinger into a cocked chapeau.

Champagne Brossault Rose `11.5` `F`

Champagne Brut, Booths `14` `F`

Cremant de Loire Brut Rose, Cray 1993 `16` `C`

One of the best wines at Booths. Only a delicate shade of 'onion-skin' as the French put it, a race of gourmands who would drink this wine as an aperitif or with smoked salmon. Snap up this bargain quick!

Deutz Marlborough Cuvee (New Zealand) `15.5` `E`

Considerably more refined and delicately delicious (and well priced) than the champagne of the same name.

Mont Marcal Cava 1992 `13` `D`

Mont Marcal Cava Extra Brut 1989 `13` `D`

An oddity. Rich and very toffee-ish.

Mont Marcal Gran Reserva 1989 `15` `E`

Here the maturity of the wine is an advantage. It is deep and delicious and very stylish.

Palau Brut (Spain) `14` `D`

Piper Heidsieck Brut `13` `G`

Piper Heidsieck Demi Sec `11` `F`

Prosecco Zonin `14` `C`

Seaview Rose Brut `15` `D`

Quite delicious.

BUDGENS

Budgens Stores Limited
PO Box 9
Stonefield Way
Ruislip
Middlesex
HA4 0JR
Tel 0181 422 9511
Fax 0181 422 1596

What's wonderful.

For the motorist, or someone who lives near a certain few selected Q8 and BP/Mobil petrol stations, this retailer offers the chance to fill up with something a little more fruity than lead-free 2-star. These forecourt enterprises, as yet in their extreme infancy, are called Budgens Express and there is a small range of wines on offer therein. The other wonderful thing about Budgens is that in nine years I have never had a single letter complaining about them.

What's maddening.

In nine years I have never had a single letter complimenting this retailer. Do any readers of this book buy wines here? I wish I knew.

SEE STOP PRESS SECTION AT END OF BOOK FOR LAST-MINUTE ADDITIONS TO THIS RETAILER'S RANGE.

AUSTRALIAN WINE RED

Dreamtime Mataro Grenache 1996 `12` `C`
Rather muddy, ill-defined and crude.

Penfolds Bin 389 1994 `14` `F`
Thickly textured, softly yet richly tannic, deep swirling complex acids and big big fruit. Expensive treat for the Christmas bird. I've tasted gravies less rich.

AUSTRALIAN WINE WHITE

Brown Brothers Dry Muscat 1994 `13.5` `C`
Delightful aperitif: light and flowery.

Dreamtime Trebbiano 1996 `13.5` `C`
Dreadful name – the fruit is less so.

Normans Lone Gum Chenin Blanc 1996 `14` `C`
The subtle quirkiness and oily texture make a delicious change from chardonnay.

**Rosemount Estate Hunter Valley
Chardonnay 1996** `15.5` `D`
One of the most sublimely elegant and sophisticated of Aussie's chardonnays. Classy stuff.

**Rosemount Estate Semillon/Chardonnay
1996** `14` `D`
Balanced, unbashful, excellent with fish.

Rymill Coonawarra Botrytis Gewurztraminer 1996 (half bottle)

Wonderful half bottle for desserts with its layers of honey, pineapple and ripe melony sweetness. It will also develop brilliantly in bottle for the next ten years.

AUSTRIAN WINE RED

Blauer Zweigelt 1993

Better than beaujolais for chilled drinking – drier too.

BULGARIAN WINE RED

Stara Zagora Merlot/Cabernet Sauvignon 1994

Fantastic value: rich, deep yet not too juicy or overripe, full-flavoured with a hint of freshness. Terrific value.

BULGARIAN WINE WHITE

Domaine Boyar Vintage Blend Chardonnay/ Sauvignon Blanc, Preslav 1995

Excellent proposition, both on the pocket and in the glass, for all sorts of grilled fish.

Preslav Chardonnay/Sauvignon Blanc 1995

Thoroughly appetite-arousing and food friendly. Very good balance of grape styles here.

CHILEAN WINE — WHITE

Vina Casablanca Sauvignon Blanc 1996 `15.5` `C`

Balanced and bonny. Great with charcoal-grilled prawns.

Vina Tarapaca Chardonnay 1996 `13.5` `C`

Convincing up-front but a touch loose on the finish. I'm wondering if I'm being hypercritical but it is less poised than other '96 Chilean chardonnays.

CYPRIOT WINE — RED

Keo Othello `10` `C`

Very ripe, too ripe for this tippler.

FRENCH WINE — RED

Abbaye Saint Hilaire Coteaux Varois 1995 `14` `B`

Good Provencal-like slurping here. The fruit is dotted with thyme bushes which scratch as they go down. A great food tipple.

Bourgogne Rouge Vienot 1995 `12` `D`

Cahors Marquis Rocadour 1995 `14` `C`

Rich plum fruit with a dry cherry finish. Good rustic tippling, well priced, great with food.

Chateau Bassanel Minervois 1995 `13` `C`
Very dry and austere.

Chateau de Malijay Cotes du Rhone 1995 `13.5` `C`
Rhone in the lighter style of roasted earthiness.

Claret, Budgens `13` `B`
Light and dry.

Corbieres Chateau Saint-Louis 1995 `12.5` `C`

Costieres de Nimes Fontanilles 1995 `14` `C`
Real earth, clodfuls of it, but great with lamb chops, off the
grill, rich with herbs (the wine is, too).

**Cotes du Rhone Villages Cuvee Reserve
1996** `12` `C`

Crozes Hermitage 1994 `10` `C`
Hmm . . . Words fail me . . .

Domaine St Roch VdP de l'Aude `10` `B`
Bland and inoffensive – it doesn't *go* anywhere.

Faugeres Jean Jean 1994 `12` `B`
Somewhat meagre and a touch constipated.

Gargantua Cotes du Rhone 1996 `12` `C`

Gigondas Domaine de la Mourielle 1995 `14` `D`
Soft, earthy, rich, touch leathery – this is prime gigondas for
tired feet and limbs generally.

**L'Esprit de Teyssier Bordeaux Superieur
1994** `14` `C`

Le Haut Colombier VdP de la Drome 1995

Has dryness but not a lot else to its earthiness.

Rouge de France Special Cuvee NV

Basic; indeed it's less basic than it needs to be. Couldn't we have just a little more fruit? Please?

Vin de Pays d'Agenais Rouge 1994

Vin de Pays de l'Aude

FRENCH WINE WHITE

Blanc de Blancs Special Cuvee

Bordeaux Blanc Sec 1996

Brilliant price for such clean crisp fruit. Perfect warm-weather tipple and food wine.

**Bourgogne Chardonnay Charles Vienot
1996**

Has some good warm fruit. Not at all bad for a white burgundy under a fiver/ More like this please!

**Chardonnay Dulac VdP l'Ile de Beaute
1996**

Fair richness of fruit undercut by sanely balanced acids. Great value here.

**Domaine Barroque VdP des Cotes de
Gascogne 1996**

Impishly fruity (melon, pineapple, pear) and fresh to finish. Terrific-value quaffing.

Domaine de Villeroy-Castellas Sauvignon Blanc 1996

`11` `C`

Somewhat ill-defined.

Domaine l'Argentier Terret VdP des Cotes de Thau 1995

`13.5` `B`

Very faint earthy edge to basic fruit which is not complex but neither is it overwrought.

Domaine Pascaly VdP de l'Aude

`12` `B`

James Herrick Chardonnay VdP d'Oc 1996

`14.5` `C`

Gorgeous melony fruit, crisp acidity, soft texture, lingering finish. Can you ask more of an under-a-fiver chardonnay?

Laroche Grand Cuvee Chardonnay 1995

`12` `C`

Improved in bottle a bit since I first tasted it. More excitingly textured and a deeper, creamier edge to the fruit.

Macon Ige 1996

`13.5` `C`

Hints of class – at a price.

Rully Blanc Raoul Clercet 1992

`13` `G`

Very expensive but very maturely fruity, vegetal, and ready for any sort of chicken and fish dish.

Sancerre Les Chasseignes 1994

`10` `E`

Simply very poor value.

Valblanc VdP du Gers Colombard 1995

`14.5` `B`

Fruity, simple, fun, very elegantly bottled (chic isn't the word for it) and excellent quaffing. Very good value.

GERMAN WINE — RED

Dornfelder 1994 `11` `C`
Appley, light, rather thin.

GERMAN WINE — WHITE

Bereich Bernkastel Mosel Saar Ruwer 1995 `11` `C`

Flonheimer Adelberg Auslese 1994 `13` `C`
Sweet? Almost – but as an aperitif I enjoy fruit like this (in small doses).

Rudesheimer Rosegarten Gustav Adolf Schmitt, Nahe 1995 `10` `C`

Schmitt von Schmitt Niersteiner Spatlese 1995 `13` `C`
A glass would by no means be despised if the weather was sultry and the company sexy.

GREEK WINE — RED

Vin de Crete Red, Kourtaki 1995 `13` `B`

GREEK WINE WHITE

Kourtaki Vin de Crete 1995

Crete was the place I once tasted the worst wine in the world: a heavily oxidised red retsina of such inflammability it could have usefully gone into a paraffin lamp. This white, dry example of Cretan oenology is not so vile.

HUNGARIAN WINE RED

Hungarian Cabernet Sauvignon 1994 `12` `B`

HUNGARIAN WINE WHITE

Hungarian Chardonnay 1993 `10` `B`

ITALIAN WINE RED

Avignonesi Vino Nobile de Montepulciano 1993 `12` `E`

Vastly overpriced for a stylish, dry, highly drinkable wine.

Barolo Villademonte 1992 `10` `E`

Merlot del Veneto, Ricordi 1995 `12` `C`

Rather vegetal.

Merlot del Veneto Zonin `12` `B`

Nexus Grave del Friuli San Simeone 1994 `14` `E`
Elegant, rich, warm, enveloping. But – very pricey.

ITALIAN WINE WHITE

**Colombara Soave Classico, Zenato
1995** `15` `C`
One of the cutest soaves around. Really lives up to its
name: a suave, sophisticated, flavoursome, balanced, stylish
wine.

**Frascati Superiore Casale dei Grillo
1996** `13` `C`
Has some attractive nuttiness to the fruit. Not an austere
specimen by any means.

NEW ZEALAND WINE RED

**Montana Cabernet Sauvignon/Merlot
1995** `14.5` `D`
Grass meets wet earth, but the result, though interesting, is not
exactly paydirt. A dry, vegetal wine which needs food.

Waimanu Premium Dry `5` `C`
Totally disgusting (almost – well, it gets 5).

NEW ZEALAND WINE — WHITE

Nobilo Fall Harvest Sauvignon Blanc 1996 — 11 D
One of the least compelling New Zealand sauvignons I've tasted.

Waimanu Premium Dry — 13 C
Somewhat gawky of gait but tries to please – maybe it would be more interesting if it didn't give a damn.

PORTUGUESE WINE — RED

Alta Mesa 1994 — 14 B
Decent glugging stuff – cheap enough.

Dao Reserve Dom Ferraz 1992 — 11 C
Used to be a cracker this wine, got sloppy in its old age. Pull your socks up, Dom!!

PORTUGUESE WINE — WHITE

Alta Mesa White 1994 — 14 B

ROMANIAN WINE — RED

Pietroasa Vineyards Young Vatted Cabernet Sauvignon 1995 — 16 B
Has wonderful fruity, tobacco-tinged, blackcurranty richness yet

easy-to-swallow zippiness and cheekiness. A smashing, quaffable wine which is also very food-friendly.

ROMANIAN WINE · WHITE

Tarnava Valley Chardonnay 1995   15 C

I've tasted white burgundies five times more expensive which are less profoundly fruity than this food-friendly bottle. The muscat in the blend is a brilliant sleight of winemaking skilldoggery. *[Ed note: sic.]*

SOUTH AFRICAN WINE · RED

Clear Mountain Cape Red   11 B

Clear Mountain Pinotage   12.5 C

Warm, soupy, very adolescently fruity.

Helderberg Shiraz 1996   15 C

Very soupy but softly spiced and richly flavoured on the finish. A potent competition to any Aussie shiraz – even one a few quid more.

SOUTH AFRICAN WINE · WHITE

Clear Mountain Chenin Blanc   13.5 B

Helderberg Sauvignon Blanc 1996   14 C

Rich and very thickly textured. Delicious with a whole range of foods from salmon through pasta to chicken.

SPANISH WINE   RED

Diego de Almagro Valdepenas 1993   `13.5` `B`

Amusing label – good to take it to a party. The wine inside?
Great with burnt sausages.

**Marques de Caro Garnacha Reserva
1991**   `12` `B`

Old-fashioned Spanish gut-swill.

Marques de Caro Merlot 1995   `11` `C`

Least leathery merlot I've ever tasted – more like muslin.

Palacio de la Vega Crianza 1994   `16.5` `C`

Rich, dark, textured, soft yet vivid and muscular, this is a
terrific food wine as well as offering very high-class but not
expensive tippling.

Rioja Don Marino NV   `10` `C`

Thin and appley with a touch of tired earth.

SPANISH WINE   WHITE

Moscatel de Valencia Vittore   `14.5` `B`

Very sweet and limpidly honeyed with a thickly textured level
of fruit which makes for a perfect accompaniment to Christmas
cake and pudding.

SWISS WINE   WHITE

Chasselas Romand 1996

Has the virtue of being screwcapped, so no nasty tree-bark cork
to gum up the works. Alas, the fruit in the bottle is a little
screwy, too.

USA WINE   RED

E & J Gallo Turning Leaf Zinfandel 1994   12 D

Glen Ellen Cabernet Sauvignon 1994   14 C

Smooth with a touch of ripe plums on the finish. Elegantly cut
and well polished.

Sutter Home Zinfandel 1994   12 C

USA WINE   WHITE

E & J Gallo Turning Leaf Chardonnay 1994   14 D

FORTIFIED WINE

Amontillado Sherry, Budgens

Touch of sweet fruit to the rich, off-dry style makes for an
intriguing and deliciously different aperitif.

Manzanilla La Guita

Not as bone-dry or heavenly nuttily crisp as other examples I've tasted.

SPARKLING WINE/CHAMPAGNE

Blanquette de Limoux Blanc de Blancs Divinaude `14` `E`

Deliciously rich and creamy, nutty and well-honed. Rather drink it than many a so-called grande marque champagne.

Brossault Rose Champagne `11.5` `F`

Champagne Pierre Callot Blanc de Blancs Grand Cru Avize `12` `G`

Expensive if a trifle biscuity and classic (in intention if not entirely in execution).

Germain Brut Reserve Champagne `13` `G`

Lemony and fresh to finish.

Lindauer Sparkling (New Zealand) `13` `E`

Getting expensive for the simplicity of the style.

Seppelt Great Western Brut (Australia) `14` `D`

Good price, excellent style. Elegant bubbly at a bargain price.

CO-OPERATIVE WHOLESALE SOCIETY LIMITED

CO-OPERATIVE WHOLESALE SOCIETY LIMITED
PO Box 53
New Century House
Manchester
M60 4ES
Tel 0161 834 1212
Fax 0161 834 4507

What's wonderful.

There is regular razzmatazz in the Co-op's wine department. Almost on a monthly basis there's a wine well under three quid, and I mean *well* under, which is a lip-smackin' bargain.

What's maddening.

Finding a branch which stocks the Co-op's £2.29 bargain wine of the month can sometimes tax the ingenuity of readers who find no difficulty in solving an Araucarian crossword in the *Guardian* in ten minutes and possess an advanced education in ordnance survey map reading.

SEE STOP PRESS SECTION AT END OF BOOK FOR LAST-MINUTE ADDITIONS TO THIS RETAILER'S RANGE.

ARGENTINIAN WINE RED

Argentine Malbec Sangiovese 1996, Co-op   `15.5` `C`

Has an aromatic pungency reminiscent of strawberry jam and this rich theme is carried through the fruit – except it is dry to finish. An individual, very interesting wine.

Graffigna Shiraz/Cabernet Sauvignon 1995   `15.5` `B`

Dry, tobaccoey, rich, deep, characterful – this is an excellent red for anyone's money. A superb wine for all sorts of grilled meats.

Lost Pampas Cabernet Malbec 1996   `14` `C`

Mission Peak Argentine Red NV   `13` `B`

Dry, rather austere.

Weinert Malbec 1991   `17` `E`

An expensive treat of such mature, tannic richness and lingering muscle-bound fruit that it cries out for food. Great with meat and cheese dishes. The texture is world-class. Puts scores of major bordeaux to shame. At top Co-ops only.

ARGENTINIAN WINE WHITE

Argentine Sauvignon-Torrontes 1996, Co-op   `15` `C`

Balbi Syrah Rose 1996 `13.5` `C`

Needs to be well chilled for its richness to shine through. It's certainly a good food wine – fish or meat – but for me it's a mite too cloyingly fruity as a general glugging wine. Only at Co-op Superstores.

Lost Pampas Oak-aged Chardonnay 1996 `14` `C`

Mission Peak Argentine White NV `14.5` `B`

AUSTRALIAN WINE RED

Australian Cabernet Sauvignon 1995, Co-op `14.5` `C`

Unusually brisk, dry Aussie cabernet with developed tannic softness, strength, and character. A handsome partner for roasts, grills, cheeses.

Australian Red, Co-op `12` `B`

Jammy and juicy.

Baileys Shiraz 1994 `16` `D`

Barramundi Shiraz/Merlot `14` `C`

Very juicy style with a burnt edge.

Chateau Reynella Cabernet/Merlot 1993 `17` `D`

Hardys Nottage Hill Cabernet Sauvignon/ Shiraz 1995 `13.5` `C`

Hmm . . . okay, but a fiver?

Jacaranda Hill Grenache 1996, Co-op `14.5` `C`

Kasbah Shiraz/Malbec/Mourvedre 1993 `13` `C`

Co-op Superstores only.

Kingston Shiraz/Mataro 1996 `13` `C`

Good pasta wine with its richness and pacy fruit. But it is a very fruity wine.

Leasingham Domaine Cabernet Malbec 1993 `15` `E`

Lindemans Bin 45 Cabernet Sauvignon 1994 `14.5` `D`

Woodstock Grenache 1995 `13` `D`

Cinnamon toast! Co-op Superstores only.

AUSTRALIAN WINE WHITE

Australian Chardonnay 1996, Co-op `15` `C`

Brilliant texture and combination of melony fruit and pineapple/citric acidity.

Australian White, Co-op `14` `B`

Raw, basic, good lemony edge and attractive value. And very attractive company for fish.

Best's Late Harvest Muscat 1995 `14.5` `D`

Butterfly Ridge Sauvignon Blanc/Chenin Blanc 1996   `14` `C`

The perfect grilled-fish wine. Has a rich, almost cloying depth of clinging flavour and with a mackerel, say, I'd be well satisfied. Only at Co-op Superstores.

Hardys Nottage Hill Chardonnay 1994   `17` `C`

Best vintage yet. Lovely textured, oily fruit, never overdone or blowsy and a buttery, melony finish of surefooted delivery. Terrific value for such classy drinking.

Jacaranda Hill Chenin Verdelho 1996, Co-op   `14` `C`

Kingston Colombard Chardonnay 1995   `14` `C`

Decently fruity with touches of depth to its texture which make it good with food. Only at Co-op Superstores.

Koala Creek Dry White 1996   `14` `B`

Leasingham Domaine Semillon 1993   `16` `D`

Pineapple and lime undertones to the firmly textured, buttery frontal assault of the fruit which is wonderful with squid dishes – and gently spiced Thai fish dishes. Co-op Superstores only.

Loxton Low Alcohol Chardonnay NV   `0` `B`

Murrumbidgee Estate Fruity Australian White NV   `12.5` `B`

Richmond Grove Verdelho, Cowra Vineyard 1993   `15.5` `D`

AUSTRIAN WINE — WHITE

Winzerhaus Gruner Veltliner 1995 | 13.5 | C

BRAZILIAN WINE — RED

Amazon Cabernet Sauvignon | 13.5 | C

BRAZILIAN WINE — WHITE

Amazon Chardonnay | 11 | C

BULGARIAN WINE — RED

Bulgarian Vintners' Reserve Cabernet Sauvignon, Rousse 1990 | 13.5 | C

Touch on the dull side as it ages and boringly reminisces about a glorious youth.

Domaine Boyar Pomorie Cabernet Merlot NV | 15 | B

As a general glug, and party wine, this wine has that added dimension of elegance, richness and dry food-friendliness which will keep people drinking. It is difficult to believe the quality for the money.

Lovico Suhindol Merlot Reserve 1991

A roast-lamb wine. It's rich, ripe, mature, and the tannins are completely softened.

Lyaskovets Cabernet Sauvignon 1990

A mature, perfectly weighted, hugely gluggable yet grilled meat-friendly red of class, style, depth and savouriness. The label sucks a bit but you may confidently slurp.

Rousse Cabernet Sauvignon/Cinsault
Country Wine

Russe Cabernet Sauvignon

Has a dry, wry twinkle in its eye under its soupy ripeness. Very drinkable.

The Bulgarian Vintners Sliven Merlot/
Pinot Noir

Simple slurping with decent fruit. Not much evidence of varietal oomph from the merlot but the pinot nicely pricks the palate. Terrific value.

BULGARIAN WINE WHITE

Domaine Boyar Preslav Chardonnay/
Sauvignon Blanc 1996

Utterly seductive blend of buttery chardonnay with green lime-fruited sauvignon. Superb to glug, to swig with fish, to bathe in – if you've a mind. And at £2.89 you don't need to be obscenely well-heeled. Only at Co-op Superstores.

Lyaskovets Chardonnay 1996

A rich, well-textured wine of great interest to fish grillers.

Pomorie Chardonnay Aligote

Delicious crisp simplicity with a hint of sweet ripe melon on the finish.

CHILEAN WINE RED

Chilean Cabernet Sauvignon, Curico Valley, Co-op

What polish! What hauteur! For grace, flavour, texture and effortless smoothness for the money, this is good enough to be the house red wine at a Michelin 3-star restaurant.

Four Rivers Cabernet Sauvignon 1995

Another fantastic Co-op bargain. This is no run-of-the-mill cabernet (although it has classic touches of pepper) for there is an immense flourish of bright brambly fruit on the finish. A lovely sustaining glug.

La Fortuna Malbec 1996

Rich, very dry, characterful and gently rustic. But it has already improved since I first tasted it in November 1996 and will continue to do so over the next twenty months and rate maybe 16 points or more in time. Co-op Superstores only.

Long Slim Cabernet/Merlot 1994

Improving considerably in bottle, this wine oozes class, depth, flavour, terrific fruit and tannic balance and a lingering presence of wines twice the price.

Santa Carolina Merlot 1994

Tierra del Rey Chilean Red NV

Fantabulous for the dosh. Has good evolved tannins, excellent depth of fruit with alert acidity, and a decent finish of no-hurry-to-quit demeanour. It is immensely drinkable, likeable, charming and good with food.

CHILEAN WINE WHITE

Caliterra Casablanca Chardonnay 1994

Superb rich edge to the final thrust of the elegant fruit. Impressive wine with gusto, flavour and real style.

Four Rivers Chardonnay 1996 `13.5` `C`

Loose and a touch gauche but it will perform well with food (even if at £3.99 it is rather outclassed by many other Chileans).

Long Slim White Chardonnay/Semillon 1996 `16` `B`

It has a blowsy richness of depth but this isn't entirely disreputable for the mannered acidity on the finish turns a louche wine charming – if rather brassy to begin.

Santa Carolina Chardonnay 1996 `17` `C`

I love this wine. It is so well-flavoured, rich yet never overblown, stylishly balanced and really convincingly textured. Loads of class here. Only at Co-op Superstores and Supermarkets.

Tierra del Rey Chilean White NV `15.5` `B`

Utterly delicious, rich-edged fruit of style and flavour. A cracking companion to fish, poultry, salads and animated, food-less conversation.

Vina Casablanca Sauvignon Blanc 1996 `15.5` `C`

One of the most elegant sauvignons around: stylish, prim, quietly rich, fresh and beautifully well-textured. Only at Co-op Superstores.

CHINESE WINE RED

Dragon Seal Cabernet Sauvignon 1993 `14` `C`

CHINESE WINE WHITE

Dragon Seal Chardonnay 1993 `14` `C`

ENGLISH WINE WHITE

Denbies English Table Wine 1992 `10` `C`

FRENCH WINE RED

Bad Tempered Cyril Tempranillo/Syrah NV `14` `C`

The label alone is worth giving to a wine snob. The fruit is simple, bright, soft with a hint of earthy dryness, and very drinkable.

Barton & Guestier Margaux Tradition 1992 `13` `E`

Beaujolais Villages Domaine Granjean 1995   `12` `C`

Soft and drinkable but why pay a fiver for it when the Co-op has such brilliant £2.99 wines of greater fruity excitement? Only at Co-op Superstores.

Bergerac Rouge, Co-op   `12` `B`

Somewhat dry and austere, but okay with food.

Cabernet Sauvignon VdP d'Oc, Co-op   `13` `B`

Rather dry and austere.

Cahors, Co-op   `12` `C`

Dry, reluctant to enchant. Only at Co-op Superstores.

Chateau Cissac 1986   `11` `F`

Chateau Fourtanet 1993   `14.5` `D`

Classic dryness from Castillon with superb compatibility with roast meats. Co-op Superstores only.

Chateau Pierrousselle Bordeaux 1996   `14` `C`

A terrific little bordeaux for the money with rich deep tannins. Great with grilled meats. The suppleness of the fruit nicely accompanies these tannins.

Claret, Co-op   `12` `B`

Cotes de Beaune Villages Jules Vignon 1995   `10` `D`

Cotes du Luberon, Co-op   `11` `B`

Only at Co-op Superstores.

Cotes du Rhone, Co-op   `13` `B`

Very attractive, inky-red. Not a deal of complexity and it isn't typically earthy.

Cotes du Roussillon, Co-op `15` `B`

Cotes du Ventoux, Co-op `14` `B`

Crozes Hermitage Louis Mousset 1994 `13.5` `C`

Domaine de Conquet Merlot 1994 `14` `C`

Has dryness and a certain richness which show their best with rich grilled vegetables and meats.

Domaine de Hauterive, Cotes du Rhone 1995 `13.5` `C`

Pleasant and soft – that's all there is to it.

Fitou, Co-op `13` `C`

Decent enough – with good earthy fruit and appealing tannins.

Fleurie, Mommessin 1995 `12.5` `D`

Hardys Bordeaux Rouge 1995 `13.5` `C`

An Aussie's idea of bordeaux. It isn't the classicist's. Co-op Superstores only.

Medoc Vieilles Vignes 1993 `10` `C`

Stringy and gawky.

Meffre Oak-Aged Cotes du Rhone 1995 `14` `C`

Real weight of teeth-gripping fruit which is rather juicy, curiously, on the finish. Co-op Superstores only.

Merlot VdP d'Oc, Co-op `14` `B`

Dry, somewhat restrained on the warmth it radiates, but thoroughly satisfying (and well priced) with bangers and mash.

Minervois, Co-op   13   B

Good value for large parties of pasta eaters.

Morgon, Les Charmes 1994   13.5   D

Moulin a Vent Pierre Leduc 1995   13   D

Quite classy in its own way (i.e. beaujolais). But pricey. Only
at Co-op Superstores.

Nuits St Georges, Pierre Leduc 1994   10   E

Dull and pricey. I'd rather drink Cola. Only at Co-op
Superstores.

Oak-Aged Claret, Co-op   13.5   C

Oak-Aged Cotes du Rhone 1995, Co-op   13.5   C

Pommard, Pierre Leduc 1994   10   F

Boring and expensive. Only a clot buys a wine like this at this
price. Only at Co-op Superstores.

St Emilion, Bernard Taillan (half bottle)   13   C

Valreas Domaine de la Grande Bellane
1995 (organic)   14.5   D

An organic, vegetarian wine – a rare double appeal of ethics
and ecological extremity – and it is very, very drinkable. It is a
touch smug and pleased with itself, even mannerly, but as it is
so easy to like it isn't earthy and bad-tempered. Only at Co-op
Superstores.

Vin de Pays d'Oc Cabernet Merlot   14   C

A very cherry/plum wine of simplicity, charm and direct
drinkability. Hasn't the robustness to counterpunch with rich
food, but it's an attractive mouthful, chilled too. Only at Co-op
Superstores.

Vin de Pays de l'Aude, Co-op `10` `B`

Vin de Pays de l'Herault Rouge, Co-op `14` `B`

Very, very friendly. Dry and warm wine with a juicy touch on the finish.

Winter Hill Red 1995 `15` `B`

FRENCH WINE WHITE

Alsace Gewurztraminer 1995 `15.5` `C`

It's difficult to think of a more delicious start to an evening or with a Thai take-away. It's spicy, roseate, utterly delicious. Only at Co-op Superstores and Supermarkets.

Bergerac Blanc, Co-op `11` `B`

Chablis, Les Vignerons de Chablis 1995 `12` `E`

Drinkable but frightfully expensive.

Chateau la Jaubertie Bergerac Blanc 1995 `14.5` `C`

Rich, well-textured, rather more fat than bergeracs normally are but this is all to the good. A plump, English-inspired wine.

Chateau Pierrousselle Entre Deux Mers 1996 `14.5` `C`

Quietly classy. Doesn't mess about trying to be something it isn't. It's simply a good shellfish wine.

Domaine de Haut Rauly Monbazillac 1994 (half bottle) `14.5` `C`

Fair Martina Vermentino NV `14.5` `C`

Fleur du Moulin Chardonnay VdP d'Oc 1996 `13.5` `C`

Light, floral, peachy – a simple glugging chardonnay of easy-going charm.

Hermitage Blanc, Les Nobles Rives 1992 `13` `F`

Le Galet Reserve Chardonnay, VdP d'Oc 1995 `13` `D`

Rather overpriced. Co-op Superstores only.

Les Pavois d'Or, Sauternes (half bottle) `13` `D`

Montagny Premier Cru 1995 `11` `D`

Muscadet de Sevre et Maine Sur Lie Domaine de la Maillardiere 1995 `10` `C`

No thrills here – or frills.

Philippe de Baudin Chardonnay 1994 `15` `C`

Premieres Cotes de Bordeaux, Co-op `13` `C`

Rose d'Anjou, Co-op `13.5` `B`

A delicate but assertive rose. Most attractive grilled-food wine.

Sauvignon Blanc Bordeaux, Co-op `13` `B`

VdP d'Oc Chardonnay, Co-op `12` `C`

Vin de Pays de l'Herault Blush `10` `C`

About as demanding as a piece of candy – except the pocket is asked for too much contribution.

Vin de Pays de Vaucluse Chardonnay/ Viognier NV
15.5 **B**

Fabulous well-ordered marriage of grapes and a real steal at the price. Terrific breadth to the fruit, to the texture, to the balance and to the finish – everywhere, in fact, except the price tag. A non-vintage wine but it is all fresh '96 juice. Only at Co-op Superstores.

Vin de Pays des Cotes de Gascogne, Co-op
13.5 **B**

Excellent chilled tipple.

Vin de Pays des Cotes des Pyrenees Orientales NV, Co-op
14 **B**

Perfect little grilled-food companion. Has a lilting drinkability.

Viognier VdP d'Oc 1994
13 **C**

Winter Hill White 1995
13.5 **B**

GERMAN WINE RED

Dornfelder, Co-op
13 **C**

GERMAN WINE WHITE

Bad Bergzaberner Kloster Liebfrauenberg Auslese 1994
15 **C**

Forster Schnepfenflug Riesling Kabinett 1995
12 **C**

Co-op Superstores only.

Graacher Himmelreich Riesling Spatlese 1994

14 | C

Treat with respect. Yes, the fruit is off-dry and ripe but there's some lovely sherbety acidity, deliciously citric, and this makes the wine a superb aperitif. Only at Co-op Superstores and Supermarkets.

Morio Muskat, Co-op

12.5 | B

Muller Thurgau, Co-op

10 | B

Rudesheimer Rosengarten 1994, Co-op

13 | B

GREEK WINE   RED

Vin de Crete Red, Kourtaki 1995

13 | B

HUNGARIAN WINE   RED

Chapel Hill Cabernet Sauvignon, Balaton 1994

13.5 | B

Very pleasant but it's lost its bite at three years old.

Hungarian Red, Co-op

13 | B

Very quiet, reserved, cherry-ripe and slips down easily.

Hungaroo Merlot 1995

14 | B

Dry, chewy, cherry/plum fruit of firm stylishness.

HUNGARIAN WINE WHITE

Chapel Hill Irsai Oliver 1995 `15` `B`

Hungarian White, Co-op `14.5` `B`

Terrific lemon edge to convincing up-front fruit of charm and style. Drink it on its own or with food – it's willing to please on all fronts.

Hungaroo Pinot Gris 1995 `15` `B`

Hungaroo Sauvignon Blanc 1995 `14` `C`

Faintly reminiscent of Kiwi sauvignon in its initial grassiness. An excellent shellfish stew wine – really good value.

ITALIAN WINE RED

Bardolino Le Canne, Boscaini 1995 `13.5` `C`

Lightly fruity, cherries sprinkled on plums. Only at Co-op Superstores.

Chianti 1995, Co-op `12` `C`

Very light and terribly uncompetitive.

Chianti Classico, Otto Santi 1994 `12` `D`

Co-op Superstores only.

Country Collection Puglian Red `15.5` `B`

Le Volte Ornellaia 1993 `12` `E`

Merlot del Veneto, Co-op `12.5` `C`

Monferrato Rosso `13.5` `B`

Flops all over the tastebuds like a big sloppy puppy dog.

Montepulciano d'Abruzzo 1994, Co-op `13.5` `B`

Principato Rosso, Co-op `12` `B`

Sangiovese di Toscana, Fiordaliso 1994 `15` `C`

Sicilian Red, Co-op `12` `B`

Almost sweet in its fruitiness. Good with meat and vegetable curries and Balti dishes.

Torresolada Sicilian Red 1995 `11` `B`

Valpolicella, Co-op `13` `B`

Light, and doesn't hurt the throat. But equally doesn't set the tastebuds alight.

Valpolicella Marano, Boscaini 1995 `12` `C`

Straightforward – a square peg in a square hole. How cosy and dull can you get? Only at Co-op Superstores.

**Villa Mantinera, Montepulciano de
Molise NV** `14` `C`

Vino da Tavola Rosso NV, Co-op `10` `B`

Sweet and juicy.

ITALIAN WINE   WHITE

Alasia Chardonnay del Piemonte 1995 `14` `C`

Bianco di Custoza Vignagrande 1995   `10` `C`

Co-op Superstores only.

Chardonnay Atesino, Co-op   `10` `B`

Chardonnay del Salento, 'Le Trulle' 1994   `15.5` `C`

Frascati Superiore 1995, Co-op   `12` `C`

Dull, and a touch mawkish.

Frascati Villa Catone 1994   `11` `C`

Monferrato Bianco   `13` `B`

Orvieto Secco, Co-op   `11` `C`

Unthrilling and overpriced.

Pinot Grigio del Veneto, Co-op   `10` `B`

Principato Valdadige 1995   `13.5` `B`

Good solid fresh fruit.

Sicilian White, Co-op   `13` `B`

Soave, Co-op   `12` `B`

Dullish.

Soave Monteleone, Boscaini 1996   `14` `C`

One of the most elegant soaves around: rich, balanced, very finely flavoured. Only at Co-op Superstores.

Torresolada Bianco di Sicilia 1995   `14.5` `B`

Sunny label, sunny disposition. Handsome partner for fish and for general glugging. Only at Co-op Superstores.

Vino da Tavola Bianco NV, Co-op `11` `B`

LEBANESE WINE RED

Chateau Musar 1977 `13` `G`

Chateau Musar 1988 `13` `G`

MACEDONIAN WINE RED

Macedonian Vranac/Cabernet Sauvignon 1993 `14` `B`

Not at all bad, considering how it has been in the past. It's dry, rich, decently fruity in a quiet cabernet manner, and it is easy to drink. Only at Co-op Superstores and Supermarkets.

MEXICAN WINE RED

L A Cetto Petite Syrah 1993 `14` `C`

Getting sweeter as it ages. Not, I must say, like some of us.

MOLDOVAN WINE RED

Kirkwood Cabernet Merlot 1994 `15` `B`

Very fireside-warm yet rich and with a serious message. The wine is dry yet full of itself – and this self is stylish and individual. Food-friendly and textured.

MOLDOVAN WINE   WHITE

Kirkwood Chardonnay 1995   13.5 C

Getting to the end of its shelf-life, this fruit, but still fair value.

MOROCCAN WINE   RED

Moroccan Cabernet Sauvignon/Syrah 1995   15 B

NEW ZEALAND WINE   RED

New Zealand Cabernet Merlot 1994, Co-op   13 C

NEW ZEALAND WINE   WHITE

Forest Flower Fruity Dry White 1995   11 C

Very sticky-toffee in texture and, in part, fruit.

Grove Mill Chardonnay 1995   12 E

Over priced and somewhat mild in the fruit department.

Millton Vineyard Semillon/Chardonnay 1995   12 D

New Zealand Semillon Sauvignon Blanc 1995, Co-op   14.5 C

Nobilo White Cloud 1995

PORTUGUESE WINE RED

Campos dos Frades Cabernet Sauvignon 1995

Smoky, rich, tobacco-scented, deep, dry, full of flavour and very gripping. Excellent value.

Duque de Viseu Dao 1992

Somewhat austere. Co-op Superstores only.

Quinta da Pancas Cabernet Sauvignon 1994

A delicious cabernet of elegance and style, improving nicely in bottle. Has richness and cabernet dryness but a complex woody undertone intrudes delightfully into the rich fruit adding a savoury note. It's a hugely gluggable wine of class and excellent with light meats – lamb especially. Only at Co-op Superstores.

Quinta da Pancas Cabernet Sauvignon 1995

This vintage demonstrates this purposeful estate's commitment to really stylish, warm, complex cabernets without a hint of coarseness. Great tannins, superb fruit, lovely balance and all-round compactness.

Ramada, Estremadura 1994

A simple fruit glug? Not a flawed notion but ... what about the sunny edge to the fruit? What about the smoothness? What about the sheer pleasure of it?

Star Mountain Oak Aged Touriiga 1994 `14` `C`

Very individual. Dry, earthy, quaintly exotically edged (spicy ripe figs), and immensely capable of handling rich meat and veg dishes. Only at Co-op Superstores and Supermarkets.

Vila Santa 1995 `15.5` `D`

A lovely, rich, textured wine of superbly smooth yet dry, cassis-edged fruitiness. It is classy in a home-spun way, deep, savoury, with a hint of jam, and very, very drinkable. It has an invigorating healthy kick to it. Only at Co-op Superstores.

PORTUGUESE WINE WHITE

Campos dos Frades Chardonnay 1995 `14` `C`

Some energy about the fruit which is fresh and far from clumsy but it does need food to bring out its best and most companionable qualities. Co-op Superstores only.

Fiuza Chardonnay 1995 `16` `C`

Wonderful oily chardonnay of lush texture which is held firmly by the acidity to provide a lovely balanced feel. Athletic, trim, yet muscled – this is a richly rewarding quaffing wine and a good wine with fish or poultry.

Fiuza Sauvignon Blanc 1995 `16` `C`

A brilliantly conceived wine of striking, balanced fruit. Richness and style in abundance.

Joao Pires Muscat Branco 1995 `15.5` `C`

Vinho Verde, Co-op `12` `B`

But . . . but . . . as an aperitif a glass of this spritzig, spineless gunk is most pleasant. A glass, mind you, no more.

ROMANIAN WINE RED

Classic Pinot Noir 1991

Mature yet lithe, soft, fruity, complex and, incredibly, a proper gamy pinot. Great value.

River Route Merlot 1995

Brilliant merlot: rich, aromatic, good development of fruit with the tannins, this is good with food, highly drinkable without. Staggeringly good value.

Romanian Country Red

Curious, polished fruit with a flavour of baked plum. Lovely drinkability here.

Romanian Prairie Merlot 1995, Co-op

Special Reserve Merlot, Sahateni Barrel-matured 1994

A perfect balance of rich, savoury, leather-edged fruit of astonishing texture, evolved tannins, and style and excellent acidity. This is a remarkable wine under a fiver. The polish, the quality of fruit, the layers of flavour are all on song and deeply impressive. Only at Co-op Superstores.

ROMANIAN WINE WHITE

River Route Sauvignon Blanc 1995 `13.5` `B`

Good with shellfish. Needs food.

Romanian Country White `11` `C`

**Romanian Prairie Sauvignon Blanc
1995, Co-op**
 15 B

SOUTH AFRICAN WINE RED

Cape Afrika Pinotage 1992
 14 C

A cheroot-edged wine of depth, dryness and richness – a touch expensive – but delicious with grilled meats and sausages. Only at Co-op Superstores and Supermarkets.

Cape Red, Co-op
 14.5 B

Perfectly priced, perfectly balanced red of positive charms: fruity (but no burnt rubber), good depth of flavour counterpointed in its savoury soupiness by zest acidity.

Jacana Merlot, Hugh Ryman 1995
 16.5 D

Improving beautifully in bottle, this wine. If the texture doesn't stun you with its thick, knitted multiplicity, the fruit takes your breath away with its sheer richness yet fluidity and elegance. A wonderful merlot. Co-op Superstores only.

Kumala Cinsault/Pinotage
16 B

Burnt-rubber fruit of great charm. Distinctive, soft, deliciously well-formed and stylish! Exceptional depth of flavour and lingering-finished fruitiness.

Kumala Shiraz/Cabernet Sauvignon 1996
 14 C

This is rather young and feisty at the moment – it needs a few more months in bottle to develop greater couthness. However, it still rates well for it has a briskness which is not entirely bereft of charm.

Long Mountain Cabernet Sauvignon 1995 `14` `C`

Soft and juicy but with a hint of caramelised fruit on the finish.
Drinkable and food-friendly.

Long Mountain Shiraz 1993 `15` `C`

Oak Village Cabernet Sauvignon 1992 `13.5` `C`

Oak Village Pinotage 1995 `14.5` `C`

Delicious charcoal-edged richness balanced by a flavoursome
acidic zip. Great pasta wine.

Robertson Cabernet Sauvignon 1995 `15` `B`

Now this is *stylish* jamminess and richness. That is to say this
immensely soft and deeply flavoured wine is not just puppyish
and ripe but will go well with food.

Robertson Merlot 1996 `14` `C`

A light merlot of some style, with cherry/plum fruit of standard
drinkability, and an easy, relaxed texture. Not deep or complex,
it is, nevertheless, hard to dislike. Only at Co-op Superstores.

SOUTH AFRICAN WINE WHITE

Cape Afrika Rhine Riesling 1996 `14` `C`

Touch of waxy, off-dry honey to the melony fruit makes it a
great glug. Only at Co-op Superstores and Supermarkets.

Cape White, Co-op `12.5` `B`

Somewhat less appealing than once it was. Has age withered its
freshness?

Goudini Chardonnay 1996 `15` `C`

Tasty, warm, not overstraining itself or blowsy and overrich. But it does have depth and style. Co-op Superstores only.

Kumala Chenin/Chardonnay 1995 `13` `B`

Longridge Chardonnay 1996 `10` `E`

Not worth the money by a long chalk.

Oak Village Chardonnay 1995 `14.5` `C`

Olive Grove Chardonnay 1996 `13.5` `C`

The finish is quirky, and spoils the effect for me, but I am being very critical (and this wine is £4.50). The initial fruit attack is fine, though. Only at Co-op Superstores.

Overgaauw Chardonnay 1995 `16.5` `D`

A lovely, layered, rich, harmonious, delicious wine of considerable flair and wit. The wood and fruit are in perfect step, giving a creamy richness, and the finish is textured and bright. Co-op Superstores only.

Welmoed Sauvignon Blanc 1996 `15` `C`

Elegant, gentle but with fleshy hints of rich fruit aromatically and on the finish. Co-op Superstores only.

SPANISH WINE RED

Baron de Ley Rioja Reserva 1991 `15` `D`

Expensive but a ripely fruity wine with great classiness. Oodles of flavour.

Berberana Tempranillo Rioja 1995   13 C

Needs food, I reckon, to nullify the rather ripe finish. But in approach its fruit is fleshy and attractively perfumed.

Campo Rojo, Carinena   14 B

Enate Tempranillo Cabernet 1992   16 D

Aromatic, smooth, classy, well-mannered. It's perhaps almost TOO smooth and classy for its rustic background. It has the politeness perhaps to be expected from a wine made by a man who worked at Chateau Margaux and Torres.

Gandia Cabernet Sauvignon 1993   12 C

Rather austere and costive. Doesn't give much, but is impressively distant.

Gandia Cabernet Sauvignon 1995   14 B

Only just rates 14. It sneaks in by virtue of its frontal attack of dry fruit, but the finish is a touch ho-hum.

Marino Tinto NV   14 B

Has a delicious (though simple) dry jamminess.

Marques de la Sierra Garnacha 1994   16 B

Brilliant value and simply terrific with casseroles and roasts. Has a good shroud of dry, rich tannin and an undercoat of soft berry fruit. Lovely texture, solid fruit with a hint of spice. It has a concentration of flavour and complexity which is stunning for the money.

Marquis de Monistrol Merlot 1993   14 C

Has a lovely warmth to its fruit allied to a soft developed texture of decent interwoven flavours – mainly plum. Only at Co-op Superstores and Supermarkets.

Palacio de la Vega Cabernet Sauvignon 1992
`16` `D`

Texture, warmth, richness, style, humour and personality. Dry yet full of fruit.

Rioja Tinto NV, Co-op
`16` `C`

You can spread this thickly on dry toast and chew with great satisfaction. Has depth, flavour, class, modern riojan richness and lovely texture.

Santara Cabernet/Merlot, Conca de Barbera 1994
`15` `C`

Delicious union of grapes, a perfect sum of parts, offering richness, depth and texture. A classy feel to the wine is granted by this texture which confers on the fruit a lovely meatiness. Only at Co-op Superstores and Supermarkets.

Tempranillo Oak-Aged, Co-op
`13.5` `B`

Torres Gran Sangredetoro 1989
`14` `D`

Vina Pomal Rioja Crianza 1990
`13.5` `C`

SPANISH WINE WHITE

Berberana Carta de Oro 1995
`13` `C`

Very attractive with a fish, where I'd rate it 14.5, but as a glug it takes some taste-acquiring. Only at Co-op Superstores and Supermarkets.

Castillo de Monjardin Chardonnay 1995
`14.5` `C`

The '95 vintage of this wine is somewhat muted at the moment. Little presence aromatically, fruit on the acidic side rather than mellow – but it will improve over a year in bottle. Co-op Superstores only.

Castillo de Monjardin Unoaked Chardonnay 1994
`14.5` `C`

Gandia Chardonnay Hoya Valley 1994
`15.5` `C`

A buttery version of chardonnay with a limpid, subtle citricity. Delicious fruit.

Gandia Hoya Valley Grenache Rose 1995
`13` `C`

Santara Chardonnay 1995
`16.5` `C`

This is one of the very few chardonnays under four quid which gives Chile a run for the same money: rich, perfectly developed, complex, utterly delicious. It has plot, character and wit. It's a literary gem. Co-op Superstores only.

Torres Sangredetoro 1992
`12` `C`

Valle de Monterrey Dry White Wine, Co-op
`13` `B`

USA WINE
RED

Beringer Zinfandel 1992
`14` `D`

California Red, Co-op
`13.5` `B`

A pleasant, peasant alternative to beaujolais, chianti and valpolicella.

Gallo Sonoma County Cabernet Sauvignon 1992
`14` `E`

Glen Ellen Merlot 1994

Hedges Cabernet Sauvignon/Merlot, Columbia 1994

Better than many a vaunted claret at three times the price. The fruit and tannin stride out together with purpose and style and show a real turn of delicacy yet weight on the tastebuds. A very classy wine. Co-op Superstores only.

Redwood Trail Pinot Noir 1995

Has true pinot aroma, truffley and warm, and a decent thwack of farmyardy wild raspberry-edged fruit. Better, much better, than the Co-op red burgundies at twice the price. Only at Co-op Superstores.

USA WINE WHITE

Arbor Crest Chardonnay 1995

Richness, depth, flavour and fullness. Very classy, very expensive, very all-embracing American. Only at Co-op Superstores.

California Colombard, Co-op `13` `B`

Only at Co-op Superstores and Supermarkets.

Glen Ellen Proprietor's Reserve Chardonnay 1995 `16` `C`

Developing more vegetality as it ages but still a richly textured, plump chardonnay of flavour, depth and real engaging fruitiness. It offers a lovely glass of wine to all the senses.

Hedges Fume Chardonnay, Columbia 1995 `12` `D`

Expensive, ill-balanced, and only a force to reckon with at £3.29. Co-op Superstores only.

Sebastiani's White Zinfandel 1995 `10` `C`

Stowells of Chelsea California Blush (3-litre box) `12.5` `B`

Price has been adjusted to show equivalent per bottle.

SPARKLING WINE/CHAMPAGNE

Barramundi Sparkling (Australia) `15.5` `D`

Brown Bros Pinot Noir/Chardonnay NV `14.5` `E`

Terribly posh feel to this wine. Better than scores of champagnes. Only at Co-op Superstores.

Codorniu Premiere Cuvee Brut (Spain) `14` `D`

Marino Cava del Mediterraneo `16.5` `C`

An absolute block-buster of a bottle: delicate, lemony, classically fresh, clean and elegant and just so ridiculously well-priced it makes you think twice and drink time and time again (and at £3.99 a bottle you can afford it).

Moscato Spumante, Co-op `14.5` `C`

Sweet as a kitten but nowhere near as hairy. The richness is not cloying and a glass is the perfect weekend start to the day – with the morning papers.

Sparkling Saumur, Co-op `13` `D`

Veuve Honorain Blanc de Noirs Champagne NV `13.5` `E`

An elegant bubbly of dry fruitiness – perhaps not as lemonic as it might be.

CO-OPERATIVE PIONEER

CO-OPERATIVE PIONEER
Sandbrook Park
Sandbrook Way
Rochdale
OL11 1SA
Tel 01706 891649
Fax 01706 891207

This is the first year that the Pioneer branch of the Co-operative Society has had its own section in this book. Time alone will reveal what is most wonderful and what is most maddening about this retailer, but they have yet to demonstrate either characteristic to my complete satisfaction. The entries in their section do not represent a great many wonderful bargains under £3, but this may change in the future. Watch this space.

SEE STOP PRESS SECTION AT END OF BOOK FOR LAST-MINUTE ADDITIONS TO THIS RETAILER'S RANGE.

ARGENTINIAN WINE   RED

Bright Bros Argentine Red, Mendoza 1997   `14.5` `B`

This is a bright red wine like lipstick: it leaves a bright red mark on the consciousness. A touch devious? Crude? Yes, but very soft and sensual.

Bright Brothers Mendoza Cabernet/ Malbec 1996   `14` `C`

Rich, dry, well-priced, but it does need food to set it alight.

Valle de Vistalba Cabernet Sauvignon 1994   `14` `C`

Dry, flooded with flavour, well-textured, good with food. Touch pricey, perhaps, but there's no doubting its excellent food-compatibility.

Vicuna Peak Malbec/Tempranillo   `15` `C`

Great gobbets of dry fruit, concentrated and polished, impact on the tastebuds here. Great with casseroles and roast vegetables with melted cheese.

ARGENTINIAN WINE   WHITE

Bright Bros Argentine Dry White, Mendoza NV   `14.5` `B`

It seems basic as it approaches the palate but once safely tucked away down the gullet a gorgeous creamy feeling suffuses the soul.

Etchart Torrontes Cafayate 1996 `15.5` `C`

Spicy, warm, giving and immensely well-dispositioned to create
a feeling of everything's-all-right-with-the-world.

Vicuna Peak Chenin Semillon 1996 `14` `B`

Rather a muted richness but an interesting construct – either
to rouse a jaded palate or consummate a marriage with food.

AUSTRALIAN WINE   RED

Australian Dry Red Wine (3 litres) `14` `B`

A really dry Aussie red of some perkiness, personality and
well-compacted flavour. Great with food. Not your usual soppy
Aussie red at this price. Note the price band has been adjusted
to show the equivalent for a single bottle.

Barramundi Shiraz/Merlot `13` `C`

Very juicy style with a burnt edge.

Chateau Tahbilk Cabernet Sauvignon 1992 `E`

Expensive but far from the soft and insidiously puppyish Aussie
reds which now proliferate. This one has some dry authority to
its soft rich fruit and it compares well with the best cabernets
on offer. Yes, it costs. But it delivers.

Duck's Flat Dry Red Wine `5` `C`

Awful filth. Australia would produce a richer red fermenting
the bones of Ned Kelly.

Hardys Nottage Hill Cabernet Sauvignon/ Shiraz 1995

Okay – but pricey. Wish it was £3.49. It's lost its bite.

Jacob's Creek Shiraz/Cabernet 1995 `13.5` `C`

Reliable if not exciting. Getting pricey this close to a fiver.

Kingston Grenache, Murray Valley 1995 `13` `C`

A warm soupy broth.

Leasingham Domaine Cabernet/Malbec, Clare Valley 1995 `15` `E`

Lovely stuff. Chocolate-edged soft fruit, a faraway hint of cigar, this is terrific – an Aussie in very stylish mood.

Lindemans Cawarra Dry Red 1996 `12` `C`

Dry red about sums it up. Australia struggles to convince at this price.

Lindemans Cawarra Shiraz/Cabernet Sauvignon 1996 `14` `C`

Savoury, dry (but amply rich and fruity on the finish), gently relaxing and softly meaty. Selected stores.

Orlando Ruby Cabernet/Shiraz 1995 `13.5` `C`

Whizz-bang shower of fruit explodes out of the bottle. Not a subtle wine, this one.

Penfolds Koonunga Hill Shiraz Cabernet 1995 `14` `D`

Very tasty, very rich. Very sparky stuff.

Penfolds Rawsons Retreat Bin 35 1995 `13.5` `C`

Respectable rather than raunchy.

Rosemount Estate Shiraz/Cabernet 1996 `15.5` `C`

So soft and slip-downable it may be a crime.

AUSTRALIAN WINE WHITE

Duck's Flat Dry White `10` `C`

Possibly the most duck-like Aussie white I've tasted. Flat? It's horizontal all the way.

Hardys Nottage Hill Chardonnay 1996 `15` `C`

This elegant style of Aussie chardonnay is light years ahead of the blowsy blockbusters of yesteryear.

Jacob's Creek Dry Riesling 1996 `14` `C`

Curious soft fruit with a hint of spice. Excellent summer aperitif.

Jacob's Creek Semillon/Chardonnay 1996 `13` `C`

Lindemans Bin 65 Chardonnay 1996 `15.5` `C`

Elegant, purposeful, balanced, finely wrought and handsomely textured. A textbook Aussie chardonnay.

Lindemans Cawarra Dry White 1996 `12` `C`

Throws up an interesting debate: what is a dry white wine? Surely not this – to a French palate or to mine.

Lindemans Unoaked Cawarra Chardonnay 1996 `13` `C`

Orlando Colombard/Chardonnay 1996 `13.5` `C`

Not a gracious wine but decently fruity and effective with food.

Penfolds Bin 202 Rhine Riesling 1996   14.5   C

Interesting softish fruit with a crisp pineapple tang. Will develop well in bottle over the next year.

Penfolds Rawsons Retreat Bin 21 Semillon/Chardonnay/Colombard 1996   15.5   C

Loaded with flavour and rich layers of fruit, it is nevertheless difficult to justify paying more for a wine of this style.

Peter Lehmann Chenin Blanc 1996   13.5   C

Rather a touch expensive for the waxy simplicity of the fruit – which is fresh and reasonably engaging if not exciting.

Peter Lehmann The Barossa Semillon, 1996   14.5   D

Has a lush richness, beautiful cool texture and a solid finish. A truly flavourful wine. Great with all sorts of grilled food.

Preece Chardonnay, Michelton 1995   14   D

Nutty and highly drinkable. Touch expensive for the style, which is certainly not old-style, flood-gate chardonnay. Nevertheless, has commendable elegance.

Rosemount Estate Semillon/Chardonnay 1996   14   D

Elegance personified.

BULGARIAN WINE   RED

Cabernet Sauvignon, Rousse 1991   12   B

Light and eager.

141

Domaine Boyar Vintage Blend Oriachovitza Merlot & Cabernet Sauvignon Reserve 1992

`15` `C`

Superbly approachable fruit with hints of herbiness to the dryness.

Lovico Suhindol Merlot 1994

`14` `B`

Dry, rich, velvety. Good value.

Merlot/Pinot Noir Country Wine, Sliven

`12` `B`

Vintage Blend Cabernet Sauvignon/Merlot, Iambol 1996

`15` `B`

Rich, dry, invigorating, loaded with fruit of classic proportions. Brilliant value for grills and roasts.

BULGARIAN WINE   WHITE

Aligote & Muskat Rousse Country White

`10` `B`

I confess to finding it as muddled as a plot of a late Iris Murdoch. Though it must be said in its defence, it is a lot easier to swallow.

Domaine Boyar Chardonnay, Preslav

`11` `B`

Mawkish, sentimental, made for readers of Barbara Cartland.

Domaine Boyar Vintage Blend Chardonnay/ Sauvignon Blanc, Preslav 1995

`14` `B`

Excellent proposition, both on the pocket and in the glass, for all sorts of grilled fish.

CHILEAN WINE   RED

Bisquertt Cabernet Sauvignon 1995   15   C

Lovely texture and a lingering fruitiness of some concentration and class.

Bisquertt Merlot 1995   13.5   C

That lingering quality Bisquertt wines have makes them attractive but for the money I'd like more attack up-front.

Casa Porta Cabernet Sauvignon 1996   16   C

The rich fruit has a black, mysterious, almost charcoal edge to it (tannins). It's lovely.

Cono Sur Cabernet Sauvignon Reserve 1995   14.5   D

Classy, very classy, rich, thick, beautifully textured, ripe and rampant yet never clumsy. Lovely wine of great style.

Tocornal Chilean Red   13   B

Tocornal Merlot   14   C

Fruity, dry, rich and solidly compacted on the finish.

Undurraga Cabernet Sauvignon 1996   14   C

A dry, blackcurranty cabernet, not classically peppery but soft, with a gentle tannic undertone, and a soft rich-edged finish.

Undurraga Merlot 1995   14   C

Not tasting so well as it was last winter. Seems rather mild and unadventurous.

Undurraga Pinot Noir 1995   14   C

Not exactly classic pinot but it is firmly in the camp of wines it is a great pleasure to quaff with or without food. Piles on the richness and flavour most agreeably.

Valdezaro Cabernet Sauvignon 1996

A good solid pasta wine or, to appreciate fully the wine's soft fruit, drink by itself.

CHILEAN WINE WHITE

Bisquertt Chardonnay 1996

Rampant on the tastebuds but not clumsily shod. It steps neatly, fruitily and richly with intent.

Bisquertt Sauvignon 1996

Touch expensive at 50p more than other Chileans and the fruit is somewhat unsure of itself. Tasted in Chile I found it elegant. Tasted in the UK, where readers of this book will drink it, I found it had travelled ill and is not such exciting company.

Casa Porta Chardonnay 1996

Delicate, decisive, decidedly Chilean. It has elegance and real style, never overstated, thanks to the richness of fruit, never flashy, to be beautifully counterpoised by the acidity.

Tocornal Chardonnay

Nicely textured and rounded with a hint of soft fruits but it finishes confidently fresh.

Tocornal Chilean White

Unusually numb and unexciting for a Chilean.

Undurraga Sauvignon Blanc 1996

Valdezaro Sauvignon Blanc `15` `C`

This is more like Chile! Ripe yet delicate, rich yet not blowsy, balanced and elegant yet full of flavour and freshness and terrifically well priced.

Vina Porta Chardonnay 1995 `14` `D`

Overshadowed a touch by more splendidly fruity Chilean chardonnays at less money. This has respectable rather than exciting fruit.

ENGLISH WINE   WHiTE

Chapel Down Summerhill Oaked White `12` `C`

A pound more than it should be and even then, you might wonder if it offers sufficient fruit.

Lamberhurst High Ridge Fume 1994 `7` `C`

Absurdly pretentious in label, price and dull fruit.

Summerhill Dry White `11` `C`

Ouch (£3.99?).

FRENCH WINE   RED

Beaujolais 1996, Co-operative `13` `B`

Reasonably well-textured fruit here.

Cabernet Sauvignon VdP d'Oc, Co-operative `13` `B`

Cheap and reasonably cheerful slurping here.

Chateau Cissac 1986 `11` `F`

Dry, but at this price I want more excitement and far more enrichment.

Chateau Gallion Bordeaux Rouge 1996 `13.5` `C`

Pleasant little claret. I said pleasant, not peasant.

Coteaux du Languedoc Les Caves St Romain 1995 `13` `B`

Ripe and as down to earth in price as it is in fruit.

Cotes du Rhone Louis Yerard 1996 `12` `B`

Domaine de Borios St Chinian 1995 `11` `B`

Rubbery and odd – made in the beaujolais style.

Domaine Sette Piana, VdP de l'Ile de Beaute `10` `B`

Characterless, dry, dusty.

Domaine St Roch VdP de l'Aude `10` `B`

Bland and inoffensive – it doesn't *go* anywhere.

Gamay VdP des Cotes du Tarn, Co-operative `11` `B`

Gigondas Domaine de Mourielle 1995 `14` `D`

Soft, earthy, rich, touch leathery – this is prime gigondas for tired feet and limbs generally.

La Baume Syrah/Grenache VdP d'Oc 1995 `15` `C`

Has packed into its rich concentration of flavours a decided herbiness reminiscent of Midi sun and languor. Decidedly drinkable without being too juicy – indeed, it has a dry edge of some class.

Merlot VdP d'Oc, Co-operative `11` `B`

Cherries here, not very ripe though.

Minervois 1995, Co-operative `12` `B`

Soft and cherryish.

Prestige Medoc 1994 `13` `C`

Dry and stalky.

Prestige Oak-aged Claret 1994 `12.5` `C`

Finishes austerely.

VdP de l'Aude Rouge, Co-operative `11` `B`

Fruity all right. Nowt else to it.

Vin de Table de France Rouge `13.5` `B`

Simple, reasonably fruity and red – difficult to claim more for its straightforward drinkability. But the price? The price is delicious.

FRENCH WINE   WHITE

Chenin Blanc 'Les Fleurs', VdP du Jardin de la France `10` `B`

Sweet with a hint of earthworm.

Cuckoo Hill Viognier 1995 `14.5` `C`

A convincing, well-textured wine of class and style. The fruit is plump and apricoty but dry.

James Herrick Chardonnay 1996 `14.5` `C`

More lemonic than previous vintages and less like the Old World style – but it will, I feel, pull itself round more richly over the next nine months.

Laperouse Blanc, VdP d'Oc 1995　15　C

Rich, invigorating fruit, a mite soft but not in any blowsy sense.

Premieres Cotes de Bordeaux 1995, Co-operative　13　C

Neither so sweet it can handle rich pud nor so complex it can excitingly be sipped by itself. Perhaps a bunch of grapes might suffice. But overall this is a Lieb-lover's wine and on the pricey side for such simplicity.

Rhone Valley Cotes du Luberon 1996　15　B

A classic French dry white to go with trout, pike, perch and other freshwater fish. The price is as clean and unadulterated as the crisp fruit. It isn't rich or complex but it is strikingly unpretentious and honest. Grilled squid and prawns might go with it, too.

Rhone Valley VdP de Vaucluse White　13.5　B

Another steely freshwater-fish white wine in the Co-op's collection. Australian chardonnay lovers will find it as unappealing as a Vanessa Feltz fan would regard Kate Moss.

Sauvignon/Semillon Le Chateau de Duras Blanc　13.5　C

Odd specimen – it seems to be old-fashioned French fruit but there's a hint of a concession to New World liberality. Very ripe wine.

Vin de Table de France Sec　10　A

Dull as can be. Really not worth £1.95 of anyone's money.

GERMAN WINE — WHITE

Binger St Rochuskapelle Kabinett, Langenbach 1995 — 13.5 B

Excellent price for such minerally fruit. A glass, well chilled, before eating would please me at any rate.

Carl Reh Bereich Bernkastel — 11 B

Mosel Deutscher Tafelwein — 13 B

Not as horribly sweet as many a Lieb and better priced.

Weinberg Hock — 9 B

The sort of all-scaffolding wine which does Germany's reputation no good. It needs bricks and mortar to stand up to being lived in.

GREEK WINE — RED

Mavrodaphne of Patras NV — 13 C

A wine for seasonal slices of cake e.g. of the Christmas variety.

Vin de Crete Red, Kourtaki 1995 — 13 B

GREEK WINE — WHITE

Kourtaki Vin de Crete 1995 — 11 B

Crete was the place I once tasted the worst wine in the world:

a heavily oxidised red retsina of such inflammability it could have usefully gone into a paraffin lamp. This white, dry example of Cretan oenology is not so vile.

HUNGARIAN WINE RED

Chapel Hill Cabernet Sauvignon, Balaton 1994 13.5 B

Very pleasant but it's lost its bite at three years old.

Frontier Island Merlot, Szekszard 1995 12 B

Frontier Island Ripe Fruity Red, Kiskoros 1995 12 B

HUNGARIAN WINE WHITE

Badger Hill Barrel Fermented Chardonnay 1994 14 C

Clean, some good fruit.

Chapel Hill Irsai Oliver, Balaton Boglar 1996 15 B

Best vintage yet for this delicate, floral aperitif. It is a brilliant warm-weather, back-garden (or front for that matter) bottle.

Frontier Island Chardonnay, Neszmely 1995 10 B

Choppy waters here. Chardonnay? Were the grapes picked at high tide?

Frontier Island White 1995 `11` `A`

Talcum-powder fruit – rather stumbling.

Nagyrede Estate Muscat Ottonel 1996 `13` `B`

A pleasing little aperitif for refined and easily distorted, tender palates.

ITALIAN WINE RED

Chianti Tenuta del Poggio 1995 `10` `B`

Leone di San Marco Merlot, VdT del Veneto `10` `B`

Rialto Lambrusco Rosso dell'Emilia `13.5` `B`

Fizzy, fresh and cherry/plum ripe. Try it with cold meats.

Sicilian Rosso `13` `B`

Some ripeness and polish to the fruit.

MEXICAN WINE RED

L A Cetto Petite Syrah 1993 `14` `C`

Getting sweeter as it ages. Not, I must say, like some of us.

MOROCCAN WINE RED

Moroccan Cabernet/Syrah `15` `B`

Rampant, racy, rich, soft, easy to love, great with casseroles.

Moroccan Red 14 B

Warm and packed with soft, never harsh rays of sunshine. Terrific with bangers and mash.

NEW ZEALAND WINE RED

Timara Cabernet/Merlot 1995 13.5 C

Hints of grass to the rich herby fruit. Good with meat dishes.

Waimanu Premium Dry Red 5 C

Totally disgusting (almost – well, it gets 5).

NEW ZEALAND WINE WHITE

Cooks Chardonnay, Gisborne 1996 13.5 C

Fails to convince, after a reasonable start, on the finish.

Forest Flower Fruity Dry White 1995 13.5 C

Just fails by a whisker to garner more points. Sound texture and fruit – the finish pales.

Timara Chardonnay/Semillon, Montana 1995 13.5 C

Expensive for the style which is fruity yet fresh. There is a hint of butter, grass and cobnut and it's well organised if in muted rather than dazzling array. Grilled fish suits it best.

Villa Maria Private Bin Chardonnay, Marlborough 1996 13.5 D

Falls a little short of what a six-quid-plus chardonnay should be.

Villa Maria Private Bin Sauvignon Blanc, Marlborough 1996 `15` `D`

Delicate grassy notes to the richly restrained fruit. Elegantly and finely cut.

Waimanu Muller Thurgau/Sauvignon 1996 `13.5` `C`

Needs fish to unhook its flavour and spread it effectively on the palate. Without food, it seems mean.

PORTUGUESE WINE   RED

Bright Brothers 'Old Vines' Estramadura 1995 `13.5` `C`

Soft and ripe.

Campos dos Frades Cabernet Sauvignon 1995 `15` `C`

Smoky, rich, tobacco-scented, deep, dry, full of flavour and very gripping. Excellent value.

PORTUGUESE WINE   WHITE

Campos dos Frades Chardonnay 1995 `14` `C`

Some energy about the fruit which is fresh and far from clumsy but it does need food to bring out its best and most companionable qualities.

Fiuza Sauvignon Blanc 1996 `16` `C`

Gorgeous, rich, inviting aroma. Big opulent fruit of textured tautness yet suppleness. Soft finish. Lovely glug.

ROMANIAN WINE   RED

Classic Cabernet Sauvignon, Dealul Mare 1991   `13.5` `B`

Ripe, very ripe, with a dry undertone. Needs food to bring out its real personality.

Pinot Noir Prahova 1993   `15.5` `B`

What a thundering bargain! Fruity, dry, superbly structured, it has flavour, tannins and balance. Terrific casserole wine.

River Route Merlot 1996 (3 litres)   `13.5` `B`

Decent enough tipple, dry with a hint of soft leather, at 50p a glass. Note the price band has been adjusted to show the equivalent for a single bottle.

Special Reserve Cabernet Sauvignon, Prahova 1990   `15.5` `B`

Fabulous bargain here. A wine loaded with flavoursome, well-textured fruit, rich tannins and acidity, and the whole package is integrated, bold, classy and superbly well priced. One of the best red bargains on this retailer's shelves.

ROMANIAN WINE   WHITE

Classic Sauvignon Blanc 1996   `11` `B`

Funny idea they have of classics in Romania.

River Route Pinot Grigio 1996   `13.5` `B`

One of those Romanian whites bottled in Germany which its

bottlers could do worse than emulate. It has a peachy richness which never turns too soft but keeps a clear, clean undertone.

Romanian Sauvignon Blanc (3 litres) `8` `B`

The least typical sauvignon blanc I think I've ever tasted. Certainly deserves to be put in a box but not one with a tap. Note the price band has been adjusted to show the equivalent for a single bottle.

Tarnava Valley Chardonnay 1995 `15` `C`

I've tasted white burgundies five times more expensive which are less profoundly fruity than this food-friendly bottle. The muscat in the blend is a brilliant sleight of winemaking skilldoggery. *[Ed note: sic.]*

SLOVENIAN WINE RED

Dragonja Merlot 1994 `11` `B`

SOUTH AFRICAN WINE RED

Beyerskloof Pinotage 1996 `13.5` `C`

Not as richly compelling as previous vintages.

Bovlei Pinotage 1995 `12` `C`

Bovlei Shiraz 1994 `12` `C`

Light yet juicy.

Cape Cinsault/Ruby Cabernet (3 litres) `13.5` `B`

Dry wine with a hint of sagebrush. Note: the price band has been adjusted to show the equivalent for a single bottle.

Kumala Ruby Cabernet/Merlot 1996 `14.5` `C`

Fruit all the way. It cascades with flavour.

Landema Falls Cape Red `13` `B`

Light and fruity.

Landskroon Pinotage 1995 `14` `C`

Rich, textured, burnt-rubbery, yet delicious.

Long Mountain Cabernet Sauvignon 1995 `13.5` `C`

Dry and rich, deep and reasonably well-balanced.

Wide River Ruby Cabernet, Robertson Winery 1997 `14` `C`

Imagine eating a ripe pear/peach/nectarine whilst behind the next tree in the orchard someone puffed on a mild cheroot.

SOUTH AFRICAN WINE WHITE

Drostdy-Hof Steen Chenin Blanc 1996 `14` `C`

Steen *is* chenin blanc, so the label helpfully translates, and the fruit equally translates well on the palate where it speaks of a very muted peachiness with a hint of citricity to the acidity. A delicately delicious wine.

Goiya Kgeisje Sauvignon Blanc/Chardonnay 1996 `15.5` `B`

Possibly the crispest, cleanest white wine for under £3 around. It runs a stream of liquid steel across the tongue, both livening the pre-prandial appetite and accompanying the seafood which follows.

Kumala Chenin Blanc/Chardonnay 1996

The '96 was one of the perkiest whites on this retailer's shelves: rich, cool, fresh to finish but never tart, with lots of initial flavour from eager-to-please fruit. An excellent quaffing wine for the money which also enjoys food. The 1997, which I tasted unfiltered, I cannot rate but it was less balanced, less acidically well polished, but will develop in bottle, possibly advantageously, during winter 1997.

Namaqua Chenin 1996

Party wine for serious academics of the grape.

Namaqua Classic Dry White (3 litres)

Fruity and well worth 46p a glass. Note the price band has been adjusted to show the equivalent for a single bottle.

Robertson Winery Wide River Sauvignon Blanc 1997

Delicious fruit here, really impressive and delicately classic for the money. It is richly textured but never overripe or overeager and the acidity is knife-edge clean and fresh. A terrific wine for the money. A wine of warmth, style, poise, and very refreshing personality.

Van Loveren Spes Bona Chardonnay 1996

Soft, edgily rich and rather laid-back. A casual wine rather than a deeply serious one.

SPANISH WINE — RED

Abadia de Altillo Rioja 10 C

Alta Oaked Tempranillo   `13.5` `B`

Rounded, ripe, and has some polish. Good for a party of pasta eaters.

Bataneros Tempranillo, Valdepenas 1996   `11` `B`

Campo Rojo, Carinena   `14` `B`

Fruity and fresh, well-developed and flavoursome. A bargain at the price.

Casa Morena   `11` `B`

Has a ripe compost-heap aroma: leave the bottle open a few months, and you can grow herbs and vegetables in it. But the fruit if drunk quickly passes unaggressively down the throat.

Castillo de Liria Valencia, Gandia   `13.5` `B`

Decently fruity and drinkable.

Don Cortez Red   `10` `B`

Used by the Spanish Inquisition to extract confessions.

Gandia Hoya de Cadenas Reserva, Utiel-Requena 1989   `15` `C`

Raspingly rich and food-friendly. Very ripe, textured, mature, and plummy to finish.

Gandia Hoya Valley Cabernet Sauvignon, Utiel Requena 1994   `13.5` `B`

A very soft and approachable cabernet.

Gandia Hoya Valley Merlot, Utiel Requena 1994   `14` `B`

Hints of vegetality only enhance the dry plummy fruit.

Gandia Hoya Valley Tempranillo 1992   B

La Mancha, Co-operative 13.5 B

The perfect Party Red. It carries its card boldly with a hint of nicotine on its fingers.

Vina Albali Reserva 1989 15 C

Takes its time but when it finally trickles down the throat the impression is of great, soft, rich fruit, perfectly firm yet ripe.

SPANISH WINE WHITE

Alta Oaked White 14 B

Some cleanly decent fruit which has a faint, very faint, echo of sticky toffee.

Castillo de Liria Moscatel de Valencia   C

Delicate yet very rich and honeyed. Waxy, subtle lemon/marmalade edge. Great with fresh fruit.

Puente Viejo NV 12 C

Like drinking bruised plums. Very ripe and rich.

**Vinas del Vero Barrel Fermented
Chardonnay, Somontano 1995**   D

This is a wine! Elegantly wooded, finely textured, delicious from nose to throat, it enjoys fish, chicken, vegetables and soups. It is also, with its aromatic, creamy fruit, very pleasant to sip whilst listening to sexual overtures. Or Bach's.

URUGUAYAN WINE RED

Castol Pujol Tannat 1994

Somewhat expensive and not as rampant as previous vintages, but a perfect grilled-food bottle.

URUGUAYAN WINE WHITE

Castel Pujol Chardonnay 1996

Rich and rolling. Gathers pace as it floods over the tongue and finishes slightly off-balance.

Castel Pujol Sauvignon Blanc 1996

Needs food. The fruit seems niggly without.

USA WINE RED

Blossom Hill Californian Red

Deer Valley Cabernet 1994

Convincing translation of Californian herbs and sunshine.

Deer Valley Merlot 1994

E & J Gallo Turning Leaf Cabernet Sauvignon 1994

Warm and possessing some depth but uncompetitively priced compared with Chile or South Africa. But you're getting better, Gallo, so stick at it! You might just make a terrific wine at a dirt-cheap price one day.

E & J Gallo Turning Leaf Zinfandel 1994 | 12 | D |

Not bad, but very overpriced at nigh on six quid. Anodyne and characterless, it lacks the oomph of real red zin. It fails to finish with either verve or vivacity. If it was £3.29 it would be a good buy. A partially turned new leaf.

Gallo Sonoma Cabernet Sauvignon 1992 | 15 | E |

Only just fails to make it higher. It is expensive – but it is gently impressive, if rather ripe.

Redwood Trail Pinot Noir 1994 | 14 | C |

Not bad for a pinot noir from California. Good truffley aroma and soft rich fruit.

USA WINE   WHITE

Deer Valley Chardonnay, Monterey County 1995 | 14.5 | C |

Rich, very forthcoming, utterly quaffable to savour, and it has that ineffable Californian edge of warmth and cosy living. It seems to stretch lazily over the tastebuds in a deliciously fruity way.

E & J Gallo Turning Leaf Chardonnay 1994 | 14 | D |

Classy and rich. Not especially elegant or finely balanced as great California chardonnays are but it's good with chicken.

Sutter Home California Chardonnay 1995 | 13.5 | C |

Creamy, very attractively flavoured fruit of some elegance and charm. It just doesn't convince me of its integrity.

Talus Chardonnay 1995   14   D

Is it sweet on the finish or just over-friendly? A lushly agreeable wine of big jammy fruit but it's never gawky or too bruised – rather it's ripe and full of itself yet totally convincing.

SPARKLING WINE/CHAMPAGNE

Bouvet Ladubay Saumur NV (France)   14.5   E

Elegant and delightfully lemony.

Cava Brut, Co-operative   14   C

Delicious dryness, freshness and elegance.

Cavalier Blanc de Blancs Brut Vin Mousseux (France)   12   C

Cavalier Demi-sec Vin Mousseux (France)   10   C

Gallo Brut   10   D

Rialto Moscato Spumante (Italy)   10   C

Sweetie for sweet young things.

Seaview Brut Rose   15   D

Elegant, purposeful tippling.

Veuve Noiziers Brut Champagne   13.5   E

Light and delicate with a hint of fruit on the finish.

KWIK SAVE STORES LIMITED

KWIK SAVE STORES LIMITED
Warren Drive
Prestatyn
Clwyd
LL19 7HU
Tel 01745 887111
Fax 01745 882504

What's wonderful.

The best thing about this retailer is that it finds decently fruity inexpensive red wines. Some readers buy their everyday drinking reds nowhere else.

What's maddening.

When this retailer mucks a reader about who takes back a wine because it is faulty (that is to say, tainted by its tree-bark seal) and tries to fob him off with excuses rather than offering an immediate refund, then I get shirty. True, this only happened once last year on the basis of my correspondence but I get the distinct impression that Kwik Save staff are not as on the ball about duff wine as they should be.

SEE STOP PRESS SECTION AT END OF BOOK FOR LAST-MINUTE ADDITIONS TO THIS RETAILER'S RANGE.

ARGENTINIAN WINE RED

Balbi Vineyard Malbec Syrah 1995 `13` `B`

AUSTRALIAN WINE RED

Lindemans Cawarra Shiraz Cabernet 1996 `14` `C`
Soupy richness and flavour make it highly drinkable.

Pelican Bay Australian Red Wine NV `14.5` `B`
Soft, slightly soupy, but good chilled or at room temperature
with loads of foods and different moods.

Pelican Bay Shiraz Cabernet 1996 `12` `C`
Odd leathery aroma, fruit respectable if not exciting, finish
matter-of-fact.

Penfolds Bin 2 Shiraz/Mourvedre 1995 `15.5` `D`
Rich, dry, stylish, this has fluidity of fruit yet tannic firmness of tone. Love the screwcap!

**Penfolds Koonunga Hill Shiraz Cabernet
1995** `14` `D`
Very tasty, very rich. Very sparky stuff.

AUSTRALIAN WINE WHITE

Lindemans Bin 65 Chardonnay 1996 `15.5` `C`

Delicious combination of butter, hazelnuts and melon under-cut by a perfectly weighted uptide of acidity.

Pelican Bay Dry White `13.5` `B`

The softness of the finish rather mitigates against the initial fruity crispness. Somewhat awkward in feel, this wine.

Pelican Bay Medium Dry White `12` `B`

An Australian Liebfraumilch – well, they've imitated every other major wine style in Europe.

Penfolds Koonunga Hill Chardonnay 1996 `15.5` `C`

Best vintage for years: aromatic, rich, balanced, food-friendly.

Penfolds Koonunga Hill Semillon/ Sauvignon Blanc 1996 `15.5` `C`

One of the best vintages ever from Koonunga Hill: rich melon fruit, nicely crafted, with pert citric acidity. A balanced wine, soundly priced.

South Eastern Australia Colombard Chardonnay 1996 `14` `B`

Ripe, very fruity, excellent thirst-quencher.

BULGARIAN WINE RED

Domaine Boyar Cabernet Sauvignon 1995 `12` `B`

Domaine Boyar Lovico Suhindol Cabernet Sauvignon/Merlot `14.5` `B`

Cherry-ripeness with a leathery dryness. Immensely drinkable.

Domaine Boyar Merlot/Cabernet 1996 `15` `B`

Dry, very charcoal-edged fruit and hugely food-friendly.

Domaine Boyar Reserve Gamza 1993 `12` `B`

Domaine Boyar Reserve Merlot 1993 `14` `B`

Soft yet dry and hinting at savoury richness.

BULGARIAN WINE WHITE

Domaine Boyar Preslav Chardonnay/ Sauvignon Blanc 1996 `16` `B`

Utterly seductive blend of buttery chardonnay with green lime-fruited sauvignon. Superb to glug, to swig with fish, to bathe in – if you've a mind. And at £2.89 you don't need to be obscenely well-heeled.

Khan Krum Riesling-Dimiat `12` `B`

Preslav Vintage Blend Chardonnay/ Sauvignon 1995 `14` `B`

CHILEAN WINE   RED

Deep Pacific Merlot Cabernet Sauvignon, Rancagua Region 1996   `15.5` `B`

Unusually mintily herbaceous Chilean with a gorgeously textured, slightly underripe plum fruit of depth, class and real lingering style. Great fruity lilt on the finish.

White Pacific Sauvignon Chardonnay, Rancagua Region 1996   `15` `B`

Brilliant value for such elegance and demure fruitiness. Has style, balance, subtle flavour and real class.

ENGLISH WINE   WHITE

Denbies 95   `13.5` `B`

Excellent fish-and-chip wine. Good price; reasonable crisp fruit.

Denbies Table Wine 1995   `12` `B`

Not bad – an English wine for £2.99.

FRENCH WINE   RED

Beaujolais, Dubessy 1996   `13.5` `B`

The right price (under £3.50) for a standard beaujolais and exactly the right level of ripe, fresh fruit. Well done, Kwik Save!

Cabernet Sauvignon VdP d'Oc 1996 | 16 | B

The best red from France for £2.79 on Kwik Save's shelves. It has character, flavour, balance and bite. Brilliant value!

Claret Cuvee V E 1996 | 12 | B

Corbieres Domaine Virginie 1995 | 13.5 | B

Soft and pliable and very anxious to please. It's a pleasure to slurp.

Cotes du Rhone, Dubessy 1996 | 10 | B

On the sweet and sweaty side.

Domaine de Bruyeres Cotes de Malepere 1995 | 12.5 | B

Les Forges VdP de l'Aude 1996 | 11 | A

Sweetish and rather tarty.

Les Oliviers VdT Francais | 13 | A

A pleasant cherry-fruited, cherry-cheeked wine of light appeal.

Rouge de France, Selection Cuvee V E | 13 | B

A cheap and cheerful party wine.

Skylark Hill Merlot, VdP d'Oc 1996 | 14 | B

Rich yet not cloying, stylish without being pretentious.

Skylark Hill Shiraz VdP d'Oc 1996 | 13 | B

Skylark Hill Very Special Red VdP d'Oc | 15 | B

Gentle rubbery undertone to the fruit which is compact and well presented. Excellent balance of fruit, acid and acidity. A really attractive quaffing wine.

FRENCH WINE — WHITE

**Blanc de France Vin de Table Selection
Cuvee** — 13 — B

Bordeaux Sauvignon Cuvee V E 1996 — 14 — B

Good rich aroma, decently balanced fruit, and a solid finish. A proper fish wine at an inviting price.

Les Oliviers VdT Francais — 13 — A

Incredibly cheap, hardly cheerful.

Muscadet Donatien Bahuaud 1996 — 13 — B

This is the price muscadet ought to be. But I'd also like a mite more zip.

Rose de France Selection Cuvee V E — 12 — B

Can make a case for itself served while the drinker is sat by a bowl of moules marinieres in the south of France on a hot summer day.

Skylark Hill Chardonnay VdP d'Oc 1996 — 15.5 — B

Nice one! An enlivening combo of melony fruit and lemony acidity. A standard recipe, perhaps, but not always so elegant at this price.

**Skylark Hill Very Special White, VdP
d'Oc 1996** — 15 — B

Some richness unsoiled by sullenness makes this wine if not very special then highly drinkable and a pleasure on the pocket.

**Stowells of Chelsea Vin de Pays du Tarn
(3-litre box)** — 14 — B

Crisp and clean as it starts work then it waves goodbye with a pleasant fruity lilt. Good to glug, good with grub. Price has been adjusted to show equivalent per bottle.

GERMAN WINE WHITE

**Bereich Mittelhardt Riesling Auslese,
St Ursula 1993** `14` `C`
Chilled, this is a brilliant off-dry aperitif.

**Kenderman St Laurens Medium Blend,
Pfalz 1996** `10` `B`

**Niersteiner Spiegelberg Kabinett,
Rheinhessen, St Ursula 1996** `10` `B`

Piesporter Michelsberg, K Linden 1996 `13.5` `B`
Try it chilled, just a glass or two, in an armchair with a book or the papers or just the cat on your lap. Now – don't you feel better already?

GREEK WINE RED

Mavrodaphne of Patras NV `13` `C`
A wine for seasonal slices of cake i.e. of the Christmas variety.

GREEK WINE WHITE

Kourtakis Retsina NV `14` `B`
I love retsina. It's a brilliant grilled-fish wine. This one is oily and cricket-bat flavoured.

HUNGARIAN WINE WHITE

Hungarian Chardonnay `11` `B`

ITALIAN WINE RED

Chianti Cecchi 1996 `12` `B`
Slobbery fruit.

Gabbia d'Oro VdT Rosso `11` `B`
Sweet (almost). A 'sort-of' wine rather than a full-blooded one.

Montepulciano d'Abruzzo, Venier `11` `B`
Sweet.

Silvano Rosso Sicilian Red 1996 `12` `B`
Some touches of depth under the sweet fruit.

Valpolicella Venier `12.5` `B`
Glug it chilled.

ITALIAN WINE WHITE

Gabbia d'Oro VdT Bianco `13` `B`
Soft, clutching at fruitiness, simple – and drinkable.

Silvano Bianco Sicilian White B

Some pert freshness and flavour here. Inviting price.

Soave Venier 15 B

Is it the cheapest soave? Certainly it must be the nattiest for the money: clean, crisp, nutty, brilliantly drinkable.

PORTUGUESE WINE WHITE

Rose de Cambriz 13.5 A

Serve very well chilled. Drink on hot evenings.

ROMANIAN WINE RED

Val Duna Merlot 1996 10 B

SOUTH AFRICAN WINE RED

Impala Cape Red 1996 14.5 B

Chill it (for fish), throw it at charcoal-grilled sausages, pour it out (chilled) for your guests – this wine aims to please.

Impala Pinotage, Western Cape 1996 14 C

Good, rich, gentle fruit which turns satisfyingly vibrant and savoury on the finish.

SOUTH AFRICAN WINE WHITE

Impala Cape White 1996 `14` `B`

An excellent, rich-edged wine for more fish dishes including Thai food.

Impala Chenin Chardonnay 1996 `14` `B`

Good nutty fruit on the finish is the final emphasis of a dry, charmingly constructed wine.

Jade Peaks Chenin Blanc 1996 `14.5` `B`

Crisp, melony, hints of mineral acidity, this is an excellent grilled-fish wine and general quaffer.

SPANISH WINE RED

Berberana d'Avalos Tempranillo Rioja 1996 `13.5` `B`

Needs sausages and mash to spark it into life.

Tempranillo/Cabernet Sauvignon Carinena NV `15` `B`

Brilliant value. A biscuity, textured, rich, dry and deliciously fruity red of style and vigour yet mature calmness.

SPANISH WINE WHITE

Castillo de Liria Moscatel, Valencia `15.5` `B`

Brilliant-value pud wine. At this price, it's a must for Christmas pud and cake.

Con Class Rueda NV `14` `B`

A food wine of individuality and flavour. Has a curious tang of dry toffeed fruit which to this palate at least is expressive of no known item of fructiculture.

USA WINE RED

California Cellars Red `11` `B`

E & J Gallo Cabernet Sauvignon 1994 `12.5` `C`

Somewhat sweet undertone makes it a very untypical cabernet.

E & J Gallo Dry Reserve NV `13` `C`

Interesting texture and old wellie fruit. Be okay with food. No elegance.

E & J Gallo Ruby Cabernet 1995 `13` `C`

Soft, rubbery and gently drinkable. A good beginner's red.

Gallo Sonoma County Zinfandel 1993 `14` `E`

Rich, ripe, very alive with solid fruit character hinting at spice. Expensive.

Paul Masson Carafes `10` `B`

USA WINE WHITE

California Cellars White `11` `B`

Paul Masson Carafes `10` `B`

SPARKLING WINE/CHAMPAGNE

Bonnet Brut Heritage Champagne   12   F

Lambrusco Bianco '4'   8   A

Lambrusco Rose '4'   6   A

Cherryade's got more personality.

Lambrusco Rosso '4'   8   A

Has some charm – not for earthlings though.

Champagne Brut, Louis Raymond   14.5   E

Excellent value. Light, lemony and properly priced.

MARKS & SPENCER

MARKS & SPENCER
Michael House
57 Baker Street
London
W1A 1DN
Tel 0171 935 4422
Fax 0171 487 2679

What's wonderful.

No one cares more about getting it right than this obsessed bunch of perfectionists and that is why M & S has a higher proportion of its range under synthetic cork than anyone else.

What's maddening.

Getting into this retailer's head office to attend a wine tasting is like trying to get into the home supporter's end of Old Trafford wearing full Chelsea kit. I wait for the day I return to my bicycle, chained up outside, only to find a security man has taken it to pieces in his zeal.

SEE STOP PRESS SECTION AT END OF BOOK FOR LAST-MINUTE ADDITIONS TO THIS RETAILER'S RANGE.

ARGENTINIAN WINE   RED

Oak Aged Mendoza Malbec 1992   15   D

Has hints of melted chocolate to its dry, rich fruitiness. A
mature wine, it needs food.

AUSTRALIAN WINE   RED

Bin 505 Shiraz Cabernet 1995   14   C

Ripe and very rich, almost too rich, like fruit cake and custard.
Can't imagine what food it goes with. Smoked kangaroo?

Coonawarra Winegrowers Shiraz 1995   12   E

A plethora of plum and soft berried fruit of such squashed
jamminess, you gasp. Could it be an invalid's soup?

Honey Tree Shiraz Cabernet 1996   13.5 D

It's so all-over friendly and soppy you can't get a word in
edgeways (let alone food).

McLaren Vale Cabernet Sauvignon 1994   16   D

Beautiful example of McLaren Vale fruit: herby, soft, rich,
aromatic, smooth yet with lots of flavour and a discreet, well-
mannered personality.

Pheasant Gully Riverina Shiraz   13   C

Ridge Coonawarra Cabernet Sauvignon
1995   13   E

Too expensive for the jam in the jar. What's going on with

Aussie reds? You can't possibly take more than a glass – you need a lot of friends to get through a bottle.

Rose Label Orange Vineyard Cabernet Sauvignon, Rosemount Estate 1993 | 14 | F

The perfume of spiced plums with ripe fruit to match. The tannins seemed detached from this middle-of-the-palate presence and only strike as the wine disappears, most deliciously, down the gullet. It won't get any better with age, so it must be drunk now. But it is very expensive.

Rosemount Estate Shiraz 1994 | 14 | D

Rosemount Estate Shiraz, South Australia 1995 | 13.5 | D

Plum and strawberry jam. Where's the tannin gone to? Oh, it's there. You just can't appreciate it under all that jam.

South East Australian Shiraz 1995 | 15 | C

Rich, ripe and soft but with enough tannins to keep from going soppy and gooey. Puppyish, yes, but it can be brought to heel and go well with food.

AUSTRALIAN WINE WHITE

Australian Medium Dry, South Eastern Australia | 13.5 | C

If it gets Gran off Lieb then it's worth the extra quid.

Haan Chardonnay, Barossa Valley 1996 | 15.5 | E

Very fancy salmon and lobster wine – has perfume, pace, potency and polish.

Honey Tree Semillon Chardonnay, Rosemount Estate 1996 `15` `D`

A delicate sipping wine of opulent texture, mild perfume, discreet fruit, fine balance and gentle, soothing manner. Not a bottle for rich food, it makes for refined tippling nevertheless.

Lindemans Bin 65 Chardonnay 1996 `15.5` `C`

Elegant, purposeful, balanced, finely wrought and handsomely textured. A textbook Aussie chardonnay.

Pheasant Gully Colombard Chardonnay `12.5` `C`

Rose Label Orange Vineyard Chardonnay, Rosemount 1995 `16.5` `F`

Beguiling perfume of woodsmoke and baked croissant, fruit which is both ripe and gently textured (ogen melon with a hint of fig and nuts) and a somewhat discreet finish of gentility and charm. An expensive treat which needs a fully alert and studious palate to catch every nuance. Robust food will kill it. Smoked salmon or mildly grilled fish will enhance it.

Rosemount Estate Chardonnay, Hunter Valley 1995 `16` `D`

Rich, creamy, smoky edge to the fruit which is beautifully shaped and poised – for take-off over nose, tastebuds, throat and mind.

South East Australian Lightly Oaked Chardonnay 1996 `16` `C`

Lovely rich, oily texture, well-buttered flavour of deep, satisfying, handsomely poised fruitiness which somehow manages to be never less than calm, unfussy and very stylish. A most unusually elegant Aussie chardonnay.

South East Australian Semillon/Chardonnay | 14.5 | C

Vine Vale Chardonnay, Barossa Valley 1996 | 14.5 | E

Classy, rich, balanced, individual. Has style all the way through it.

BULGARIAN WINE · RED

Bulgarian Vintners Cabernet Sauvignon, Svischtov 1992 | 13.5 | B

Very ripe and soft for such a comparatively middle-aged wine. I suspect it's past its best.

CHILEAN WINE · RED

Alta Mira Cabernet Sauvignon 1996 | 17 | C

Quite brilliantly priced and poised. The fruit is aromatic, rich and deep but has good tannins. There is an echo of cassis to it but mostly it's rich plums deliciously textured and well finished. Superb wine.

Carmen Reserve Merlot 1995 | 17 | D

Magnificence for little money: superb fruit of great elegance, floral and fruit complexity (herbs, violets, plums and raspberries) and caressing texture.

Carmen Vineyards Cabernet Sauvignon Reserve 1995 | 16 | D

Texturally fruity, aromatically all a delight. Somewhat coy, so robust food is out, but an elegant delight.

Carmen Vineyards Central Valley Cabernet Sauvignon 1995 `16` `C`

Rampant, ripe, dry, all-over stylish and very, very finely flavoured and delicious. Subtle smoky blackcurrant is its theme and it's deliciously played.

Carmen Vineyards Central Valley Merlot 1995 `16.5` `C`

Packed with flavour – like a jamjar crammed to the brim with soft rich fruit – but has depth, character, style, aplomb and a rousing finish. A strikingly savoury wine of polish and texture – the essence of leather-soft, luxuriously appointed merlot.

Carmen Vineyards Maipo Cabernet Sauvignon Reserve 1995 `16.5` `D`

Chocolatey, raspberryish, dry yet full of rounded fruit flavours, great tannic balance, superbly textured and perfectly weighted to go from nose to throat with insidious ease. A lovely wine.

Casa Leona Cabernet Sauvignon 1995 `15` `C`

Brilliant soft gentle fruit with a brushed suede edge of finesse.

Casa Leona Cabernet Sauvignon Reserve 1995 `16.5` `C`

A chocolate-lover's dream wine. Fattening, full, rich, deep, dry, complex, it's like an elixir of fruity layers – textured and fine.

Casa Leona Merlot 1996 `16` `C`

Soft, aromatic of old club chairs, dark cherry fruit, very vivid, beautifully textured and richly finished.

Casa Leona Merlot Reserve 1995 `16` `C`

Very soft and almost sweet on the finish, so potent is the immediacy of fruit. Beautiful texture, though, and a book-worm's bottle.

CHILEAN WINE WHITE

Carmen Vineyards Gewurztraminer Sauvignon 1996 `15` `D`

Spicy and daft, irreverent, full of flavour – great with oriental food and giving to stick-in-the-muds: 'My God! What is this yummy confection?!'

Casa Leona Chardonnay 1996 `13.5` `C`

Casa Leona Chardonnay Reserve 1996 `16.5` `C`

Wonderful value under a fiver: opulent, luxurious, rich, flavour all the way to the tip of your toes.

Lontue Chardonnay 1996 `15` `C`

Quiet, demure, delicate, delicious and thoroughly drinkable. Okay, so it is quiet – but when you want to be, this wine is a highly civilised companion.

Lontue Sauvignon Blanc 1996 `14.5` `C`

Delicious, calm, classy, fresh, hints of ripe fruit, balanced, exceedingly drinkable.

ENGLISH WINE WHITE

Leeford's Vineyard English Wine 1995 `10` `C`

Expensive, unbalanced, awkwardly fruited and quite oddly conceived. I cannot think anything but sentiment puts this wine on M&S shelves.

FRENCH WINE   RED

Beaujolais Sapin 1996   13.5 C

This has improved in bottle somewhat. Nice soft touch on the palate. It's drinkable even if it is a touch overpriced.

Bordeaux Matured in Oak, AC Bordeaux 1993   12 D

Bourgogne Rouge Tastevinage 1993   11 D

Some gamy inclination but little style as it limps its way home.

Cepage Counoise VdP d'Oc, Domaine Jeune 1996   15.5 C

This is, as likely as not, the only 100 per cent counoise grape variety wine on sale at a British supermarket. Counoise? Hardly famous, it pops up as 2 per cent of a few Chateauneuf-du-Papes. In this manifestation it is strikingly soft yet alive with ripe tannins and has a huge weight of brambly fruit in the mouth. A very intriguing wine of class, style and delicious eccentricity.

Chateau de Santenay, Mercurey 1994   10 E

So dull I'd rather drink pineapple juice.

Chateauneuf-du-Pape, Quiot 1995   13 E

It's good, but I'd rather drink Counoise (qv) at half the price.

Classic Claret Chateau Cazeau 1995   13.5 C

Domaine de Belle Feuille Cotes du Rhone 1995   11 C

Domaine St Pierre VdP de l'Herault, Domaines Virginie 1996

Very ripe and raunchy. Youngsters will like it.

Fitou, Domaine de Tauch Oak Aged 1993

Although one can't escape the nagging suspicion that this wine is a polite, anglicised Fitou made specifically for the orderly palates of M&S customers, there is a lot of soft, deliciously drinkable fruit here. Warm, ineffably plumply textured and willing, this is an attractive glug of immediate charm.

Fleurie Sapin 1996

Very drinkable. Has sufficient character and style to make you forget it's a beaujolais. And then you see that eight-quid price tag!

French Country Red VdP des Pyrenees-Orientales, Vignerons Catalans 1996

Full Red, Cotes du Roussillon Villages (1 litre)

Gold Label Cabernet Sauvignon VdP d'Oc, Domaines Virginie 1995

Soft and very delicious with sufficient depth of warm plummy fruit and finely knitted tannin to make it a brilliant glugging wine and a bottle to go with roasts and casseroles.

Gold Label Pinot Noir, Domaines Virginie VdP d'Oc 1994

House Red Wine

Margaux 1993

Merlot Moueix 1993 13 D

Moueix St Emilion 1993 13 E

Pinot Noir VdP d'Oc 1994 13.5 C

This would, it strikes me, be a ten-quid bottle (or much more) if it said Volnay on the label. But it doesn't. It says Vin de Pays d'Oc – Hicksville to the uninformed.

Syrah 'Domaine de Mandeville' VdP d'Oc 1996 14.5 C

Syrah like young beaujolais but much tastier and better with food. A real satisfying glug here.

FRENCH WINE   WHITE

Chablis 1995 12.5 D

Chablis Premier Cru, Grande Cuvee 1991 13 F

In spite of its divine aroma and lovely fruit as it initially strikes the palate, the finish doesn't live up to its prior billing.

Chardonnay 'Domaine de Mandeville', VdP d'Oc 1996 14.5 C

Delicate fruit (hints of melon) with a lovely lemonic, nutty finish. Cannot take pungent food, but great with salad and grilled prawns, and fish cakes.

Cotes de Gascogne Vin de Pays, Plaimont 1996 14 B

Very refreshing – in the glugging style of fruitiness.

French Country White Vin de Pays, Vignerons Catalans 1996

`13` `B`

Reasonable price but lacks bite on the finish.

Gold Label Chardonnay VdP d'Oc, Domaines Virginie 1996

`14` `C`

Mild-mannered and can meet the in-laws without upsetting anyone.

House White Wine

`12.5` `B`

Jeunes Vignes, La Chablisienne 1994

`12` `D`

Montagny Premier Cru, Cave de Buxy 1995

`14.5` `D`

Distinguished, superbly well-textured and rich with classy overtones. A truly excellent white burg.

Petit Chablis 1996

`13.5` `D`

Clean, mineral-edged, very fresh and lively.

Rose de Syrah VdP d'Oc, Domaines Virginie 1996

`14` `C`

The cosmetic edge is saved from complete tartiness by the crisp acidity. Excellent with grilled fish.

Sancerre Les Ruettes 1996

`13` `D`

Lemony, simplistic, very drinkable – at £3.99.

Vin de Pays du Gers White, Plaimont 1996

`14.5` `B`

Well-priced, well-fruited, well-adjusted all round. Nice pear/pineapple touch on the finish.

Viognier 'Domaine de Mandeville', VdP d'Oc 1996

`15` `C`

Gentle apricot fruit, whistle-clean and fresh, with an excellent balanced finish of subtle peach and a vague hint of lime.

Vouvray Domaine de la Pouvraie 1996

`15` `C`

Medium-bodied, slightly off-dry. But a brilliant aperitif. The fruit has a wet-wool edge to it and the acidity also saves the wine from sweetness. It will improve in bottle, if laid down, for several years. Delicious prospect for AD 2000 and beyond.

White Burgundy, Caves de Lugny 1995

`11` `C`

GERMAN WINE   WHITE

Hock, Tafelwein 1996 (1 litre)

`11` `C`

Somewhat dull.

Liebfraumilch, Klosterhof 1996

`12.5` `B`

If you must drink Lieb, this is as good as any – and decently priced. A glass, well chilled, as an aperitif would be a not unattractive prospect.

ISRAELI WINE   WHITE

Galilee Golan Chardonnay 1994

`13.5` `D`

Expensive curiosity. Has texture and flavour but is too expensive and finishes with its style cramped. But a most respectable stab at chardonnay from an unlikely source. If it was £3.99 it would be more winning.

ITALIAN WINE RED

Canfera Single Vineyard VdT di Toscana 1994

Interesting texture but the cherry-ripe fruit is adolescent and the finish mawkish. It would be a good wine at £3.99.

Castel del Monte 1996

Wins my label of the year award. It's charmingly kitsch-rustic. This beautifully echoes the fruit in the bottle.

Chianti Roberta Sorelli 1995

Almost cherry-sweet on the finish. A mild red which would be better chilled – and drunk with grilled meats and fish.

Collina d'Oro NV `13.5` `C`

Old and figgy-rich – good with food.

Italian Red Table Wine (1 litre) `11` `C`

Pretty dull.

Merlot del Veneto, Casa Girelli NV `12` `B`

Montepulciano d'Abruzzo, Girelli 1996 `13` `C`

At its best with pasta.

Tesoro Rosso NV `14.5` `C`

Rich and earthy, deliciously dry with a soupy richness, well held back by tannin and acidity.

Villa Cafaggio Chianti Classico 1995 `13` `D`

Has an uncharacteristic sweetness on the finish. Spoils the attempt to build a classy wine.

ITALIAN WINE WHITE

Bianco di Custoza 1996 `14` `C`

Expensive but very classy fish wine with a modern, fresh structure yet with enough personality and quiet depth to go far with food.

Bianco di Puglia 1996 `13.5` `B`

Clean, fresh, very respectable – not a lot of excitement but young and well served with good clean fruit. Good with fish and chips.

Cardillo Bianco di Sicilia 1996 `15.5` `B`

A brilliant aperitif tipple. Has soft, almost cosy fruit, pinned back by pert acidity from being overrich. Gorgeous flavour and style.

Casale Romano Malvasia/Chardonnay Lazio 1996 `14` `C`

Worth the entrance money for the touch of luxuriously opulent fruit on the fresh clean edge.

Chardonnay delle Tre Venezie `12` `C`

Frascati Superiore DOC (Estate Bottled) 1996 `13` `C`

Good flavour – but a mite expensive.

Italian White Table Wine (1 litre)   `14` `C`

Clean, flinty, fresh, demure, refreshing. A perfect fish wine.

Orvieto Classico 1996   `14` `C`

Crisp and nutty – almost elegant. Good with spaghetti alla vongole.

Pinot Grigio delle Tre Venezie   `13.5` `C`

MEXICAN WINE   RED

Parras Valley Cabernet Sauvignon/ Merlot 1994   `14` `C`

Interesting vegetal aroma leads to some delicious fruit which is truly impressive. Very highly polished wine of dry, wry classiness.

NEW ZEALAND WINE   RED

Kaituna Hills Cabernet/Merlot, Marlborough 1995   `13.5` `C`

Certainly arouses the palate and the nose. But whether it's a sympathetic arousal I'm not convinced. The vegetality is what gets to you. And the ragged edge to the texture.

Saints Hawkes Bay Cabernet Merlot 1994   `14.5` `D`

Touch of vegetality and pepper on the aroma which is carried through to the fruit. A dry yet highly strung wine which is best with meats and vegetable dishes.

NEW ZEALAND WINE WHITE

Kaituna Hills Gisborne Chardonnay 1996 | 14.5 | D

Rich, well-textured (melon spread thickly on velvet), well-balanced, well-priced, attractive all round.

Kaituna Hills Gisborne Chardonnay Semillon 1996 | 14.5 | C

Great shellfish wine. Warm, soft fruit on the tongue which arrives through an aromatic entrance suggesting something leaner, meaner and more mineral-intensive. Still, it's very tasty, attractively balanced.

Kaituna Hills Marlborough Sauvignon Blanc 1996 | 15 | D

Lovely grassy edge to firm, well-defined fruit of flavour and class.

Saints Gisborne Chardonnay 1995 | 13.5 | D

Delicious as it shakes the tastebuds but not impressive in the throat.

SOUTH AFRICAN WINE RED

Cabernet Sauvignon Coastal Region KWV 1993 | 13.5 | C

You won't believe cabernet can be made this puppyish and all-over-your-tongue friendly.

Shiraz Coastal Region KWV 1993 `14.5` `C`

Shiraz wearing its jazzy outdoor clothes: soft, colourful, bursting with personality.

Stellenbosch Merlot 1996 `14.5` `C`

Tasty, nicely leathery, dry but soft and ripe, and a lovely savoury edge to the fruit.

SOUTH AFRICAN WINE WHITE

Cape Country Chenin Blanc 1997 `13.5` `C`

Cape Country Colombard 1997 `14` `C`

Peardrops and ripe melon. Good warm-weather glug.

Madeba Dry White 1996 `12` `C`

Rather blowsy and ripe. Needs a rich fish dish on the side.

Madeba Reserve Chardonnay/Sauvignon Blanc 1996 `13.5` `C`

Rather rich. Food necessary here.

McGregor Chardonnay 1997 `13` `C`

Comes over very cosmetic as air gets to it in the mouth.

McGregor Chenin Blanc 1997 `12.5` `C`

Perderburg Cellar Sauvignon Blanc 1996 `13` `C`

Hints of grass up-front but not much of a lawn out back – it finishes weakly.

SPANISH WINE   RED

Gran Calesa Costers del Segre 1992

Savoury, rich, vibrant, dry yet softly voluptuous and fruity on the finish, this is lovely textured wine of great charm and flavoured, aromatic warmth.

La Mancha Tempranillo Cabernet Sauvignon 1996   14   C

This wine is good value, with its dry, rich character, well trimmed with its usual vanilla.

Las Falleras Utiel-Requena 1996   13.5   B

Very ripe and soft. Good adolescent glug.

Marques de Romeral Gran Reserva Rioja 1988

Flabby and knock-kneed, it seems pitiful to pit it against food let alone fork out seven quid for it.

Penascal Vino de Mesa Tinto N V   13.5   C

Like putting your nose in a make-up bag. If you can take that, you can swallow the price.

Rioja Bodegas AGE   14   C

One of the new-age (no pun on the maker's name intended) riojas with solidity and character, drinkability and soft texture without entirely losing the feel of the style.

Roseral Rioja Crianza, Bodegas AGE 1994

Dry, edgily rich, nicely textured – bring on the roast lamb!

Tempranillo Rioja, Bodegas AGE 1994 `14.5` `C`

Rioja fans' dream of a red: vanilla-textured, rapaciously fruity in the throat and accommodating with chorizo and chicken stew.

SPANISH WINE WHITE

Conca de Barbera Macabeo/Chardonnay 1996 `14` `B`

Good melon output which is deliciously complemented by pineapple and pear acidity.

Las Falleras Rose Utiel-Requena 1996 `12` `B`

Las Falleras Utiel-Requena 1996 `15.5` `B`

The best white wine for the money at M&S. It's nutty and demurely finished, has a nice smack of fruit in the middle and goes down a refreshed yet expectant throat (expectant for more).

Moscatel de Valencia NV `16` `C`

A brilliant honeyed pre-prandial passion-arouser. Or drink it with fruit and blue cheese.

Rioja Roseral 1996 `12` `C`

Awkward flinch on the finish.

URUGUAYAN WINE RED

Uruguayan Merlot 1996   `C`

Real bite! Lots of flavour, depth, fruit, tannin, vigour, acidity and a brilliant texture to round it all off. Terrific food wine as well as a great grilled-food glugger!

Uruguayan Tannat 1996 `14.5` `C`

Warm, rustic, slightly woody aroma leads to full rich fruit with a very dry finish. The centre of the fruit is ripe plum as if oven-warm. Individual flavour all round.

URUGUAYAN WINE WHITE

Uruguayan Chardonnay 1996 `13.5` `C`

Fresh with a nutty finish. Very attractive. Touch pricey for the style, though.

Uruguayan Chardonnay/Viognier 1996 `15` `D`

Individual, almost quirkily rich and frisky with a spicy edge – and quite quite delicious.

Uruguayan Sauvignon/Gewurztraminer 1996 `13.5` `C`

Interesting, even though the sauvignon well dominates the gewurz, and there is a hint of spice to the fresh fruit.

USA WINE RED

Canyon Road Cabernet Sauvignon 1995 `13.5` `D`

Bit soft and soupy.

Canyon Road Chardonnay 1996 `15` `D`

Cool style here plumped by some rich fruit.

FORTIFIED WINE

Cream Sherry 14 C

Fino Sherry 16 C

Delicate yet slyly fruity. A fino to bring wine lovers back to sherry?

Medium Amontillado Sherry 13 C

Rich Cream Sherry 15.5 C

SPARKLING WINE/CHAMPAGNE

Asti Spumante Consorzio 13 D

Bluff Hill Sparkling Wine (New Zealand) 15 D

Elegant and fruity.

Bottle Fermented Blanc de Blancs 1994 (Australia) 13 E

Has a subtle soap edge. I'm not sure at this price I want to clean my tongue in this way.

Cava Brut (Spain) 16 C

I'd rather engage my tastebuds with this soft yet finely finished cava than any number of champagnes priced five times higher.

Champagne Chevalier de Melline, Premier Cru Blanc de Blancs `12` `G`

Champagne Orpale 1985 `10` `H`

Medium Dry Cava (Spain) `14` `C`

Sweet, good with grandmas.

Oudinot Brut Champagne `16` `F`

This is one of the softest, most deliciously fruity champagnes at any supermarket anywhere. It has a delicate citric finish to complete its charms.

Oudinot Rose Champagne `17` `F`

Delightful rose – it justifies its soppy colour and steep price by being aromatically enticing, fruity in a most gentle way, with a finish of finesse.

Rosato Spumante (Italy) `12` `C`

Seppelt Chardonnay Blanc de Blanc Bottle Fermented Brut 1994 (Australia) `15` `E`

Delicate and delicious. As good as bubbly gets at this price.

Veuve de la Lalande Brut `10` `C`

Veuve de la Lalande Rose `12` `C`

Veuve de Medts, Premier Cru Brut (France) `14.5` `G`

Vintage Cava Brut 1993 `15` `D`

Very delicate and nicely put together. Delicious aperitif.

Vintage Champagne, St Gall, Premier Cru Brut 1990 `13` `G`

Vintage Oudinot Grand Cru 1989 ┃ 13.5 ┃ ┃ G ┃

Yarden Blanc de Blancs Bottle Fermented
Brut NV (Israel) ┃ 13.5 ┃ ┃ E ┃

Very elegant. As good as a cava – but, alas, at twice the price.

WM MORRISONS SUPERMARKETS

WM MORRISONS SUPERMARKETS
Wakefield 41 Industrial Estate
Wakefield
W Yorks
WF1 0XF
Tel 01924 870000
Fax 01924 921250

What's wonderful.

This is the northern supermarket group whose higher management starts to run a temperature and feel genuinely ill if it sees a rival selling something for less. And there's never any bullshit here either. What's fancy are the price tags and how fanciable they make the wines; many of these tags come attached to some highly drinkable specimens. These aren't special bargains, on offer for a limited period. Neither are they on–off parcels of wine, on sale for a week or so. At Morrisons there is great value on the wine shelves every day of the year.

What's maddening.

Morrisons is a leanly run organisation. The only fat you see here is firmly adhering to the bacon rinds. It doesn't wear a suit and a lurid tie and spout inanities.The wine department was run, leanly and cleanly and solely, by one man for many years until he recently acquired an assistant buyer (lean as a willow staff she). But this hasn't made much difference to the load it adds to my life. You see, other supermarkets hire London hotels and lay out the wines on firmly starched tablecloths for me to taste. They number the wines and the numbers correspond to a list, with prices all neatly appended. Morrisons don't run to this sort of palaver. I'll come home after a day spent tasting at one of those starched white hotels and there will be the Morrisons tasting: all six or seven cases of it nonchalantly stacked against the basement door. I have to lug the cases inside before I get my bike stored away. I have to unpack all those wines. True, they have prices on the back on little yellow stickers (inexpensively printed) but Linda will have to log all the wines, they will fill my tiny kitchen, and I will faithfully give up a sunny Saturday and the company of my kids to taste them. My reward is some terrific bargains I hope my readers will delight to buy and slurp. But all that humping! At times Morrisons makes me feel like a stevedore.

ARGENTINIAN WINE   RED

Balbi Vineyard Mendoza Rouge 1995   15.5   B

AUSTRALIAN WINE   RED

Barramundi Shiraz/Merlot   13   C

Zips across the tastebuds very smartish.

Coldridge Shiraz/Cabernet Sauvignon 1996   13   C

The Aussie version of peasant plonk. Thus, it lacks the backbone of Spanish, Italian and southern French peasants who do not bend over backwards to please – as does this soft, somewhat soppily fruity wine. Anyway, Australian peasants all drink beer.

Jamiesons Run Coonawarra Red 1994   13.5   E

Rich and soupy. Food will murder it.

Lindemans Bin 45 Cabernet Sauvignon 1995   13   D

I suppose one can imagine toying with a glass, but the wine tries to be liked so unimaginatively, it's embarrassing. I prefer more character in wine, as in people – especially at this price.

Lindemans Bin 50 Shiraz 1994   13.5   D

Expensive for the style, which is puppyishly fruit.

Penfolds Bin 35 Shiraz Cabernet 1994   15.5   C

Penfolds Rawsons Retreat Bin 35 1995   13.5   C

Respectable rather than raunchy.

AUSTRALIAN WINE — WHITE

Coldridge Chenin Blanc/Chardonnay 1996 `13` `C`

Very prettily perfumed fruit with a cosmetic edge. Pleasant enough tipple when the weather turns warm.

Lindemans Bin 65 Chardonnay 1996 `15.5` `B`

Delicious combination of butter, hazelnuts and melon undercut by a perfectly weighted uptide of acidity.

Lindemans Hunter River Semillon Bin 455 1994 `13` `C`

I've tried hard to rate it higher but the finish lets it down. It fails to grip.

Penfolds Rawsons Retreat Bin 21 Semillon/Chardonnay/Colombard 1996 `15.5` `C`

Wyndham Estate TR2 Medium Dry White Wine 1995 `11` `C`

Sweet and sour-faced wine of oddly disconcerting charms.

AUSTRIAN WINE — WHITE

Lenz Moser Gruner Veltliner 1995 `13` `B`

BRAZILIAN WINE — RED

Amazon Cabernet Sauvignon `13.5` `C`

BRAZILIAN WINE   WHITE

Amazon Chardonnay   `11` `C`

BULGARIAN WINE   RED

Bear Ridge Gamza NV   `12` `B`

Bulgarian Reserve Merlot 1991   `15` `B`

Lovely dry old thing. Like drawing a thin leather curtain over
the tastebuds. Great value.

**Twin Peaks Reserve Cabernet Sauvignon
1993**   `13` `C`

BULGARIAN WINE   WHITE

Bulgarian Reserve Chardonnay 1993   `14` `C`

Great maturity and flavour which coats the tastebuds and makes
the wine a treat with chicken.

CHILEAN WINE   RED

**Castillo de Molina Cabernet Sauvignon
1995**   `16` `C`

Terrific flavour, depth, texture, structure, weight of fruit, and
just beautiful flavour.

Entre Rios Chilean Red   `15.5` `B`

Gato Negro Cabernet Sauvignon 1996   `15` `B`

Brilliant richness of attack, really clogs the tastebuds and won't be shifted. Terrific glug, terrific food wine.

Stowells of Chelsea Chilean Merlot
Cabernet (3-litre box)   `10` `C`

Price has been adjusted to show equivalent per bottle.

CHILEAN WINE   WHITE

Castillo de Molina Chardonnay 1995   `16` `C`

Gorgeous texture and richness, great depth and oodles of flavour. Yet it's dry, sophisticated and witty. Chilean chardonnay really is something else.

Castillo de Molina Chardonnay Reserva
1996   `16` `C`

Very elegantly attired, rich and characterful, this is a splendid example of how mature in feel a young Chilean chardonnay can surprisingly be. It hums with flavour and it is irresistibly drinkable.

Castillo de Molina Sauvignon Blanc 1996   `13` `C`

Entre Rios Chilean White   `15` `B`

Gato Blanco Sauvignon Blanc, Lontue
Valley 1996   `15.5` `B`

Brilliant, crisp, textured fruit of length, style, elegance and subtlety. It is excellent with fish, excellent value, excellent all round. It is high-quality sipping (if you must consume your white wine this way).

Stowells of Chelsea Chilean Sauvignon Blanc (3-litre box) · 15.5 · B

Price has been adjusted to show equivalent per bottle.

ENGLISH WINE · WHITE

Three Choirs Estates Premium 1996 · 12 · C

Expensive for the style, which is ordinary. Not one of Three Choirs' classic vintages on this evidence.

FRENCH WINE · RED

Bourgogne 1994 · 10 · D

It is true that expensive, rough burgundy like this goes surprisingly well with a roast hen, but you still have to part with seven quid for the wine and then there's the small matter of the hen. Seven quid is better spent elsewhere at Morrisons than here.

Cellier la Chouf, Minervois · 14 · B

Chais Cuxac Cabernet Sauvignon VdP d'Oc 1995 · 13.5 · C

Dry and a touch wrinkled at the edges. But excellent with food.

Chateau de Flaugergues Coteaux du Languedoc 1995 · 14 · D

Dry, rich, very dry and full of herb-packed brambly fruit. Lovely elegant food wine.

Chateau de Lauree Bordeaux Rouge 1995 `14` `C`

Goodness! Drinkable, more than drinkable, claret at this price. What's the world coming to?

Chateauneuf-du-Pape Domaine du Vieux Lazaret 1995 `14` `E`

Lot of money, lot of flavour and richness. Savoury and soupy.

Claret, Morrisons `13` `B`

Dry, very dry (but not dry like Clive Anderson). But also soft (but not as soft as Clive Anderson).

Corbieres Les Fenouillets 1995 `15` `B`

£2.95! Doesn't seem credible. What do you do, Stuart, smuggle bottles out under your jumper? Why put up with the ferry port fracas, dear reader, when there's this number lying fruity and dry on Morrison's shelves?

Cotes du Rhone Villages, 1995 `14` `C`

Cotes de Saint Mont, Bastz d'Autan 1995 `16.5` `C`

The essence of Midi warmth! A terrific rich dark wine of great tannic depth and flavour. Wonderful with robust meat and vegetable dishes. Terrific style and character from the tannat grape.

Cotes du Ventoux 1995 `14` `B`

Good lip-smackin', throat-throbbin' savoury finish to some decently rustic fruit.

Cotes du Luberon 1995 `14.5` `B`

One of Morrison's best grilled meat reds: a characterfully dry wine of substance and acute drinkability. Complex? No. Rich? Not especially. True to itself? Absolutely.

Cotes du Rhone (half bottle)

Usefully fruity wine in a bottle sized to suit the modest tippler.
A dry, approachable wine of simple charms. Also available in
75cl–1.5litre sizes.

Cotes du Rhone, Morrisons `13` B

Very soft and approachable.

Cotes du Roussillon, Morrisons `15` B

Ridiculously down-to-earth in everything including, felicitously,
price. It is dry, soft, gently rounded at the edges and has some
degree of character. It is perfectly brilliant value for parties.

Domaine du Crouzel Corbieres 1995

The soft, love-to-meet-you level of southern French red. More
raunch please! (Goes best with lunch, raunch.)

Fox Mountain Syrah/Merlot VdP d'Oc 1996 `15` B

Light but rich, soft but gently hairy, flavourful yet lithe. An
excellent quaffing bottle.

Julienas 1996

La Source Cabernet Sauvignon VdP
d'Oc 1994

La Source Merlot VdP d'Oc 1995 `14` B

Soft and approachable with a ripe cherry finish. Not a textbook merlot.

La Source Syrah VdP d'Oc 1995 `14` B

Simple, tasty, eminently acquirable and drinkable, well fleshed
out on the finish. A good food and glugging red.

Le Millenaire Cotes du Roussillon Villages 1994
`13.5` **B**

Margaux 1994
`11` **E**

The label says it all really. 'Margaux!' it shouts. That stands for bullshit, bumptiousness, blather and bad value.

Marquis de l'Estouval, VdP de l'Herault 1995
`13` **A**

Montregnac Bergerac 1994
`13` **B**

Oak Matured Claret 1995
`14` **C**

Decent age, decent fruit, a general decency of dry claret style. Excellent with grilled and roast meats.

Regnie, Duboeuf 1994
`12` **D**

Renaissance Buzet 1994
`14` **C**

St Emilion, Morrisons
`13` **C**

Touch expensive for the reluctance of the sun to shine on the grapes.

Stowells of Chelsea Claret Bordeaux Rouge (3-litre box)
`13` **C**

Price band has been adjusted to show equivalent per bottle.

Tradition Coteaux du Languedoc NV
`15.5` **B**

Amazingly well-turned out for the money: rich, softly textured and ripe, dry (good tannins), balanced and has some real hints of class. The alert palate might even detect, yawn yawn, the hint of chocolate in it. A chump chop will soon see off subtleties like this, leaving you mere tasty fruit.

Vin de Pays de l'Aude Red (half bottle)   13   A

Has hints of dry scrubland which give the appley fruit some suggestion of its provenance. Also available in 75cl–1.5litre sizes.

Winter Hill VdP de l'Aude 1995   15   B

FRENCH WINE   WHITE

Cascade Sauvignon Blanc Bordeaux 1996   13   B

Cheap, marginally cheerful.

Chais Cuxac Chardonnay VdP d'Oc 1996   15   C

A superbly well-balanced chardonnay of style and class. It has real depth to its fruit, no blowsiness or textured coarseness, and it has great versatility with food: soups, salads, chicken and fish. It is staggeringly good value when compared with some of the burgundian stuff.

Chateau de Lauree Bordeaux 1995   12.5   B

Chateau Saint Galier, Graves 1995   14   C

Classy, mineral-edged fruit here. Good choice for fish and grilled prawns, etcetera.

Cotes du Luberon 1996   14.5   B

Fresh-faced, clean, youthful, crisply turned out and a little nutty. Can you imagine a more congenial companion for grilled fish?

Cotes du Roussillon   11   B

Has a flat finish which is not expressive of wit or style.

Entre Deux Mers 1996 `13.5` `B`

An excellent, decently clean, crisp fish wine. Certainly be good with moules, say, or crab cakes.

Fox Mountain Sauvignon/Chardonnay, VdP d'Oc 1996 `13` `B`

Ginestet Graves Blanc 1994 `13` `C`

J. P. Chenet, Cinsault Rose 1995 `12` `B`

La Source Chardonnay VdP de l'Aude 1996 `14` `B`

Languedoc's most engaging under-three-quid chardonnay. Has bite, balance and some hints of richness.

La Source Sauvignon Blanc VdP d'Oc 1996 `15` `B`

Ah! The many virtues of this splendid little wine. Let me count the ways it thrills me: 1. The smell. 2. The fruit. 3. The price. 4. The plastic cork. A wine of plasticity, price and proper sauvignon fruit.

La Source Syrah Rose VdP d'Oc 1995 `13` `B`

Le Millenaire Cotes du Roussillon 1994 `12` `C`

'M' Muscadet Sevre et Maine `12` `B`

Also available in half bottles at £1.69 (at time of going to press).

Macon-Villages Domaine Jean-Pierre Teissedre 1994 `13` `C`

At nigh on a fiver, it's asking a lot. However, it does have some blunt character to it of warm vegetality but as a specimen of delicious fruit, chardonnay at that, to compare it with similarly priced specimens of the same grape from Chile, South Africa, Languedoc and southern Italy is to find this wine lacking.

Meursault Pierre Matrot 1990 `8` `F`

Montregnac Sauvignon, Bergerac 1995 `12` `B`

This is reasonable enough, for a French sauvignon at £3.30, but compare it with Gato Blanco at the same price, same grape and you see the gulf which separates the ordinary from the truly classy.

Muscadet Sevre et Maine, Morrisons `12` `B`

Has something in its fruit and acidity which rings a bell (i.e. reminds the ancient tippler of the excellence of muscadet when Napoleon was the French Republic's head barman) but it's only an echo.

Pinot Blanc Vin d'Alsace Preiss Zimmer 1995   `C`

Rich, dry but with a hint of smoke and creamy (like echoes, really). Needs oriental meat dishes, I reckon, to really shine.

Pouilly Fume Pierre Guery 1995 `10` `D`

Insipid and uninspired. Morrisons only stock it because there are still clots in the world who see the words 'Pouilly Fume' on the label and think 'Wow!' Let us pity these poor creatures.

Rameaux de France Ile de Beaute Chardonnay 1994   `B`

Curiously vegetal and coyly rich. Needs food – crude food, no frills.

Rose d'Anjou, Morrisons `14`

The label speaks true! It *is* fruity and elegant as claimed and it is a perfect glugging wine, well chilled. I would add it's cheap – for a decent rose – and it has a beautiful plastic cork.

213

Sauvignon de St Bris, Marquis de Bieville 1996
`15` `C`

Stands up to all sorts of breezy shellfish and fish dishes because it is so brilliantly concentrated with a lush, grassy undertone.

Terret Vin de Pays Lurton 1994
`12` `B`

Tradition Gewurztraminer Vin d'Alsace, Preiss-Zimmer 1995
`14` `D`

Expensive but worth the entrance money for the quirkily exotic edge of smoky spiciness to the fruit. Brilliant with oriental food.

Vin de Pays de l'Aude White (half bottle)
`13.5` `A`

It's simplicity itself but has some crisp charm and a level of fruit to tickle anyone's palate. Also available in 75cl–1.5litre sizes.

Vouvray Jean Michel 1996
`13` `C`

Off-dry, soft, quietly honeyed. Good with fresh fruit.

Winter Hill White 1995
`13.5` `B`

GERMAN WINE
WHITE

Bereich Bernkastel 1996
`11` `B`

Flonheimer Adelberg Kabinett Johannes Egberts 1995
`13` `B`

Franz Reh Auslese 1994
`12` `C`

Franz Reh Kabinett 1994
`11` `B`

Franz Reh Spatlese 1993 `13` `B`

Sweet – good with fresh fruit and goat's cheese.

Mosel Light & Flinty `11` `B`

Light I get. Missed the flinty.

Seafish Dry Rheinhessen 1995 `12` `B`

Tries so hard to be liked! It is, however, somewhat of a dull dog – even at £3.09.

Stowells of Chelsea Liebfraumilch (3-litre box) `12` `B`

Price has been adjusted to show equivalent per bottle.

Urziger Wurzgarten Riesling Auslese, Ewald Pfeiffer 1993 `15` `D`

Rich and honeyed yet delicate, aromatic, minerally and lovably grapey. A pud wine, yes, or blue cheese and great with fresh fruit.

Weinheimer Sybilenstein Beerenauslese (half bottle) `14` `C`

Still young but a stunning accompaniment to strawberries or raspberries if you fancy laying it down until next summer. Oodles of honeyed fruit here.

Zimmermann Riesling NV `13.5` `C`

More zip than its rivaner cousin, it has the citricity of riesling with some of its subtle richness – but in a dry form. It's just so ridiculously uncompetitively priced at £3.99!

Zimmermann Rivaner NV `13` `C`

Not a bad stab at grape crushing. A glass, chilled, after a day at the coal face would be acceptable enough – you could employ the remainder as a foot bath (but I'm being very cruel to a decent wine here – besides, your feet would have to be abnormally tiny).

GREEK WINE   RED

Mavrodaphne of Patras   `11` `C`

GREEK WINE   WHITE

Kourtaki Vin de Crete 1995   `11` `B`

Crete was the place I once tasted the worst wine in the world: a heavily oxidised red retsina of such inflammability it could usefully have gone into a paraffin lamp. This white, dry example of Cretan oenology is not so vile.

HUNGARIAN WINE   RED

Chapel Hill Pinot Noir   `10` `B`

Thin as a politician's excuse.

HUNGARIAN WINE   WHITE

Chapel Hill Irsai Oliver   `13.5` `B`

A simple, delicious muscaty aperitif.

Chapel Hill Pinot Noir Blanc 12 B

With pinot noir failing to make great red wine in certain areas it's tempting to applaud anyone leaving out the skins to create a white wine. This drinker's clapping, however, is muted.

ITALIAN WINE RED

Barbera d'Alba, Feyles 1993 13.5 D

Adventurous wine. Goes where other wines dare not tread: over £5, and to where figs grow and prunes dry in the sun.

Barbera Piemonte 1996 10 B

Chianti 1996, Morrisons 10 C

Chianti Classico Uggiano 1995 13 C

A soupy, jammy chianti of a curious style. It's probably at its best with pastas with rich meaty sauces.

Chianti dei Colli Fiorentini Uggiano 1991 11 C

Chianti dei Colli Fiorentini Uggiano 1994 14 C

Has greater acidity and bite than other Uggiano chiantis, perhaps its particular provenance is the reason and this gives it a lighter, zippier feel in the mouth with muted earthiness. An attractive glug and versatile food wine (chicken, roasts, pastas).

Chianti Riserva Uggiano 1991 14 D

The most expensive Uggiano offering and rightly so: it's an impressive, correctly Tuscan red of rich dry flavours which summon up hints of the most hearty aspects of the landscape and cuisine of its native region. It would be excellent with lamb roasted with rosemary. It also goes brilliantly with dishes using Parmesan cheese.

Chianti Uggiano 1995 `14` `C`

Better than its Classico big brother (and over a quid less). Has typical Tuscan earthy overtones to a decent level of rich plummy fruit.

Eclisse VdT di Puglia Rosso `14.5` `B`

Merlot del Veneto, Vigneti del Sole 1996 `13.5` `B`

Cheap, cheerful, lightly fruity company. Probably best chilled with a fish stew.

Montepulciano d'Abruzzo Vigneti del Sole 1995 `13.5` `B`

Valpolicella, Morrisons (half bottle) `12` `A`

Has some warmth. But so does a three-bar electric fire. Also available in 75cl–1.5litre sizes.

ITALIAN WINE WHITE

Ca'Fornari Soave Classico Costeggolia 1995 `13.5` `C`

Dry fruit which works best with fish or shellfish. It's a touch austere drunk by itself.

Eclisse White `12` `B`

Fish and chips? Might work with it.

Frascati Superiore 1996 `12.5` `A`

Has a gentle energy and bite to its meagre fruit. Also available in 75cl–1.5litre sizes.

Orvieto Classico Uggiano 1995 `13.5` `B`

A clean, fresh wine of decency and good citizenship, but it might just exhibit a bit more character.

Pinot Grigio delle Venezie 1996 `13` `B`

Hum, not bad with spaghetti alla vongole.

Soave (half bottle) `12` `A`

Not especially suave (or smooth or polite), but then that's misnomers all over . . . Also available in 75cl–1.5litre sizes.

Stowells of Chelsea Chardonnay (3-litre box) `13.5` `C`

Price band has been adjusted to show equivalent per bottle.

MOROCCAN WINE RED

Cabernet Syrah `14` `B`

Not as rampantly rich and savoury as it has been, but it's still soft and highly drinkable – and well able to cope with a range of meaty dishes. It's a jammy wine of warmth and subtle richness.

NEW ZEALAND WINE WHITE

Montana Reserve Barrique Fermented Chardonnay 1996 `14` `E`

Expensive for a piece of wood.

PORTUGUESE WINE   RED

Bairrada Reserva, Borges 1994   `13.5` `C`

There's a hiccup to the fruit as it finishes in the throat when you'd prefer to supply your own satisfied hiccups. This might disappear with food, but it mars an otherwise reasonable show.

Dao Meia Encosta 1994   `11` `C`

Soveral Tinto de Mesa   `10` `A`

Val Longa Country Wine NV   `14` `B`

PORTUGUESE WINE   WHITE

Val Longa Country Wine NV   `10` `B`

Vinho Verde   `10` `B`

Not a vast array of charm on display here unless you wish to acquire a candle holder.

ROMANIAN WINE   RED

Classic Pinot Noir 1994   `14.5` `B`

More drinkable, tasty, rich and satisfying than dozens of red burgundies at five times the price.

Romanian Country Red `12` `B`

Interesting combination of fruit concentrate and tar. A gooey wine.

ROMANIAN WINE WHITE

Classic Sauvignon Blanc 1995 `13.5` `B`

Curiously rich sauvignon of interest to kitchens serving smoked salmon.

Romanian Late Harvest Chardonnay 1985 `15` `C`

This is improving nicely in bottle and is now one of the most unusual, intriguing and best-value pudding wines around. Lovely aroma, honeyed sweet fruit and a rich finish of lime and pineapple. Brilliant stuff.

SOUTH AFRICAN WINE RED

Bottelary Winery Pinotage, Stellenbosch 1995 `13.5` `C`

Bovlei Winery Merlot 1995 `15.5` `B`

Cracker for the money: warm, rich, aromatic, reasonably deep and gently leathery (leather with some degree of polish to it) and very well balanced. It is excellent company for roasts, cheeses and vegetables, pastas, risotti and sausages.

South African Red, Morrisons `15` `B`

Thoroughly warm and friendly and unspeakably drinkable – if you don't mind the mollycoddling it gives the throat on the way down. It has a kind of linctus effect.

SOUTH AFRICAN WINE   WHITE

Bovlei Winery Sauvignon Blanc 1996   14.5   B

Deliciously nutty and fresh – great accompaniment to all fish dishes.

Cape Country Chardonnay 1996   12   C

Somewhat muddy fruit of uncertain direction.

Faircape Chenin Blanc 1996   14   B

Good tippling here. Trips neatly over the tongue with gentle lemonic steps, crisp and positive, and its style is very suited to all fish dishes. There is a faint floral quality to it, never intrusive but absolutely delicious.

Faircape Sauvignon Blanc 1995   13   B

Namaqua Colombard Chardonnay 1996   13   B

Curious rich undertone. Will work with food, though.

South African White Crisp and Fruity, Morrisons   13.5   B

Doesn't quite come up to scratch on the finish, though it has reasonable attractive fruit lightly fleshed out in the modern manner.

Stowells of Chelsea Chenin Blanc (3-litre box)   12   B

Price has been adjusted to show equivalent per bottle.

SPANISH WINE   RED

Bodegas Navajas Rioja 1995, Morrisons   `15.5` `C`

Light yet tobaccoey and rich-edged and delightfully drinkable.
A delicious wine of quiet class.

**Clos d'en Ton Cabernet Sauvignon Costers
del Segre 1996**   `14` `D`

Extremely elegant, smooth, flavourful and typical yet delicious.

Good Spanish Red   `13.5` `B`

At £2.59 (at time of writing – hand steady as a rock after
grasping its seventieth glass of the day), this wine is no pain
to acquire and no pain to drink. True, its price tag generates
more excitement than its fruit but let us not gainsay the fruity
softness of the wine which is commendably soupy.

**Remonte Navarra Crianza Cabernet
Sauvignon 1992**   `15.5` `C`

Rioja, Morrisons   `14` `C`

Rubbery and fruity – odd yet engaging.

Rioja Navajas Reserva 1990   `14` `D`

Minty, stylish and decently fruity – but at six quid it requires
more. And it provides more (albeit a touch of it): texture and
fair fruit.

**Stowells of Chelsea Tempranillo (3-litre
box)**   `14` `B`

Price has been adjusted to show equivalent per bottle.

Torres Sangredetoro 1994   `16` `C`

Best vintage yet for some while of this old warhorse. Has gently spicy, warmly textured fruit, ripe and rich but deliciously coated with a dry tannic shellac. Great with casseroles, etc.

SPANISH WINE WHITE

Bodegas Navajas Rioja 1995, Morrisons C

Real flavour and edgy richness here. Great with all manner of foods – including tandoori fish.

Solana Torrontes Treixadura 1994 15 C

You might think twice before spending the touch over four quid needed to acquire this eccentricity, but if you want something different, exotic and delicious, then hesitate not. Local peasant grape vinified into something crisp and flavourful for grilled, poached and even raw fish.

URUGUAYAN WINE RED

Castel Pujol Las Violetas Tannat 1994 C

Big yet friendly, instantly fruity yet deep.

USA WINE RED

Blossom Hill, California 10 C

Californian Red NV, Morrisons 13 B

Not as good as it once was – almost a sweet edge to the fruit here.

Nathanson Creek Merlot 1995 14 C

Soft, rich, ripe and compellingly fruity. Good texture.

Parducci Petite Sirah 1994 13 D

Lot of money, but interesting: soft, ripe, rich, aromatic, and . . . gooey.

Sutter Home Cabernet Sauvignon 1994 13 C

Sutter Home Zinfandel 1994 13.5 C

Zippy yet rich – zin's great double act.

Willamette Oregon Pinot Noir 1993 13.5 E

USA WINE   WHITE

Blossom Hill, California 10 C

Californian White NV, Morrisons 13 B

Some richness here. Needs food.

Glen Ellen Proprietor's Reserve Chardonnay 1995 16 C

Developing more vegetality as it ages but still a richly textured, plump chardonnay of flavour, depth and real engaging fruitiness. It offers a lovely glass of wine to all the senses.

Sebastiani White Zinfandel 1995 10 C

Sutter Home California Chardonnay 1995 15 C

One of the best under £5 California chardonnays around. Knocks the Gallo product into a cocked stetson. Class and flavour at a reasonable price.

Willamette Valley Chardonnay, Oregon 1993
`14.5` `E`

A lot of money but a lot of fruit: mature, rich, rampantly deep and gummy (and yummy), it is a ripe, full wine of savouriness, texture and old-style (in the best sense of the word) burgundian rusticality yet finesse.

FORTIFIED WINE

Rozes Ruby
`13` `C`

Rozes Special Reserve
`14` `D`

Tasty stuff. Some classy texture.

Rozes Tawny
`12.5` `C`

SPARKLING WINE/CHAMPAGNE

Asti Spumante Gianni (Italian)
`13` `C`

Sweet thing for the sweet-toothed (or sweet-toothless).

Cava Brut 1993, Morrisons
`15` `D`

Classic dryness, class, style and really impish fruit of real charm.

Fita Azul Vinho Espumante (Portugal)
`8` `C`

Stuart, where did you find this extraordinary specimen? It tastes as if vinified from the underwear of disgraced ex-Tory MPs. (Mind you, having said that, this bubbly is easier to take than some of the latter group's vile whoppers.)

Nicole d'Aurigny Brut Champagne `13.5` `E`

If you must buy champagne, buy this. At less than a tenner, it's not a steal but with the general obscenity called champagne pricing this one, at least, isn't too rude.

Paul Herard Blanc de Noirs Brut
Champagne (half bottle) `14` `D`

Paul Herard Blanc de Noirs Demi Sec
Champagne `14` `F`

This is a lovely bottle of bubbly. it's not remotely too sweet or too dry. Great with smoked fish.

Raimat Sparkling Chardonnay (Spain) `15` `D`

Seaview Brut `14` `D`

Seaview Brut Rose (Australia) `15` `D`

Has flavour and some depth without forgetting its job: to refresh the palate.

Seppelt Great Western Brut `15` `C`

SAFEWAY PLC

SAFEWAY PLC
Safeway House
6 Millington Road
Hayes
UB3 4AY
Tel 0181 848 8744
Fax 0181 573 1865

What's wonderful.

Safeway has adopted a pioneering attitude to some of the wine styles of Romania and Hungary and the results have been inexpensive wines with generous levels of fruit. No retailer spends more time fretting about getting its customers interested in newer and different wines and it has regular Wine Fairs where there are stunning bargains on offer.

What's maddening.

I wish this retailer was a bit crazier, a bit more instinctive. Last year, for all the right reasons , it spent vast sums on redesigning certain aspects of its wine display and yet, to my mind, I don't believe it made as much of an impact as it should have. And the reason is because Safeway lives up to its name: the safe way. I do not offer this witless pun because I have a wooden head but because I have a soft heart. I would like to see the store's talented wine department, headed by a gifted and resourceful woman, be even more successful. As successful as it deserves to be.

SEE STOP PRESS SECTION AT END OF BOOK FOR LAST-MINUTE ADDITIONS TO THIS RETAILER'S RANGE.

ARGENTINIAN WINE   RED

Alamos Ridge Cabernet Sauvignon, Mendoza 1994   14   C

Dry bordeaux style without the austerity. Selected stores.

Balbi Vineyard Malbec 1996   15   C

Mendoza Red 1996, Safeway   15.5   B

Terrific value for money here. A dry yet rollingly rich-edged wine which reserves its best speech for the final curtain.

ARGENTINIAN WINE   WHITE

Alamos Ridge Chardonnay, Mendoza 1996   15.5   C

Complex, individual, hints of controlled richness, great balance, firm acidity. An excellent chardonnay of style and character. Selected stores.

Balbi Syrah Rose 1996   13.5   C

Ripe and rich and ready for anything. Certain drinkers will happily drown in it.

AUSTRALIAN WINE   RED

Australian Oaked Shiraz 1996, Safeway   14   D

Rich and very soft. Like soup charged with fruit alcohol.

Breakaway Grenache/Shiraz, McLaren 1995

`14` `C`

There might be the odd bottle of the '95 left, but the '96 should be coming in by the time this book appears (not available for tasting at time of going to press).

Farms Cabernet/Merlot, Barossa Valley 1992

`10` `F`

Spineless and far too pricey. Top fifty stores.

Hardys Bankside Shiraz 1995

`14.5` `D`

Classy stuff – has oodles of flavour but it doesn't sag in the middle like some Aussies. It has some weight, some tannin, some character to last the course (meat or veg or cheese).

Hardys Collection Coonawarra Cabernet Sauvignon 1994

`14` `E`

Hardys Nottage Hill Cabernet Sauvignon/ Shiraz 1995

`13.5` `C`

Okay, but a fiver?

Hardys Stamp Grenache/Syrah 1996

`13` `C`

Jacob's Creek Dry Red 1993

`15` `C`

Lindemans Pyrus, Coonawarra 1993

`14` `F`

Very expensive but worthy – if not magnificent. The texture and fruit are high class but it is a touch contrived in style. Top fifty stores.

Mount Hurtle Shiraz 1994

`13.5` `E`

Another stinking red Aussie all over the tongue like squashed fruit.

Penfolds Bin 407 Cabernet Sauvignon 1993 `15` `E`

Deeply classy fruit and tannic scaffolding give the whole construct richness, ornamentation and solidity.

**Penfolds Clare Valley Shiraz/Cabernet
Sauvignon 1994** `15.5` `D`

**Penfolds Koonunga Hill Shiraz Cabernet
1992** `14` `C`

Penfolds Rawsons Retreat Bin 35 1995 `13.5` `C`

Usual decent turnout.

**Peter Lehmann Barossa Cabernet
Sauvignon 1995** `16` `E`

An expensive but very interesting, tannically well shaped cabernet. Selected stores.

**Rosemount Estate Cabernet Sauvignon
1995** `14` `D`

Stylish and drinkable but a touch expensive. Should be coming into selected stores as this book comes out.

Rosemount Estate Shiraz, 1995 `13` `E`

Very soft and, at this price, I'd like more character and feistiness. Costs less at Thresher, hence the higher rating there.

Rosemount Shiraz/Cabernet 1995 `15` `C`

South East Australia Shiraz 1996, Safeway `14` `C`

Mild but satisfying.

**South Eastern Australia Oaked Cabernet
Sauvignon 1995, Safeway** `15` `C`

South Eastern Australia Shiraz/Ruby Cabernet 1996, Safeway `15` `C`

Stoneyfell Metala Shiraz/Cabernet Sauvignon, Langhorne Creek 1994 `13.5` `D`

Dazzlingly labelled like a tonic sherry of pre-rationing days. Very ripe and squashy. Top fifty stores.

Wolf Blass Yellow Label Cabernet Sauvignon 1993 `13.5` `D`

AUSTRALIAN WINE
WHITE

Australian Chardonnay/Colombard 1996, Safeway `15.5` `C`

Lovely rich texture twitches over the tongue, flavoursome and frisky, young yet mature, and the result is classy and terrific value.

Australian Marsanne 1996, Safeway `12` `D`

Dull for the money – respectable but dull.

Australian Oaked Chardonnay 1996, Safeway `16` `C`

Love the texture! The fruit! The acidity! The sheer oily richness of the whole assembly.

Australian Oaked Colombard 1996 `13` `C`

Breakaway Grenache Rose 1996 `11` `C`

Breakaway Sauvignon Blanc/Semillon 1996 `13` `C`

Geoff Merrill Chardonnay 1994 `14` `E`

Has rich melon fruit and lime acidity. An expensive treat, still, although it is developing in bottle.

Hardys Nottage Hill Chardonnay 1996 `15` `C`

This elegant style of Aussie chardonnay is light years ahead of the blowsy blockbusters of yesteryear.

Jacob's Creek Riesling 1995 `14` `C`

Jacob's Creek Semillon/Chardonnay 1996 `13` `C`

Oxford Landing Sauvignon Blanc 1996 `14.5` `C`

Rich and well-textured and lovely to sip or glug or quaff with food.

Penfolds Organic Chardonnay/Sauvignon Blanc, Clare Valley 1996 `14` `D`

One of the classiest organic whites around: thick fruit of richness and flavour.

Penfolds Rawsons Retreat Bin 21 Semillon/Chardonnay/Colombard 1996 `15` `C`

Richly textured, warmly fruity (some complexity on the finish where the acidity is most pertinent), this is an excellent vintage for this wine.

Peter Lehmann Chardonnay/Semillon, Barossa 1995 `15` `D`

Peter Lehmann The Barossa Semillon, 1996 `15.5` `C`

Has a lush richness, beautiful cool texture and a solid finish. A truly flavourful wine. Great with all sorts of grilled food.

Rosemount Estate Chardonnay, Hunter Valley 1996

15.5 D

Elegance personified. A treat. Selected stores.

Rosemount Estate Semillon/Chardonnay 1995

15 D

Rosemount Estate Show Reserve Chardonnay 1995

16 E

Gripping texture, soft as buttered muslin. Selected stores.

BULGARIAN WINE RED

Barrel-Matured Cabernet Sauvignon, Svischtov 1993, Safeway

14.5 B

Youthful in spite of its vintage and deeply flavoured and delicious it is. Not rich but incisive all the same.

Bulgarian Country Wine (Merlot/Pinot Noir) 1996, Safeway

13.5 B

The perfect price for light cherry/plum quaffing.

Cabernet Sauvignon Reserve, Sliven 1991, Safeway

15 B

Brilliant value to go with anything from steak to aubergines with melted cheese.

Gorchivka Estate Selection Cabernet Sauvignon 1993

14 B

Vinenka Merlot/Gamza Reserve, Suhindol 1992, Safeway

14 B

The sort of wine to open and switch on the telly, lie back, and just slurp.

BULGARIAN WINE WHITE

Bulgarian Chardonnay, Rousse 1996 `14` `B`

Surprising charm here. Hints of vegetal richness and coolly displayed.

Chardonnay Reserva 1993 `15` `C`

Young Vatted Cabernet Sauvignon, Sliven 1996, Safeway `14` `B`

Rich with hints of cherry and blackcurrant. Dry edge. Good with food.

CHILEAN WINE RED

Alpaca Plain Cabernet Sauvignon, Central Valley (3-litre box) `15` `B`

Fabulous value! Possibly the cheapest Chilean red wine of classic drinkability, stylishness and rich dry fruit on the market. Price band has been adjusted to show equivalent per bottle.

Caballo Loco No 1 `13.5` `E`

Decent enough but not a tenner's worth. Top fifty stores.

Caliterra Cabernet Sauvignon 1995 `16.5` `C`

What flavour! What softness! What lingering depth of fruit! Chile, I kiss your feet.

Casa Lapostolle Cuvee Alexandre Merlot 1995 `17` `E`

One of Chile's finest merlots. It's magnificently well endowed with deftly interwoven fruit and tannin. Masterly. Top fifty stores.

Chilean Cabernet Sauvignon, Lontue 1996, Safeway

`16.5` `C`

What is the magic of Chilean red wine when it's as fine as this? Is it the texture? The chocolate edge? The creamy finish? This wine is one lovely, happy draught.

Chilean Cabernet/Malbec, Central Valley 1996, Safeway

`16.5` `C`

Superb texture and this gives great thrust to the fruit which is vivid, beautifully structured, utterly captivatingly flavourful (hints of meat, herbs and coffee) and possessed of a gorgeous finish.

Chilean Carignan, Maule Valley 1996, Safeway

`14.5` `C`

Unusually earthy Chilean red. Has bite, style, character and subtle richness. Should just be coming into selected stores when this book comes out.

Cono Sur 20 Barrels Pinot Noir, Rapel Valley 1995

`14` `E`

Starts excitingly, finishes by hitting the post. But the fruit's better than many a £30 Cotes de Beaune.

Palmeras Estate Oak Aged Cabernet Sauvignon, Nancagua 1995

`15.5` `C`

What energy and brightness here! Has textured tannins, richness and depth. Great food wine.

Valdivieso Cabernet Franc 1995

`15.5` `E`

Lovely perfume, great depth, soft, rich, warmly textured fruit. A treat. Top fifty stores.

Villa Montes Oak Aged Reserve Merlot 1994　　14　C

Collectors will like this wine. The tannins collect deliciously on the tongue.

CHILEAN WINE　　　WHITE

Caliterra Chardonnay 1996　　15　C

Castillo de Molina Sauvignon Blanc 1996　　13　C

Chilean Chardonnay 1996, Safeway　　13.5　C

Beginning to lose its freshness and bite, this '96. The '97 will be the one to go for this Christmas.

Chilean Dry White 1996, Safeway　　13.5　B

Chilean Sauvignon Blanc, Lontue 1996, Safeway　　13.5　C

Cordillera Estate Oak Aged Chardonnay, Casablanca 1996　　13.5　C

One of the few Chilean chardonnays not to really excite me.

ENGLISH WINE　　　WHITE

Stanlake, Thames Valley Vineyards 1996, Safeway　　13.5　C

Excellent looker (label-wise) but thin on fruit and crashes on the finish.

FRENCH WINE   RED

Beaujolais 1995, Safeway   `12` `C`

Beaune 1995, Safeway   `10` `E`

Beaune Premier Cru Les Epenottes 1994   `11` `F`
Top fifty stores.

Bourgueil 'Cuvee:Les Chevaliers' 1995   `13` `C`
For lovers of the cabernet franc grape in all its cherry-rich
deliciousness.

**Cabernet Sauvignon VdP d'Oc 1995,
Safeway**   `15.5` `C`
Superb warm fruit with hints of the Midi in every herby, dry
sip.

Chateau des Gemeaux, Pauillac 1992   `12.5` `D`

Chateau du Ragon, Bordeaux 1996   `14` `C`
This wine is improving nicely in bottle. It has to be enjoyed with
roasts or grills where the burnt edge will go well with the wine's
savouriness.

**Chateau la Tour de Beraud, Costieres de
Nimes 1994**   `14` `C`

Chateauneuf du Pape 1995, Safeway   `12` `E`

Claret, Safeway   `13.5` `C`
Authentic clarety fruit of dryness yet very drinkable, soft
ripeness.

Cotes du Rhone 1996, Safeway `13` `C`

Earthy backdrop to some very youthful fruit.

Cotes du Rhone Oak Aged 1995 `14` `C`

Domaine du Bois des Dames Cotes du Rhone Villages 1995 `14.5` `C`

Domaine Roche Vue Minervois 1995 `15.5` `C`

Has colour, aroma, rich fruit, dryness, balance, tannin – it all adds up to a treat for eye and throat and with grilled meats a great treat.

Domaine Vieux Manoir de Maransan 1996, Safeway `13` `C`

Very jammy wine. Nothing like as impactful as previous vintages.

French Organic Vin de Table, Safeway `13` `B`

Gevrey-Chambertin Domaine Rossignol-Trapet 1993 `11` `F`

Selected stores.

Hautes Cotes de Nuits Cuvee Speciale 1995 `12` `D`

Selected stores.

La Cuvee Mythique Vin de Pays d'Oc 1994 `16` `D`

One of the Midi's most fulfilling reds: characterful, dry, rich, multi-layered, assertive yet soft and polished, witty yet down to earth. It puts scores of fancy bordeaux to immediate shame.

Margaux 1993, Safeway `12` `E`

Has some initial arousal.

Merlot VdP d'Oc 1996, Safeway　13.5　C

Merlot which saunters on stockinged toes rather than belts along on leather shoes.

Minervois 1995, Safeway　13　B

Rustic and ripe.

Nuits St George 1993, Safeway　10　E

Oak Aged Medoc 1993　13　C

Oak-aged Claret NV, Safeway　13.5　C

Pommard Premier Cru 'Les Fermiers' 1994　10　G

Regnie Duboeuf 1996　11　D

Richemont Montbrun Old Vine Carignan VdP de l'Aude 1995　13　D

I loved it until the finish – too sentimental. Top fifty stores.

Saint-Julien Tradition 1994　13　C

Expensive, but well-ordered and well-textured if not well-priced. There's nothing austere or forbidding about its softly conceived fruit.

St-Julien 1994 (half bottle)　11　E

Syrah VdP d'Oc 1996, Safeway　13　C

Syrah in the jammy style.

VdP de l'Ardeche 1996, Safeway　13　B

Fresh-faced and urgent.

Vin de Pays de Vaucluse 1996, Safeway 11 B

Juicy stuff. Very juicy.

Volnay Domaine Michel Lafarge 1992 10 F

FRENCH WINE   WHITE

Alsace Gewurztraminer 1995, Safeway 16 D

Spicy aroma, rip-roaring fruit of crushed rose petals with lychee hints. It's ripe but never too fruity. Elegant yet forceful. Great with oriental food.

Bordeaux Blanc Sec Aged in Oak 1996, Safeway 14 C

Primly fruity and classy. Great with shellfish.

Chablis Cuvee Domaine Yvon Pautre 1995, Safeway 10 D

Chablis Premier Cru 'Les Lechet' 1995 12 E

Makes you think at least. The price, I mean.

Chardonnay VdP d'Oc 1996, Safeway 13 C

Chardonnay VdP du Jardin de la France 1996, Safeway 14 B

Soft yet refreshing. Good chardonnay structure and personality.

Chateau de Mercey, Hautes Cotes de Beaune 1995 13 E

The quality of Mercey is rather strained at eight quid.

Chateau du Plantier Entre Deux Mers 1996 · 14.5 · C

Delightful tippling here – a wine of fresh, spring-flower fruit which never goes flabby in the throat.

Chenin Blanc VdP du Jardin de la France 1996, Safeway · 14.5 · B

Quite deliciously complex yet hugely gluggable. Has an edge of melon, cream and nuts.

Cotes du Luberon Rose 1996, Safeway · 13.5 · B

Domaine Brial, Muscat de Rivesaltes 1996 (half bottle) · 15 · C

Great stuff for the Christmas pudding. Waxy, rich and very sweet.

Domaine de l'Ecu Muscadet de Sevre et Maine Sur Lie 1996 (Organic) · 13 · D

Expensive. Selected stores.

Domaine de Rivoyre Chardonnay VdP d'Oc 1995 · 15.5 · C

Brilliance of texture, richness of fruit, poise and real class make this a bargain.

Domaine du Rey Vegetarian White Wine, VdP des Cotes de Gascogne 1996 · 13.5 · C

Crisp and clean – what else can one say of it? Not at all stores.

Domaine Latour-Giraud Meursault 1994 · 11 · F

Domaine Vieux Manoir de Maransan, Cotes du Rhone 1996, Safeway · 14 · C

A modern version of the earthy Rhone-style white – it's fruity, bustling, polished, and crisp to finish. Selected stores.

Hugh Ryman Chardonnay VdP d'Oc 1995 ·16· ·C·

Subtle, balanced, incisive, very classy, calm, impressive. Rich food will disturb it but grilled white fish is perfect.

James Herrick Chardonnay VdP d'Oc 1996 ·14.5· ·C·

Gorgeous melony fruit, crisp acidity, soft texture, lingering finish. Can you ask more of an under-a-fiver chardonnay?

Montagny 1er Cru 1995, Safeway ·12· ·D·

Philippe de Baudin Sauvignon Blanc, VdP d'Oc 1996 ·14· ·C·

Stylish little number, delightfully citric and fresh.

Premieres Cotes de Bordeaux, Safeway ·11· ·C·

Puligny Montrachet 'Les Charmes' 1995 ·12· ·G·

Drinkable at £3.99 but not £14.99.

Sancerre 'Les Bonnes Bouches' Domaine Henri Bourgeois 1996 ·11· ·E·

A lot of money, nine quid. I expect a lot of wine for it.

Sauvignon de Touraine 1996, Safeway ·13· ·C·

It's white, yes it's definitely white – and it's drinkable. Is it, though, a four-quid white? Selected stores.

Sauvignon VdP du Jardin de la France 1996, Safeway ·14.5· ·B·

Incisively crisp, flavourful and immensely quaffable.

Vin de Pays de Vaucluse 1996, Safeway ·13.5· ·B·

Clean as a surgeon's scalpel.

Vouvray Demi Sec 1996, Safeway 11 C

Very fat and fruity, sweet to finish, and no compensating acidity to give it a future.

White Burgundy 1996, Safeway 13 D

Starts out classy, ends up citric.

GERMAN WINE WHITE

Auslese 1994, Pfalz, Safeway 13.5 C

Gewurztraminer Pfalz 1995, Safeway 10 C

Hugh Ryman Almond Grove Riesling Dry, Pfalz 1993 12.5 C

HUNGARIAN WINE RED

Chapel Hill Barrique-Aged Cabernet Sauvignon 1994 15 D

Chapel Hill Cabernet Sauvignon 1995, Safeway 13.5 D

Interesting, dry, food-friendly – but expensive.

Spring Time Red, Nagyrede 1996 12 B

More like autumn in its old leafy taste.

HUNGARIAN WINE WHITE

Chapel Hill Barrique-fermented Chardonnay, Balaton 1995 15 C

Hungarian Cabernet Sauvignon Rose 1996, Safeway 13.5 B

Not as fruity as it once was but still a reasonably polished specimen. Selected stores.

Hungarian Pinot Blanc, Nagyrede 1996, Safeway 14.5 B

Matra Mountain Chardonnay, Nagyrede 1996, Safeway 14 B

Very fresh and sea-breezy style.

Matra Mountain Pinot Grigio, Nagyrede 1996, Safeway 13.5 C

Very pleasant tipple – not exciting, perhaps, but very agreeable. Selected stores.

Matra Mountain Sauvignon Blanc, Nagyrede 1996, Safeway 13 C

Another fresh, clean Safeway bottle. Selected stores.

Neszmely Estate Barrique-Fermented Sauvignon Blanc 1995 15.5 C

Riverview Chardonnay/Pinot Gris, Neszmely 1996 13.5 C

Yet another respectable, crisp, dry white at Safeway.

ISRAELI WINE RED

Carmel Vineyard Cabernet Sauvignon 1991   `13` `D`

Interesting – once you've negotiated the checkpoint of the aroma.

ITALIAN WINE RED

Amarone della Valpolicella Classico 1993   `12` `F`

A lot of money. Too much. Top fifty stores.

Barolo Terre del Barolo 1992   `12` `E`

Overpriced and underfruited. If it was £3.99 it would be fine. Hence its 12-point rating.

Casa di Giovanni 1994, Safeway   `15` `C`

Chianti 1996, Safeway   `13` `C`

Soft, not one whit coarse, and drinkable.

Chianti Classico 1995, Safeway   `13.5` `D`

Friendly enough.

Lambrusco Rosso Safeway   `11` `B`

Montepulciano d'Abruzzo 1995, Safeway   `15` `C`

Cheekily textured, ripely fruity, richly endowed but also light-seeming and very quaffable.

Montepulciano d'Abruzzo, Barrique Aged 1994   `15.5` `C`

Rosso Veronese 1996, Safeway   15 B

Superb value here. A rosy-cheeked red, hale and heartily soft and
cherry-ripe, of quite irresistible quaffability. 'It's a poppet,' says
Safeway's head wine buyer of this charmer, and she's spot on.

Salice Salento Riserva 1993   14 D

This must have food. It's too figgy and currant-edged to
quaff. But with food – anything from cheese to chicken – it
comes alive!

Sicilian Red 1996, Safeway   13.5 B

Dry yet soft and plummy.

Tedeschi Capitel San Rocco Rosso 1991   14.5 E

Tenuta San Vito Chianti 1996   13 D

An organic chianti of light fruit with a dusty finish.

Valpolicella 1996, Safeway   10 C

Young Vatted Teroldego, Atesino 1996,
Safeway   14.5 C

Hums with a soft rubbery richness, freshness and deliciously
textured finish in the throat.

Zagara Nero d'Avola 1996 (Sicily)   15 C

Terrific texture (soft), good ripe fruit and deep flavour. Selected
stores.

ITALIAN WINE   WHITE

Bianco del Lazio 1996, Safeway   13.5 B

Bianco di Custoza, Cantine Montresor 1996
`14` C

Delicious, and deliciously different without being quirky – indeed it has a silky stylishness of its own.

Casa di Giovanni Grillo, VdT di Sicilia 1996, Safeway
`15` C

Has a nutty theme from nose through tongue to throat. Delicious all the way through: crisp, gentle, classy, surprisingly elegant without any sacrifice made to its Sicilian origins.

Casa di Giovanni VdT di Sicilia 1996, Safeway
`15.5` C

Brilliant quality of fruit: soft, aromatic, nutty, rich but never overbaked. A handsome specimen.

Chardonnay delle Venezie 1996, Safeway
`13.5` C

Rich, nutty Italian, not quite baroque but pleasantly ornamental on the tongue.

Frascati Superiore 1996, Safeway
`12` C

Lambrusco Rose, Safeway
`10` B

Lambrusco, Safeway
`10` B

Pinot Grigio delle Venezie 1996, Safeway
`13.5` C

Very subtly smoky. Very drinkable.

Puglian White 1995, Safeway
`14` C

Sicilian Dry White 1996, Safeway
`13.5` B

Light, dry wine – good with sardines.

MOLDOVAN WINE — RED

Kirkwood Cabernet/Merlot 1995 `15.5` `B`

MOLDOVAN WINE — WHITE

Kirkwood Chardonnay 1995 `13.5` `C`

Getting to the end of its shelf-life, this fruit, but still great value.

MOROCCAN WINE — RED

Domaine Sapt Inour `14` `B`

Warm, soft, soupy, excellent value. Selected stores.

NEW ZEALAND WINE — WHITE

**Millton Vineyard Barrel-fermented
Chardonnay 1995 (organic)** `15.5` `E`

Expensive but very deliciously constructed of old pianos, melons, woodsmoke, satin sheets and a distant aroma of roasting herbs. It's certainly improved in bottle since last year.

Montana Sauvignon Blanc 1996 `14.5` `D`

Good grassiness smoothly mown and well tended. Loss of impact on the finish but too individual and decently fruity to rate less.

Taurau Valley, Gisborne 1996 `13.5` `C`

Fading a little.

The Millton Vineyard Semillon/Chardonnay, Gisborne 1996 `13` `D`

Clean and fresh, but a touch expensive for the overall simplicity of the style. Selected stores.

Villa Maria Private Bin Sauvignon Blanc, Marlborough 1996 `15` `D`

Classic grassy undertones to the richness of the fruit give it delicious versatility.

PORTUGUESE WINE RED

Apostolos Alentejo 1996 `13` `C`

Jam today, jam tomorrow, jam to infinitude.

Fiuza Merlot, Ribatejo 1994 `14` `C`

The odd bottle might still be left, but the '95 will be coming in any minute now – see below.

Fiuza Merlot, Ribatejo 1995 `15` `C`

Lovely savoury fumes attached to this textured, dry, deep wine.

Ribatejo 1996, Safeway `12.5` `B`

I like fruit, I really do, but . . . really!

Tinto da Anfora, Alentejo 1992 `12` `D`

Alas, not as exciting as once it was.

PORTUGUESE WINE WHITE

Bright Brothers Fernao Pires/Chardonnay, Ribatejo 1995 `15.5` `C`

Vinho Regional Ribatejo, Falua 1996 `13` `B`

SOUTH AFRICAN WINE RED

Cape Red 1996, Safeway `13.5` `B`

Jacana Cabernet Sauvignon/Merlot Reserve, Stellenbosch 1995 `15` `E`

Heavy, serious, rich, tannic, dry, not a laugh in sight. Give it to a geriatric claret lover for Christmas. Selected stores.

Kleindal Pinotage 1996, Safeway `16.5` `C`

Brilliant lingering flavour and rounded softness of tone. Terrific balance makes this wine both deep and quaffable. Humming value for money.

Rosenview Cabernet Sauvignon, Stellenbosch 1996 `14` `C`

Rosenview Cinsault, Stellenbosch 1996 `14.5` `C`

So rich and soupy you could pour it over slices of roast meat. On the other hand, you could drink it from a glass with the same general kind of fare and enjoy a luxury-textured wine. Anxious to thrill.

Rosenview Merlot, Stellenbosch 1996

13 | C

Simonsvlei Shiraz Reserve, Paarl 1996

13 | C

Curiously rubbery undertone. Needs food, this wine.

Villiera Estate Cabernet Sauvignon/Shiraz, Paarl 1995

15 | D

Has somewhat of burnt edge to the fruit on the finish which lifts the finesse of the delivery. A lovely mellow wine of aplomb and stylish intent.

SOUTH AFRICAN WINE   WHITE

Cape Dry White 1996, Safeway

14 | B

Long Mountain Chardonnay, Western Cape 1996

13 | C

Curious sticky toffee edge to the fruit.

Quagga Colombard/Chardonnay, Western Cape 1996, Safeway

13.5 | B

South African Chenin Blanc, Early Release 1997, Safeway

15 | B

Very prettily fruited, delicate and floral, young, intensely modern. Delicious appetite arouser.

Umfiki Sauvignon Blanc 1996

13 | C

Vergelegen Chardonnay, Stellenbosch 1995

16 | D

A wooded wonder: rich, deep, purposeful, hugely flavoured yet not inelegant and terrifically quaffable. One sip and you feel everything's all right with the world.

**Waterside White Colombard/Chardonnay
1996** C

SPANISH WINE RED

**Berberana Tempranillo Oak-Aged Rioja,
1995** C

**Cosme Palacio y Hermanos Rioja
1995** 16 D

One of the tastiest riojas around: dry, rich, resoundingly well packed with fruit, and beautifully textured with assertive but not aggressive tannins. Selected stores.

Don Darias 14 B

Fuente del Ritmo Reserva 1993 14 C

Beautifully polished texture and near-opulence of fruit in the mouth. Perhaps a bit pleased with itself and smug but it is smooth . . .

**Stowells of Chelsea Tempranillo (3-litre
box)** 14 B

Price band has been adjusted to show equivalent per bottle.

Valdepenas Reserva 1991, Safeway 15 C

**Young Vatted Tempranillo, La Mancha
1996, Safeway** 14 C

Good fresh rich fruit with earthy tannins. Good food wine.

SPANISH WINE WHITE

Agramont Navarra Viura/Chardonnay 1996 `16` `C`

Aromatic. fruity, rich, deep, beautifully balanced and terrific value. A very classy wine indeed.

Somontano Chardonnay 1995 `15.5` `C`

Vina Malea Oaked Viura 1995 `15.5` `B`

USA WINE RED

Fetzer Pinot Noir, Santa Barbara 1994 `13.5` `D`

Excellent pinot aroma, truffley and wild-strawberryish, but the finish is light.

Fetzer Zinfandel 1993 `14.5` `D`

Glen Ellen Merlot Proprietor's Reserve 1994 `15` `C`

USA WINE WHITE

Fetzer Barrel Select Chardonnay, Mendocino 1995 `16` `E`

Has massive texture of sufficient oleaginous deliciousness to coat a moving motor component. Any stray tongue will beg for more.

Fetzer Chardonnay Reserve 1995   16   F

Did white burgundy, Montrachet say, ever taste this good in the good old days? Nope, never. This is a white wine of great class, richness, balance, and sheer world-class finish.

FORTIFIED WINE

10 Year Old Tawny Port, Safeway   11   F

Cream Sherry, Safeway   13   C

Fino Sherry, Safeway   14   C

Fonseca Guimaraens 1982   13   G

Very soft, biscuity in texture, and rich to finish. It is, though, very expensive.

LBV 1990, Safeway   13   E

A soft approachable port, not as rich and sweet as some specimens.

Lustau Old Amontillado Sherry (half bottle)   14   B

Lustau Old Dry Oloroso Sherry (half bottle)   14   B

Ruby Port, Safeway   12   D

Taylors LBV 1991   13   F

Delicious, sweet, rich – but not as gripping as previous vintages. Will it develop if laid down for a few years? Certainly.

Vintage Character Port, Safeway   12.5   D

SPARKLING WINE/CHAMPAGNE

Albert Etienne Champagne Brut, Safeway `12` `H`

Rather raw on the finish. Top ninety-five stores.

Asti Spumante, Safeway `12` `D`

Sweet, very sweet.

**Barrel Fermented Sparkling Chardonnay
(Italy)** `15` `D`

A brilliant bubbly of class and style. Has a lovely softness yet,
paradoxically, a crisp fruity edge.

Cava Brut, Safeway `15` `D`

A delicious Cava of delicate richness and finesse.

**Chartogne-Taillet Champagne Brut Cuvee
Sainte-Anne** `12` `G`

**Edwards & Chaffey Pinot Noir/Chardonnay
1993 (Australia)** `13` `E`

Graham Beck Brut (South Africa) `13.5` `E`

J. Bourgeois Pere et Fils Champagne Brut `12.5` `F`

Lindauer Brut `13.5` `D`

Moscato Spumante, Safeway `12` `C`

Pol Acker Chardonnay Brut (France) `14` `C`

Saumur Brut, Safeway `14` `D`

Sparkling Chardonnay Brut, Safeway (Italy) `13.5` `D`

**Veuve Clicquot Champagne Yellow
Label Brut** `11` `H`

J SAINSBURY PLC

J SAINSBURY PLC
Stamford House
Stamford Street
London
SE1 9LL
Tel 0171 921 6000
Fax 0171 921 7925
Internet orders http://www.j-sainsbury.co.uk

What's wonderful.

The supermarket as institution, with a strict ethos of commercial rectitude and mercantile ethics, is a living exemplification at this august corporation headquartered on the southern approach to Blackfriars Bridge in London. Tesco is in chummy Cheshunt, Safeway's in suburban Slough, Asda's up in louche Leeds, Waitrose in boring Bracknell; but Sainsbury's HQ stands (almost) by the Thames and the Thames (almost) runs past it. The store group is bastioned close enough to the City of London – a view of the dome of St Paul's is visible via a craned neck – to throw stones at it. It is much too dignified to try – even when the wretched City deserves to be pelted.

What's maddening.

Nothing. There's nothing to get mad at Sainsbury *about*. To be sure, the idea of a world full of superstores you can only reach by car is destructive and bland out-of-season fruit and vegetables made available every season of the year adds, for me at least, no value. It used to be that winter arrived the day chicory went on sale. But all the supermarkets have rejigged the calendar in this respect and so my nostalgia pains can hardly be laid exclusively at Sainsbury's door. Wine-wise, Sainsbury is goody two-shoes. *That's* what maddening about the store. What about a bit of vulgarity, Allan?

SEE STOP PRESS SECTION AT END OF BOOK FOR LAST-MINUTE ADDITIONS TO THIS RETAILER'S RANGE.

ARGENTINIAN WINE · RED

**Mendoza Cabernet Sauvignon/Malbec
Peter Bright, Sainsbury's** `15` `B`

Mendoza Country Red, Sainsbury's `15` `B`

Lovely level of rich fruit here plus an expensive texture. Great to slurp with or without food.

Mendoza Pinot Noir/Syrah, Sainsbury's `15` `C`

Mendoza Sangiovese, Sainsbury's `14.5` `C`

Juicy, fun, light to begin but rich to finish. Selected stores.

Mendoza Tempranillo, Sainsbury's `16` `C`

Watch out, rioja! This will give tempranillo fans everywhere something to slaver over – a rich, dark, exotic beauty of depth and very warm personality. Top seventy stores.

ARGENTINIAN WINE · WHITE

Mendoza Country White, Sainsbury's `14` `B`

A curiously fruited wine for food (which it must have, it seems to me). The aroma is oddly cosmetic and talcum powdery and so is the fruit. But with a roast chicken these are assets.

**Tupungato Chenin Chardonnay Peter
Bright, Sainsbury's** `14.5` `C`

AUSTRALIAN WINE RED

Australian Cabernet Sauvignon, Sainsbury's

A deliciously approachable, gently soupy Aussie jaw-breaker with sufficient clout to tackle rich food.

Bailey's Block 1920s Shiraz 1993

Will be 20 points in three years? One of Australia's great shirazes and therefore one of the most interesting syrah representatives in the whole wide world. It explodes with flavour, leathery, cassis-like but with a figgy undertone, and the finish is rich. It has superb tannins, fruit and acid. Top twenty-five stores.

Hardys Banrock Station Mataro/Grenache/ Shiraz 1996

Restrained for an Aussie with a hint of vegetality to the fruit. It has a curious coy demeanour. Now – when did you last meet an Aussie like that?

Hardys Stamp Series Shiraz/Cabernet Sauvignon 1995

Leasingham Cabernet Sauvignon/Malbec, Clare Valley 1994

Rich, juicy, ripe, textured but so soft it's like a puppy begging to have its tum tickled. Soppy stuff really, rating only 13 at first opening. But give it five to six hours to breathe, letting the very rich tannins develop, and the wine becomes savoury, passionate, rottweilerish. Don't say you haven't been warned. Top eighty-five stores.

Leasingham Clare Valley Shiraz 1995

Intensely jammy. Smells like it, tastes like it – jam. But it has

a faintly serious savoury edge. It saves it from utter soppitude.
Top seventy-nine stores.

Lindemans Cawarra Shiraz/Cabernet Sauvignon 1996 `14` `C`

Savoury, dry (but amply rich and fruity on the finish), gently
relaxing and softly meaty. Selected stores.

Lindemans Padthaway Pinot Noir, Coonawarra 1995 `13.5` `E`

Not bad as Aussie pinot goes – but I'm not sure this raspberry-
scented vegetality and strawberry richness is worth eight quid.
Top twenty-five stores.

Lindemans Pyrus Coonawarra 1992 `15` `F`

The elegance and aplomb here are delightful to behold and
experience. Lovely texture, minty fruit and a whiplash finish
of soft, tannicky satin. A very fine wine indeed – but is it worth
£12? Top twenty-five stores only.

Penfolds Bin 389 Cabernet/Shiraz 1993 `15` `E`

Rosemount Diamond Label Shiraz 1995 `15` `D`

Such heavenly textured richness and flavour but delicate, mild
meats and vegetable dishes will suit it, not robust ones. Top
seventy stores.

Rosemount Estate Shiraz/Cabernet 1995 `15` `C`

St Hallett Cabernet Merlot 1994 `13.5` `E`

Lots of money for such squidgy fruit. A great £3.50 tipple but
not at nigh on eight quid. Selected stores.

Stowells Australian Red Mataro/Shiraz NV (3-litre box) `15` `C`

Has warmth, character, a touch of sweaty saddle-soreness (both aromatically and on the finish) and the fruit is dry, fruity and highly drinkable – at the equivalent of 64p a glass. Price has been adjusted to show equivalent per bottle.

Tarrawingee Shiraz Mourvedre, Sainsbury's

12 C

Tyrrells Cabernet Merlot, South Australia 1995

13 D

Expensive for the shortness of the excitement. Selected stores.

Wynn's Cabernet Sauvignon Coonawarra 1993

15 E

Most superior in manner: rich, dry, very deep.

AUSTRALIAN WINE WHITE

Australian Chardonnay, Sainsbury's

14.5 C

A quiet, firm chardonnay which politely whispers. But this is a great improvement on the raucous shout of yesteryear's Aussie chardies!

Australian Semillon Sauvignon Blanc, Sainsbury's

15.5 C

Beautiful hand-in-hand wine. The semillon has bite and vigour, the sauvignon svelte fruitiness of grip and style. Selected stores only.

Hardys Banrock Station Chenon/Semillon/ Chardonnay 1996

14.5 C

Most uncommonly Europeanised Aussie vino. A combination of the sauciest muscadet of yesteryear with the minerality of a Loire white, and then it finishes with something of an echo of the southern Rhone. An excellent fish wine.

Jacob's Creek Chardonnay 1996

It still rates well – in spite of sailing perilously close to a fiver.

Jacob's Creek Dry Riesling 1996

Curious soft fruit with a hint of spice. Excellent aperitif.

Jacob's Creek Semillon/Chardonnay 1996

Lindemans Bin 65 Chardonnay 1996

Elegant, purposeful, balanced, finely wrought and handsomely textured. A textbook Aussie chardonnay.

Lindemans Cawarra Colombard/Chardonnay 1996

Good but lacks pizzazz. Rather demure on the finish. Selected stores.

Lindemans Cawarra Semillon/Chardonnay 1995

The fruit has warmth, style and flavour. It is in cahoots with crisp acidity. The result is balance, personality and food-compatibility. Selected stores.

Lindemans Cawarra Unoaked Chardonnay 1996

Selected stores.

Mick Morris Liqueur Muscat, Rutherglen (half bottle)

Mount Hurtle Sauvignon Blanc 1996

Fresh, gripping, classic, clean, deliciously fruity – this is fine stuff. Top twenty-five stores only.

Penfolds Koonunga Hill Chardonnay 1996 `15.5` `C`

Best vintage for years: aromatic, rich, balanced, food-friendly.

Penfolds Koonunga Hill Semillon/ Sauvignon Blanc 1996 `15.5` `C`

One of the best vintages ever from Koonunga Hill: rich melon fruit, nicely crafted, with pert citric acidity. A balanced wine, soundly priced.

Penfolds Rawsons Retreat Bin 21 Semillon/Chardonnay/Colombard 1996 `15` `C`

Richly textured, warmly fruity (some complexity on the finish where the acidity is most pertinent), this is an excellent vintage for this wine.

Penfolds The Valleys Chardonnay, South Australia 1994 `16` `D`

Expensive but hugely expressive. It declaims with style, with tonal complexity and what it says is simple: you want total luxury, you pay for it. It's worth paying.

Rosemount Estate Diamond Label Chardonnay 1996 `15.5` `D`

Opulence vinified. Rather grand fruit, proud and rich.

Rosemount Show Reserve Chardonnay 1995 `16` `E`

One of Australia's most incisively fruity chardonnays, with huge hints of class, depth, balance and persistence. Expensive but very fine. Selected stores.

Wynns Coonawarra Chardonnay 1993 `14` `D`

Wynns Coonawarra Riesling 1996

Brilliant food wine (fish, chicken, Thai food) which is rich and fresh now but will develop well in bottle for two years. Selected stores.

BULGARIAN WINE RED

Bulgarian Cabernet Sauvignon 1995, Oak Aged, Russe Region, Sainsbury's

A soft, juicy cabernet with a touch of jam on the finish. Very fresh and perky.

Bulgarian Cabernet Sauvignon, Sainsbury's (3-litre box)

Young fruit with lots of vim and gusto allied to polished, smooth depth of flavour which is intense, gluggable, and very good with food. A delicious clean red. Price band has been adjusted to show equivalent per bottle.

Bulgarian Reserve Merlot, Lovico Suhindol 1992

Rich merlot with a hint of apple-skin. Touch of spice, too.

Cabernet Sauvignon/Merlot, Liubimetz NV, Sainsbury's 14.5 B

A characterful wine of glugging simplicity but with an undertone which hints at complexity and depth if not altogether providing it fullthroatedly.

Country Red Russe Cabernet Sauvignon/ Cinsault, Sainsbury's (1.5 litres) 15.5 D

Domaine Boyar Cabernet Sauvignon/ Merlot 1996

16   B

Calm and classy with lovely rich, warm texture. Neither peppery, too dry nor over-baked, this is a delicious quaffing cabernet of some style and class. Not at all stores.

Domaine Boyar Cabernet Sauvignon Reserve, Iambol 1992

16   C

Real class in a glass here. The texture is mouth-watering, let alone the aroma and the fruit (warm and cassis-like).

Domaine Boyar Special Reserve Cabernet Sauvignon, Suhindol 1991

16   C

Bigger and juicier than many of its compatriots, this has richness but also an echo of real, old-style cabernet depth and the result is very impressive. Top seventy stores.

Domaine Boyar Vintage Blend Oriachovitza Merlot & Cabernet Sauvignon Reserve 1992

15   C

Superbly approachable fruit with hints of herbiness to the dryness.

JS Bulgarian Merlot, Oak Aged, Rousse

13.5   B

Glugging merlot, pure and simple.

CHILEAN WINE   RED

Canepa Winemaker's Selection Zinfandel, Maipo 1996

16.5   C

Has real structure: fruity, spicy-edged, agreeably weighty without coarseness and it has a rich savoury finish of velvety concentration. Selected stores.

Casablanca Cabernet Sauvignon, Santa Isabel Estate 1995

16.5 | E

Wonderful aroma of ripe blackcurrant leading to a juicy flutter of fruit on the palate and a final thwack of richness as the wine descends. Very classy, this wine. Has Chilean chutzpah with French-inspired insouciance. Top twenty-five stores.

Chilean Cabernet Sauvignon/Merlot, Sainsbury's

15.5 | B

Chilean Merlot, Sainsbury's

14 | C

Concha y Toro 'Casillero del Diablo' Cabernet Sauvignon, Maipo Valley 1995

15.5 | C

One of the most elegant cabs you can hail. Takes your tastebuds for a very comfortable trip.

La Palma Reserve Cabernet/Merlot 1995

17 | C

Spicy, rich, textured, deep, thought-provoking, dry but enormously (yet delicately) fruity, this has complexity and style in every drop. Top seventy stores.

Mont Gras Cabernet Sauvignon Reserva 1995

16.5 | D

Catering chocolate, raspberry and cassis combine to cause the instincts to say 'no, not another glass', but you cannot resist such rich complexity. Top twenty-five stores.

Mont Gras Merlot Reserva 1995

16 | D

Brilliancy of texture, flavour, balance and sheer style. A trifle ruffled (easily) with rich food, it is soothing company with roast fowl, plain. Selected stores.

Quinta las Cabras Merlot, Rapel 1996

16.5 | B

Astonishing price for such soft, ripe classy, beautifully textured wine. Not complex, can't take rich food, but it has to be the cheapest high-class Chilean quaffing red around. Sublimely cheering wine.

Santa Carolina Merlot, 1996   16   C

Very soft merlot, almost jammy, but good to glug while cooking the Sunday lunch (which I am doing now) and even to add to the gravy. Selected stores.

Santa Carolina Merlot Reserva, Maipo Valley 1993   15   D

Santa Rita 120 Pinot Noir, Casablanca 1995   15   C

Hints of farmyard and wild raspberry as you smell the wine lead to soft, rich fruit of flavour and real pinot depth. Selected stores.

Valdivieso Cabernet Sauvignon, Lontue 1996   16.5   C

What a price for such vivacious complexity and youth! The quality of the fruit and the winemaking is world-class. The flourish, the cheek, of the wine is incredible. A magnificent, rich, chewy finish of spicy cassis!

Valdivieso Cabernet Sauvignon Reserve 1995   17   D

Savoury, rich, beautifully integrated tannins and fruit, and such finesse controlling the power! This is a tremendously well-flavoured wine. Top twenty-five stores.

Valdivieso Merlot, Lontue 1996   16.5   C

A delicious merlot, no mistake, which begins juicy and ripe and then turns seriously complex and clinging. Huge clash of flavours here: spiced damsons predominate. Top seventy stores.

Villa Montes Merlot Gran Reserva, Oak Aged, Curico 1995 `15.5` `C`

Echoes of cough linctus, such is the initial richness. But it turns soft and fruity as it develops on the tongue.

Villa Montes Oak-Aged Cabernet Sauvignon Gran Reserva, Curico 1992 `15` `D`

Mature yet sprightly and poised as it dances with plummy nicety over the tastebuds. Top seventy stores.

Vina Casablanca Cabernet Sauvignon, Santa Isabel Estate 1996 `18.5` `E`

In texture, richness, ripeness, balance and sheer deliciousness of fruit this is a great cabernet of sublime drinkability and style. It has guts yet finesse, flavour yet ineffability, utter class in every drop from nose to throat. An experience evoking sheer joy. Top fifty-three stores.

CHILEAN WINE WHITE

Casablanca Barrel Fermented Chardonnay, Santa Isabel Estate 1995 `18` `E`

Expensive but very fine. Beautifully woody fruit with controlled white burgundy-style vegetality but the fruit is so rich, textured, complex and deep it seems never to depart the tastebuds. Top twenty-five stores.

Casablanca Chardonnay 1996 `16.5` `D`

The combination of elements in a wine this good, at such a reasonable price, must have other chardonnay growers tearing their hair out. It is fruity yet elegant, fresh but complex, rich yet delicate. Selected stores.

Chilean Chardonnay, Sainsbury's `14` `C`

Muted on the finish but certainly rates as a worthy wine up-front.

Chilean Sauvignon Blanc, Sainsbury's `15.5` `C`

Crisp, flavourful, beautifully balanced, effortlessly classy.

Concha y Toro Casillero del Diablo
Sauvignon Blanc 1995 `15` `C`

Clean yet with hints of richness. Terrific freshness of approach. Selected stores.

Santa Carolina Chardonnay, Lontue
1996 `17` `D`

A hugely seductive aroma, superb texture to the rich fruit and a vivid lingering finish. Ripe, complex, youthful yet mature, this is a world-class wine. Top seventy stores only.

Santa Rita Chardonnay, Estate Reserve
1996 `16` `D`

A cool chardonnay, not overblown or too ripe. Has crispness and tone, and a citric undertone. Selected stores.

ENGLISH WINE WHITE

Denbies Estate English Table Wine,
1992 `10` `C`

Lamberhurst Sovereign Medium Dry `10` `B`

FRENCH WINE   RED

**Antonin Rodet Gevrey Chambertin
1994**   `10` `G`

Vastly underfruited. Hugely overpriced. Top sixty stores.

Beaujolais, Sainsbury's   `12` `C`

**Beaujolais-Villages, Les Roches Grillees
1995**   `12` `C`

Bordeaux Rouge, Sainsbury's   `14.5` `B`

Brilliantly priced claret of some class. Dry and flavourful.

**Bush Vine Grenache, Coteaux du
Languedoc 1995**   `14` `C`

**Cabernet Sauvignon Syrah VdP d'Oc,
Sainsbury's**   `14` `B`

**Cabernet Sauvignon VdP d'Oc, Caroline
Beaulieu 1996**   `15` `C`

A rich heap of fruit with a keen-edged yet old-style classic
cabernet richness.

Cabernet Sauvignon VdP d'Oc, Sainsbury's   `14` `C`

**Chateau Belgrave Grand Cru Classe Haut
Medoc 1994**   `11` `G`

Meaty aroma, brisk tannins overlaying peppery cabernet and
hints of leather (from, I guess, merlot). However, this is just
an impression. The tannins soon gobble the fruit, within an
hour of opening, and so it's witless with food.

Chateau Calon-Segur Grand Cru Classe St Estephe 1993 `15` `G`

Rich, chocolatey, well-evolved, tannicky, Calon-Segur has always drunk well young. This has richness, no coarse tannins, firm texture, a whiff of Medoc classiness. Will last for five to seven years but improve for only three more. Not at all stores.

Chateau de la Tour Bordeaux Rouge 1995 `13.5` `D`

Good polished texture and soft fruit. An adult drink.

Chateau de Peyrat Premieres Cotes de Bordeaux 1994 `13` `D`

Tries hard.

Chateau Ferriere 3e Cru Margaux 1993 `13` `G`

Vastly overpriced. Top twenty stores.

Chateau La Vieille Cure, Fronsac 1990 `17` `E`

Sainsbury's deliberately held back stocks of this 1990 (selling '92 and '93 ahead of it) and the result is a superbly mature claret of perfect weight and balance. Lovely soft tannins and very rich delivery to the throat. Top seventy stores.

Chateau Lynch Bages, 5e Cru Classe Pauillac 1991 `G`

Chateau Marsau, Cotes de Francs 1995 `15` `D`

Touch light but lots of dry, tannic fruit up-front and a lovely herby finish. Excellent with food. Selected stores.

Chateau Pavie Macquin Grand Cru Classe Saint Emilion 1992 `G`

Ludicrous amount of money to pay for a bottle of wine unless the stuff courses down your veins and sets your cuticles alight. This one gets about as far as the elbow. Not at all stores.

Chateau Tassin, Sichel Bordeaux Rouge 1995
14.5   C

A simple glugging claret on one level but it hints at greater depth than this and the finish is profound. Good value here. Selected stores.

Chiroubles Duboeuf 1995
13.5   C

Tasty – after a fashion. It's just its casual attitude that stops it being rated higher. Selected stores.

Claret Cuvee Prestige, Sainsbury's
13   C

Touch austere on the finish but fruity up-front. Needs food to really charm.

Claret, Sainsbury's
12.5   C

Soft and approachable with a hint of dry, stalky claretyness.

Clos Magne Figeac, Saint Emilion 1993
16   E

Serious cedar wood aroma invites you in and then doesn't disappoint as you relax in the very richly endowed fruit which offers beautifully smooth tannic/acid balance. This wine is improving well in bottle. Top 150 stores.

Comte de Signargues Cotes du Rhone Villages 1994
14   D

Interesting double-faced wine of seeming fruity lightness but it packs a dry tannic wallop on the finish. Selected stores.

Corbieres, Sainsbury's (3-litre box)
13.5   B

Price band has been adjusted to show equivalent per bottle.

Cotes du Rhone, Sainsbury's
13.5   B

Simple fruity glugging.

Crozes Hermitage, Cave de Tain l'Hermitage 1994 | 16 | D |

A genuine Crozes Hermitage for under a tenner! Lovely syrah wine here, resonant with brambly fruit (in a great fruity vintage), dry, very deep-throated, not hugely long but extremely drinkable. It's everything an Aussie shiraz (syrah) isn't: youthful yet full of character. Selected stores.

Crozes Hermitage Les Jalets, Jaboulet Aine 1994 | 14.5 | E |

Surprisingly forward, ripe and ready. Only hints of earth and bramble. Possibly 16.5 in three to four years' time.

Cuvee Prestige Cotes du Rhone, Sainsbury's | 13 | C |

Domaine du Pujol Minervois, Cave de la Cessane 1995 | 16.5 | C |

What a delightful wine. It is the essence of drinkability and food-compatibility: dry, rich, characterful, gorgeous. Not at all stores.

Domaine Rio Magno Pinot Noir, VdP l'Ile de Beaute 1994 | 12 | C |

Fitou Chateau de Segure, 1994 | 14 | C |

Textured, warm, ripe yet dry, rich. Delightful stuff. Selected stores.

Fleurie La Madone, 1995 | 13 | E |

Hermitage Monier de 'La Sizeranne' 1991 | 14.5 | G |

Julienas Chateau des Capitans 1995 | 11 | D |

Light but not fantastic. Selected stores.

**La Baume Cabernet Sauvignon, VdP d'Oc
1994, Sainsbury's**　　

Dry, rich, gently peppery and deep – this is class cabernet.

**Le Second Vin de Mouton Rothschild,
Pauillac 1993**　　

An expensive joke played on asses' heads.

Merlot Bankside Gallery, VdP d'Oc 1995　　

Chocolatey, thick, beautiful textured tannins integrated with the fruit. This is a class merlot of stunning quality for the money. Selected stores.

Minervois, Sainsbury's　　

Moulin a Vent, Cave Kuhnel 1994　　10　E

**Nuits St-Georges 'Aux Meurgers' Domaine
Bertagna 1994**　　10　G

If one's aspiration is ditchwater, this bottle is ascendant. For the common-sense tippler, however, £15 for this dull wine is sheer effrontery.

Red Burgundy, Sainsbury's　　

Has some character, but I'm not so sure I like the price.

**St Joseph Le Grand Pompee, Jaboulet
Ainee 1994**　　

A lot of money for a Rhone of uneasy texture and somewhat moody fruit. Top seventy stores.

St-Marc Reserve Shiraz, VdP d'Oc 1996　　

Herbier, spikier, thornier than the Aussie equivalent – and much more able to take on rich food. Selected stores.

Syrah/Mourvedre VdP d'Oc, Sainsbury's   15.5   B

With its splendid taint-free plastic cork (looking for all the world like tree-bark) this specimen of boot leather and scrub is light and full-bodied, rich yet not fat, fruity yet agile and soft in the mouth. A splendid little country wine of character, style and wit at a down-to-earth price. Top 120 stores.

Vacqueyras Brotte 1993   15.5   D

Juicier style than previously but the finish is still brilliant. Top seventy stores.

Valreas Domaine de la Grande Bellane 1996   13.5   D

Aromatic, soft, fruity, organic. Selected stores.

Vin de Pays de l'Ardeche, Sainsbury's   13.5   B

Vin de Pays de l'Aude Rouge, Sainsbury's   16   B

Remarkable character and wisdom in a wine so young, chirpy and cheap. Has depth and richness, properly modulated, and an integrated earthy edge. Dry, decisive, daring.

Vin de Pays des Bouches du Rhone, Sainsbury's   13   B

Vin Rouge de France Dry Red Wine, Sainsbury's (3-litre box)   12   B

Fairly ordinary stuff. Might be better chilled. Price band has been adjusted to show equivalent per bottle.

Vosne Romanee 'Les Beaumonts' Domaine Bertagna 1994   10   G

Top nineteen stores.

Vougeot Clos Bertagna 1994   9   G

Total waste of space on Sainsbury's shelves. Selected stores.

FRENCH WINE WHITE

Alsace Gewurztraminer, Sainsbury's 14 D

Rich, almost cloyingly so, with a scent of crushed rose petals and a spiciness on the fruit. Very musky, thick stuff. Selected stores.

Blanc Anjou Medium Dry, Sainsbury's 12 B

Bordeaux Blanc Cuvee Prestige, Sainsbury's 11 C

Bordeaux Blanc, Sainsbury's 12 C

Bordeaux Sauvignon Blanc, Sainsbury's 14 B

Can't ask fairer than this. It's clean, crisp, decisive, great with fish.

Cabernet Rose, VdP du Jardin de la France 1996 12.5 C

Top sixty-nine stores.

Chablis 1er Cru Montee de Tonnerre, Brocard 1993 13.5 E

Chardonnay Bankside Gallery, VdP d'Oc 1995 15.5 C

Elegant, classy, stylish, balanced, sanely priced. Selected stores.

Chardonnay Maurel Vedeau, VdP d'Oc 1996 16 C

A rich, warmly textured chardonnay of depth, flavour, style, great food-compatibility – and the price is brilliant! Selected stores.

Chardonnay VdP d'Oc, Sainsbury's
(3-litre box)

Price has been adjusted to show equivalent per bottle.

Chateau Les Bouhets Bordeaux Blanc 1995

A touch more elegant than the own-label offering but then it's a quid more. Solid fish hitter. Selected stores.

Chenin Blanc, VdP du Jardin de la France, Lurton 1996

Needs a spicy fish cake to come alive. Selected stores.

Classic Selection Chablis Domaine Sainte Celine 1995, Sainsbury's

A perfectly drinkable chablis. Why does it not rate more? The price is of a magnitude which demands a more vivid concentration of fruit.

Classic Selection Muscadet de Sevre et Maine Sur Lie 1996, Sainsbury's

Is muscadet trying harder? Certainly crisper – mercifully so. Selected stores.

Classic Selection Pouilly Fuisse 1995, Sainsbury's

Selected stores.

Classic Selection Pouilly Fume 1996, Sainsbury's

Decent rather than exciting. Selected stores.

Classic Selection Sancerre 1996, Sainsbury's
14 D

Not quite classic stuff, but nearly. Has some richness to the finish and a gentle mineral edge to the acidity.

Domaine de Grandchamp Sauvignon Blanc, Bergerac 1996 `14` `D`

At the rich end of sauvignons. Not grassy or lean but fruity with a crisp echo only. Selected stores.

Domaine de la Tuilerie Rose, VdP d'Oc Ryman 1996 `13` `C`

Domaine de Sours Bordeaux Rose 1996 `14` `C`

More generous than many reds, it has elegance to its fruit. Selected stores.

Grenache Rose VdP de l'Ardeche, Sainsbury's `12` `B`

La Baume Chardonnay, VdP d'Oc 1995, Sainsbury's `16.5` `C`

Magnificent cool class. Sheer satin, deep fruit (but never blowsy or overripe), this is a high-class act at a great price.

Macon Chardonnay, Domaine les Ecuyers 1995 `16` `D`

Terrific price for such authentic, delicious white burgundy. Knocks the store's chablis, for example, into a cocked chapeau. The wine is rich, handsomely textured, ripe, gently vegetal and finishes with aplomb. Great with food or mood. Selected stores.

Menetou Salon Domaine Henri Pelle 1996 `14` `D`

Crisp, impishly fruity and classily gooseberryish. Selected stores.

Moulin des Groyes, Cotes de Duras Blanc 1995 `13.5` `C`

This is one of those wines which taste wonderful sipped in the summer sun in a cafe a few hundred yards from the vineyard. Travel seems to make it coy and uncommunicative.

Muscadet Sevre et Maine, Lurton 1996 `13.5` `C`

Decent Muscadet at a reasonable price. Great with shellfish and fish soups/cakes. Selected stores.

Muscadet Sevre et Maine Sur Lie, La Goelette 1996 `12` `C`

Ho hum.

Muscat de Beaumes de Venise, Sainsbury's (half bottle) `14` `C`

Quatre Terroirs Chardonnay VdP d'Oc 1995 `15` `D`

Lovely gentle fruit, charming, demure and classy. Stylish wine altogether. Top ninety-five stores.

Quincy Clos des Victoires 1996 `14` `D`

So much better value than sancerre which it resembles. Has flavour and style and class. Top seventy stores.

Reserve Saint Marc, Sauvignon Blanc VdP d'Oc 1996 `14` `C`

Refined but with an impudently fruity finish. Not at all stores.

Sauvignon Blanc VdP du Jardin de la France, Lurton 1996 `14` `C`

Classic sort of shape for a sauvignon, clean, crisp and subtly herbaceous, but this specimen has a lovely fruity lilt on the finish. Selected stores.

Sichel Selection Graves Blanc 1995 `14` `C`

Has an imposing, somewhat cosy, level of fat fruit but not

entirely a concomitant level of balancing acidity. It seems
overstuffed as a result but is classy, good for rich seafood dishes
with ravishing sauces, and not obscenely priced.

Touraine Sauvignon Blanc, Sainsbury's   10   B

Vin Blanc de France Dry White Wine, Sainsbury's (3-litre box)   11   B

Price band has been adjusted to show equivalent per bottle.

Vin de Pays de l'Aude Blanc, Sainsbury's   14   B

Simple, fruity, crisp, well-managed. Good fruit, good price,
terrific little glug or with fish.

Vin de Pays des Cotes de Gascogne, Domaine Bordes 1995   15   C

Vouvray la Couronne des Plantagenets 1996   15.5   C

A brilliant off-dry aperitif or one to lay down for five or six
years.

White Burgundy, Sainsbury's   13.5   D

A thoroughly decent white burgundy of some style.

GERMAN WINE   WHITE

Black Foil Rivaner/Riesling 1996   14   C

More spine here gives the wine more posture on the palate –
better-balanced and fruitier.

Blue Nun Liebfraumilch   13   C

Not as yucky as most Liebs but pricier than comparable,

forwardly-fruity off-dry wines from elsewhere. Decent aperitif next summer, perhaps. Selected stores.

Fire Mountain Riesling 1996 `12` `C`

Starts with some intent to please but simpers on the finish. Needs food to really come to life.

Hock, Sainsbury's `10` `A`

Liebfraumilch, Sainsbury's `10` `B`

Mainzer St Alban Kabinett, Rheinhessen 1995 `13` `C`

Amusing aperitif. Won't shock your guests or thrill them but it might tickle them.

Mainzer St Alban Spatlese, Rheinhessen 1994 `13.5` `C`

This has a sweet tone but is far from a honeyed dessert style. Best as a palate-arouser, I think. Selected stores.

Mosel, Sainsbury's `12` `B`

Niersteiner Gutes Domtal, Sainsbury's `11` `B`

Oppenheimer Krotenbrunnen Kabinett, Sainsbury's `12` `B`

Palatinarum Riesling, Zimmerman Graeff 1995 `12.5` `C`

Rather expensive for the simplicity of the lemony fruit. Nice with grilled prawns, though. Top seventy stores.

Piesporter Michelsberg, Sainsbury's `12` `B`

GREEK WINE RED

Kourtakis VdP de Crete Red

Earthy, drinkable, food-friendly, well-fruited. Fun yet will work with a beef casserole. Selected stores.

GREEK WINE WHITE

Retsina, Sainsbury's 14 B

Old cricket bats soaked in fruit juice. Has a certain devil-may-care freshness. Needs Greek food to be friendly.

HUNGARIAN WINE WHITE

Hungarian Irsai Oliver, Sainsbury's

Tokay 5-Puttonyos 1988

I find this over-priced and too medicinal in character. With a streaming cold, and in bed, it might prove congenial.

ITALIAN WINE RED

Barrique Aged Cabernet Sauvignon
Atesino 1995

Touch green and peppery but will soften and develop well in bottle. Brilliant with food with its concentrated blackcurrant.

Castelgreve Chianti Classico Riserva 1991 $\quad$ 15.5 $\quad$ D

Cortegiara Amarone della Valpolicella
Classico, Allegrini 1991 $\quad$ 15 $\quad$ E

Apples and cherries to smell, it turns juicy and then rich and roasted as it descends. Magical effect on the arteries, this wine – really summons up the blood! Top seventy stores.

Lambrusco Rosso, Sainsbury's $\quad$ 12 $\quad$ B

Lambrusco Secco Rosso 'Vecchia-Modena' $\quad$ 14 $\quad$ B

Merlot Corvina Vino da Tavola del Veneto, Sainsbury's $\quad$ 14.5 $\quad$ B

Montepulciano d'Abruzzo, Sainsbury's $\quad$ 15 $\quad$ B

Rosso di Verona, Sainsbury's $\quad$ 11 $\quad$ B

Sangiovese di Toscana, Cecchi 1996 $\quad$ 13 $\quad$ C

What a flirtatious little beast! So juicy!

Sicilian Nero d'Avola & Merlot, Sainsbury's $\quad$ 15 $\quad$ C

Sicilian Red, Sainsbury's $\quad$ 14 $\quad$ B

The essence of dry yet fruity, simple yet flavourful, dry, everyday swigging wine.

Squinzano Mottura 1994 $\quad$ 14 $\quad$ B

Selected stores.

Teroldego Rotaliano Geoff Merrill, Sainsbury's $\quad$ 12 $\quad$ C

Selected stores.

Valpolicella, Sainsbury's `11.5` `B`

Vino Nobile di Montepulciano, Cecchi 1991 `14` `D`

ITALIAN WINE — WHITE

Bianco di Verona, Sainsbury's `13` `B`

Chardonnay del Salento Vigneto di Caramia 1996 `16` `D`

One of the classiest southern Italian chardonnays around: rich, giving, textured, ripe but not rampant, it's silky and quite delicious. Selected stores.

Cortegiara Chardonnay, Garganega 1996 `14` `B`

Light but appley with hints of richness. Clean and fresh with an underlying crispness, it represents solid, if not inspired, value.

Cortegiara Pinot Grigio 1996 `12.5` `C`

Cortese del Piemonte 1995 `15` `C`

Frascati Secco Superiore 1996, Sainsbury's `13.5` `C`

As frascatis go, this is not one to dismiss entirely.

Garganega Vino da Tavola del Veneto, Sainsbury's `13.5` `B`

Inzolia & Chardonnay (Sicily), Sainsbury's `14` `C`

Lambrusco Bianco Medium Sweet, Sainsbury's `10` `B`

Lambrusco Rosato, Sainsbury's `10` `B`

Lambrusco Secco, Sainsbury's `8` `B`

Le Trulle Chardonnay del Salento 1996 `15.5` `C`

Delicious, gentle, rich, smooth and very well-balanced. Top 100 stores only.

Lugana San Benedetto, Zenato 1996 `15.5` `D`

Makes you purse your lips, sigh with pleasure, and think everything is all right with the world. Selected stores.

Pinot Grigio Atesino, Sainsbury's `13` `C`

Dry, fresh, would suit crustacea.

Pinot Grigio Collio, Enofriula 1996 `15.5` `D`

A classic pinot grigio: gently peachy, mineral, crisp yet full of life. A lovely wine. Top ninety-four stores.

Soave, Sainsbury's `11` `B`

Soave Superiore 1996, Sainsbury's `13` `C`

Has some cosy fruit.

Trebbiano di Romagna, Sainsbury's `14.5` `B`

Tuscan White, Cecchi `13` `B`

Verdicchio dei Castelli di Jesi Classico 1996, Sainsbury's `15.5` `C`

It is rare for an under-£4 Italian white to rate so highly in my book but this specimen wins out because it is quintessentially first-class Verdicchio Classico, not one whit New Worldish, and it strikes with a delicious no-holds-barred freshness, bite and supreme nuttiness.

LEBANESE WINE   RED

Chateau Musar 1989   `12` `E`

Looks and smells like a light game and mushroom sauce.
The fruit is creaky and sweet – a touch toothless. Top
ninety stores.

MACEDONIAN WINE   RED

Macedonian Cabernet Sauvignon 1996   `13` `B`

Jammy stuff – spread thinly. Top twenty-six branches only.

Macedonian Country Red 1996   `13.5` `B`

Some reasonable plummy depth with a fresh finish. Selected
stores.

MACEDONIAN WINE   WHITE

Macedonian Chardonnay 1996   `13` `B`

Decently well short of three quid but the fruit is a little well
short too, alas.

NEW ZEALAND WINE   WHITE

**Montana Sauvignon Blanc, Marlborough
1996**   `14.5` `D`

More grassy and fresh than previous vintages. Typical Marlborough fruit – a solid example.

Nobilo White Cloud 1996 `13` `C`

Sanctuary Chardonnay, Marlborough
1996 `16` `D`

Rich and ripe, echoes of cream-puffs and smoked melon tarts. Brilliant with prawns. Selected stores.

Sanctuary Sauvignon Blanc, Marlborough
1996 `15.5` `D`

Nettly and grassy to smell – a scent picked up by the whistle-clean fruit. An elegant, typical Kiwi wine of style and class. Great with shellfish. Selected stores.

Villa Maria Private Bin Chardonnay,
Marlborough 1996 `13.5` `D`

Falls a little short of what a six-quid-plus chardonnay should be.

Villa Maria Private Bin Sauvignon Blanc,
Marlborough 1996 `15` `D`

Delicate grassy notes to the richly restrained fruit. Elegantly and finely cut.

PORTUGUESE WINE RED

Cabernet Sauvignon Ribatejo, Sainsbury's `13` `C`

Do Campo Tinto, Sainsbury's `14.5` `B`

Portuguese Red Wine, Sainsbury's `13` `B`

PORTUGUESE WINE — WHITE

Do Campo Branco Peter Bright, Sainsbury's 14 B

Do Campo Rosado, Sainsbury's 12 B

Portuguese Rose, Sainsbury's 8 B

Santa Sara Barrel Fermented Reserve 1995 16 C

Complex, exciting, rich (layers of melon with a nutty overcoat), beautifully textured, warm, full and fruity yet very elegant. Terrific tipple. Top eighty-five stores only.

Sauvignon Blanc Ribatejo 1995, Sainsbury's 15.5 C

Smoky, rich, deep, utterly deliciously priced. This is a terrific wine for the money. Excellent with fish and chicken dishes.

Sauvignon Blanc Rueda, Lurton 14 C

A lovely texture of calm, quiet, understated richness. Delicious fish wine. Selected stores.

Vinho Verde, Sainsbury's 12 B

ROMANIAN WINE — RED

Idle Rock Merlot Reserve 1996 15 C

Greater vigour and richness with the merlot, and a softer, warmer texture and finish. Deliciously quaffable stuff. Top forty-five stores.

Idle Rock Pinot Noir Reserve 1996 | 13 | C

Savoury aroma, reasonable fruit (not especially pinot-like) and a finish of dry reluctance. Top forty-five stores.

Romanian Pinot Noir Dealul Mare, Sainsbury's | 14.5 | B

SOUTH AFRICAN WINE — RED

Bellingham Merlot 1995 | 14.5 | D

Lovely warmth and richness here, with that leathery edge. More expensive than it was but developing nicely in bottle. Delicious. Selected stores.

Fairview Cabernet Sauvignon, Paarl 1995 | 15 | D

The usual high-class act from this estate, though I tend to feel this cabernet is more a glugger than previous vintages. The texture is soft, the fruit aromatic and gently rich.

Fairview Pinotage, Paarl 1995 | 17 | C

Baked-biscuit fruit of great richness, fruitinesss, charm, superb texture and great depth. Lovely flavour here which you feel you could drink for ever. Top seventy stores.

Jacana Pinotage, Stellenbosch 1995 | 16.5 | D

One of the pinotage tribe which is deliciously anxious to please with its up-front fruit and richness. Soft, ripe, aromatic and keen.

South African Cabernet Sauvignon/Merlot Reserve Selection, Sainsbury's | 15.5 | C

Sublimely soft, rich fruit of great class, perfect balance, with great charm. Selected stores.

South African Cape Red Wine, Sainsbury's 13.5 B

South African Pinotage, Sainsbury's 14 C

**South African Reserve Pinotage 1995,
Sainsbury's** 14 D

Pinotage as civilised and charming, and soft, not one bit beastly.
Top 100 stores.

**South African Reserve Selection Merlot
1995, Sainsbury's** 16 D

Superbly gripping structure which is soft, gently leathery, firm
yet very supple. A beautifully textured, dry wine of some class.
Top seventy stores.

**South African Ruby Cabernet/Cinsault,
Sainsbury's** 14 C

Soft, almost soppy, frisky as a young pup and huge fun to slurp
with friends. Top seventy stores.

Swartland Merlot Reserve 1996 16 C

Snap it up before every merlot maniac in Britain grabs hold of
it. Rich, dark, savoury, lingering, deep, food-friendly yet great
by itself, this is a fiver very well spent. Selected stores.

**Vergelegen Cabernet Sauvignon,
Stellenbosch 1995** 16.5 D

This creeps stealthily and deliciously insidiously from nose to
throat like some richly exotic secret agent of Bacchus determined
to titillate but only at the finish produces its finest, mysterious,
rich, enigmatic moment. Its flavour lingers like a wanted guest.
Top twenty-five stores only.

SOUTH AFRICAN WINE WHITE

Cape Dry White Wine, Sainsbury's `14` `B`

Cape Medium White Wine, Sainsbury's `14` `B`

Danie de Wet Grey Label Chardonnay, Robertson 1996 `13` `D`

Didn't thrill me as much as previous vintages. Selected stores.

Jacana Chardonnay 1996 `15.5` `D`

Utterly delicious and a captivating blend of Old World vegetality and woody aroma, and New World intensity of fruit, plump texture and clean finish. Classy, complex, characterful.

South African Chardonnay, Western Cape, Sainsbury's `15` `C`

Riches for the tongue but not poverty for the pocket. A well-balanced wine of flavour and style at a very good price.

South African Colombard, Sainsbury's `14` `B`

South African Reserve Selection Chardonnay 1996, Sainsbury's `14.5` `C`

Nicely balanced, edgily rich, creates a nice warm feeling in the throat, and it's food-friendly. Selected stores.

South African Sauvignon Blanc Reserve Selection 1995, Sainsbury's `16` `C`

Terrific price for such flavoursome elegance and rich-edged style. Great class here. Top seventy stores.

South African Sauvignon Blanc, Sainsbury's `13` `B`

South African Sauvignon Blanc/Chardonnay, Sainsbury's `15` `C`

Springfield Estate Sauvignon Blanc 1996 `14.5` `C`

Curiously delicious crisp wine with a fruity edge of ripe melon and pear. Selected stores.

Thelema Sauvignon Blanc 1995 `15.5` `E`

Vergelegen Chardonnay 1995 `16` `D`

Very classy stuff. Lovely controlled use of wood, fine depth of fruit, complex structure. A delicious bottle of wine at a fair price. Top twenty-five stores.

SPANISH WINE RED

Classic Selection Rioja Reserva 1990, Sainsbury's `14` `E`

Rich, dry, personable, this is good company for a meat dish – though I'm uncomfortable with £7.45 for such a wine. By the time this book appears in the autumn of 1997 the new '91 vintage will be phasing in (not tasted as yet).

Conde de Siruela Crianza, Ribera del Duero 1991 `12` `D`

Has an aroma like a freshly turned allotment. The fruit is a touch cabbagey, too. Works out best with rich food. Selected stores.

Dama de Toro, Bodegas Farina 1994 `16` `C`

Rich, ripe, rampant – yet dry, characterful, and very jammy yet never soft or soppy. A very flavourful, assertive wine of great depth and hugely well-adapted food-compatibility. Extremely well-priced. Selected stores.

El Conde Oak-Aged Vino da Mesa, Sainsbury's
14 B

Jumilla, Sainsbury's
15.5 C

Brilliant on-form wine of jammy drinkability and rich, tonally complete structure which allows the wine to finish with a great hearty flourish of fruit. Terrific value and quaffability with food versatility.

Navarra, Sainsbury's
15 B

What fantastic value! Real rich, classy fruit shrouded in dryness.

Navarra Tempranillo/Cabernet Sauvignon Crianza 1994, Sainsbury's
16 C

Beauteous texture of ruffled velvet and this, with the aroma and the depth of fruit, makes for a remarkably stylish wine for the money.

Orobio Rioja Reserva 1990
14 D

Rioja Reserva Vina Ardanza 1989
14 E

Expensive, very expensive. Top forty stores.

Santara Cabernet Merlot, Conca de Barbera 1994
16 C

Develops licorice and dry herb flavours as it opens up on the tastebuds. Certainly as mature as it needs to be, the wine has an opulence, a flippant depth of richness and a wonderful savoury finish. Superb value for money.

Valencia Oak Aged, Sainsbury's
14.5 B

Quite delicious. It begins brisk and dry, then turns really rich and compellingly gluggable.

SPANISH WINE   WHITE

Navarra Cabernet Sauvignon Rosado 1996, Sainsbury's   `13.5` C

Selected stores.

Santara Chardonnay 1995   `16.5` C

This is one of the very few chardonnays under four quid which gives Chile a run for the same money: rich, perfectly developed, complex, utterly delicious. It has plot, character and wit. It's a literary gem.

USA WINE   RED

California Red, Sainsbury's   `13` B

E & J Gallo Turning Leaf Cabernet Sauvignon 1994   `13.5` D

E & J Gallo Turning Leaf Zinfandel 1994   `12` D

Gallo Sonoma Cabernet Sauvignon 1992   `15` E

Mature and impressive.

South Bay Reserve American Cabernet Sauvignon   `14` D

Love the touch of warm, tannic fruit on the finish. Real class in a glass here. Selected stores.

South Bay Vineyards American Pinot Noir   `13.5` C

Classic aroma but the finish sucks.

USA WINE   WHITE

California White, Sainsbury's   `12` `B`

E & J Gallo Turning Leaf Chardonnay 1994   `14` `D`

Fetzter Bonterra Chardonnay 1995   `14.5` `E`

Lovely musk of melon aroma, rich and inviting, which leads to unhurried fruit of charm and poise, finishing the melony fruit with vague hints of pineapple and firmer hints of lemon. A fine, well-textured wine.

South Bay Vineyards American Chardonnay, California   `12` `C`

Not hugely overwhelming for a fiver.

Sutter Home White Zinfandel 1995   `12` `C`

FORTIFIED WINE

1985 Vintage Port Quinta Dona Matilde, Sainsbury's   `15` `G`

Very rich and soft and the sweetness is controlled and fine. Great with Christmas cake and rich cheeses. Top sixty stores.

Aged Amontillado, Sainsbury's (half bottle)   `13.5` `B`

Lifts a blue mood – in about five seconds. Selected stores.

Blandy's Duke of Clarence Malmsey Madeira   `13` `E`

**Cantine Pellegrino Superiore Garibaldi
Dolce Marsala (half bottle)** `14` `D`

Cream Montilla, Sainsbury's `14` `B`

Dow's Extra Dry White Port `14` `E`

Worth trying to ferret out a bottle, but Sainsbury's tell me they may be discontinuing this line.

Fino Sherry, Sainsbury's `14` `C`

Classic dryness for nutty conversations.

Manzanilla, Sainsbury's `12` `C`

Matusalem Sherry (half bottle) `14` `E`

Sainsbury's may be discontinuing this line, so if you can't find it that could be why.

Medium Dry Amontillado, Sainsbury's `12` `C`

Medium Dry Montilla, Sainsbury's `14` `B`

Moscatel Pale Cream, Sainsbury's `15` `C`

Old Oloroso, Sainsbury's (half bottle) `16` `B`

The quintessence of sherry: quirky, rich, nutty, full of wit, great to simply sip while warm words fill the room. Selected stores.

Pale Cream Montilla, Sainsbury's `13` `B`

Pale Cream Sherry, Sainsbury's `14` `C`

Pale Dry Amontillado, Sainsbury's `15` `C`

Pale Dry Montilla, Sainsbury's `13.5` `B`

Palo Cortado, Sainsbury's (half bottle) `15` `B`

Very rich and off-dry. A lovely cold weather aperitif. Selected stores.

Pellegrino Marsala `14` `B`

Rich Cream Sherry, Sainsbury's `14.5` `C`

Sainsbury's 5 Year Old Sercial (half bottle) `14.5` `E`

Sainsbury's LBV 1989 `13.5` `E`

Sainsbury's Ruby `13.5` `D`

Sainsbury's Tawny `14` `D`

Taylors LBV, 1989 `14.5` `E`

SPARKLING WINE/CHAMPAGNE

Angas Brut Rose (Australia) `15` `D`

Asti, Sainsbury's `11` `C`

Blanc de Noirs Champagne Brut, Sainsbury's `14.5` `F`

One of the best-value champagnes around – if you like a forward, fruity style.

Cava Rosado, Sainsbury's `15` `C`

Cava, Sainsbury's `16` `D`

Superb delicacy of tone, restrained richness, citric pertinacity and overall balance.

Champagne Alfred Gratien NV   13 G

An elegant hint-of-lemon bubbly which is rashly overpriced.

Champagne Extra Dry, Sainsbury's   15 F

The more elegant style, fully successful in its stylistic ambition, and very, very classy.

Chardonnay Brut Methode Traditionnelle, Sainsbury's (France)   14.5 D

Demi Sec Champagne, Sainsbury's   10 E

Gallo Brut   10 D

Lindauer Special Reserve   14 E

Classy and stylish. Better than many more expensive champagnes. Top seventy stores.

Madeba Brut, Robertson (South Africa)   14 D

Nice warmth to the fruit here.

Mercier Brut   11 G

Sekt, Sainsbury's   11 C

Sparkling White Burgundy, Pinot Noir/ Chardonnay 1992, Sainsbury's   14 D

Soft with rich hints. Has some swash to its buckle, this bubbly. Top seventy stores.

Vin Mousseux Brut, Sainsbury's   12 C

Vintage Blanc de Blancs Brut 1991, Sainsbury's   14 G

You can get something extra for extra dosh here – but it is subtle. An elegant wine of some class.

Vintage Brut, Cremant de Loire 1992, Sainsbury's [14.5] [D]

Earthy, yeasty aroma rather disguises the excellence of the fruit which though with some richness is never less than dry and classic in inspiration. Selected stores.

Yalumba Pinot Noir Chardonnay [16] [E]

So much tastier and better-priced than hundreds of champagnes. Selected stores.

SOMERFIELD

SOMERFIELD
Gateway House
Hawkfield Business Park
Whitchurch Labe
Bristol
BS14 0TJ
Tel 0117 935 9359
Fax 0117 978 0629

What's wonderful.

All those £1.99 bargains sprinkled throughout the year! I love wine buyer Angela Mount, as do thousands of the *Superplonk* column readers, for this.

What's maddening.

When a reader goes into a branch of this retailer and is told, 'Sorry, love, never heard of that wine. Who did you say recommended it? Michael Fluck of the *Guardian*? Isn't that an insurance company?'

SEE STOP PRESS SECTION AT END OF BOOK FOR LAST-MINUTE ADDITIONS TO THIS RETAILER'S RANGE.

ARGENTINIAN WINE RED

La Rural Merlot 1996

Lovely soupy rich fruit, almost sweet on the finish but never soppy with it. Terrific texture and grip – but always very soft.

ARGENTINIAN WINE WHITE

Argentine White 1997, Somerfield `13.5` `B`

Some decently assembled nutty fruit.

AUSTRALIAN WINE RED

Australian Dry Red, Somerfield `13` `B`

Little cherry-ripe lad.

Australian Shiraz `13` `C`

Hardys Bankside Shiraz 1995 `14.5` `D`

Classy stuff – has oodles of flavour but it doesn't sag in the middle like some Aussies. It has some weight, some tannin, some character to last the course (meat or veg or cheese).

Hardys Banrock Station Mataro/Grenache/ Shiraz 1996

Fruity and appealing but it slips down and then disappears . . . Hallo down there! Anyone still alive?

Penfolds Cabernet Sauvignon 1996, Somerfield

`14.5` `C`

Now this is exactly what inexpensive Australian reds should be: ripe, dry, flavour-packed, soupy, rich and very quaffable but still able to take on food.

Penfolds Koonunga Hill Shiraz Cabernet 1995

`14` `D`

Very tasty, very rich. Very sparky stuff.

Penfolds Rawson's Retreat Bin 35 Cabernet/Shiraz/Ruby Cabernet 1995

`13.5` `C`

Usual decent turnout.

Rymill Cabernet Sauvignon, Coonawarra 1994

`14` `E`

Impressive Coonawarra typicity: rich, mint-edged (very subtle, this) and very softly textured, like taffeta. Not at all stores.

Somerfield Cabernet Shiraz

`13.5` `C`

South East Australian Cabernet Sauvignon 1995

`14` `C`

Mature, aromatic, brisk (i.e. some tannin on the edge of fruit which has bite) and rich, this is an excellent casserole wine.

AUSTRALIAN WINE   WHITE

Hardys Nottage Hill Chardonnay 1996

`15` `C`

This elegant style of Aussie chardonnay is light years ahead of the blowsy blockbusters of yesteryear.

Jacob's Creek Chardonnay 1996

It still rates well – in spite of sailing perilously close to a fiver.

Jacob's Creek Semillon Chardonnay 1996

Jamiesons Run Chardonnay 1996

Eight quid isn't peanuts but then peanuts do not accompany this rich wine. You need soft lights, soft music and pliant company.

Lindemans Bin 65 Chardonnay 1996

Still one of the Antipodes' best-value chardonnays: rich, elegant, stylish.

Lindemans Coonawarra Botrytis Riesling 1994 (half bottle)

A wonderfully surprising Aussie: sweet-natured, waxy, burnt-edged, rampantly rich and just great with fresh fruit, ice cream, foie gras. Or – just drink it with the Walkman curled up in an armchair. It's a lot more exotic, sexy and gorgeous than the Spice Girls. Selected stores.

Lindemans Unoaked Cawarra Chardonnay 1996

Penfolds Australian Chardonnay 1997, Somerfield

Has unusual European edginess, this specimen. That is to say the acidity dominates the fruit. Excellent! And great with food.

Penfolds Australian Dry White 1997, Somerfield

Very dry, very white.

Penfolds Rawsons Retreat Bin 21 Semillon/Chardonnay/Colombard 1996 | 15 | C

Richly textured, warmly fruity (some complexity on the finish where the acidity is most pertinent), this is an excellent vintage for this wine.

Penfolds The Valleys Chardonnay 1996 | 15 | D

Insouciance, charm, casual but stylish richness.

Rosemount Chardonnay 1996 | 15.5 | D

It's the sheer silky class of the wine which notches up the points. It's so elegant it makes you simply want to retire to the fireside with a bottle.

Rosemount Estate Semillon/Chardonnay 1996 | 14 | D

Balanced, unbashful, excellent with fish.

St Hilary Chardonnay, Orlando 1996 | 15.5 | E

Aggressive but very good company. Not elegant perhaps but it has huge lingering flavour.

BULGARIAN WINE   RED

Bulgarian Cabernet Sauvignon 1992, Somerfield | 14 | B

A bargain red for meats off a grill.

Bulgarian Iambol Cabernet Sauvignon, Domaine Boyar 1996, Somerfield | 15.5 | B

Lovely stuff! Absolute cracker of a wine with its plumpness, richness, and beautiful balance of fruit/tannin/acidity. Yum!

Bulgarian Iambol Merlot, Domaine Boyar `14` `B`

The soft, fresh, cherry-edged quaffing merlot.

Country Red Merlot/Pinot Noir, Somerfield `15` `B`

Oriachovitza Cabernet Sauvignon Reserve 1994 `15` `C`

The woodiness adds a chewy edge to the fruit and greater versatility with choice of food. Not at all stores.

Stambolovo Merlot Reserve 1990 `16` `C`

Wonderful richness and maturity yet surprisingly vigorous, warm, deep and savoury.

BULGARIAN WINE WHITE

Bulgarian Chardonnay, Somerfield `13.5` `B`

Fruity all the way through.

Somerfield Bulgarian Country White `14.5` `B`

Suhindol Aligote Chardonnay Country White, Somerfield `13.5` `B`

Goodness gracious! What value!

Suhindol Barrel Fermented Bulgarian Chardonnay 1996, Somerfield `15.5` `B`

Terrific texture and restrained opulence. Rich but clean, fresh but fruity, outstanding value.

CHILEAN WINE   RED

Canepa Reserve Merlot 1995   `13.5` `D`

Soft and very juicy with it. Unusual for a Chilean at this price.
Selected stores.

**Chilean Cabernet Sauvignon 1996,
Somerfield**   `17` `C`

Soft, savoury-chocolate fruit, firmly textured, hugely gluggable.

Chilean Red 1996, Somerfield   `16.5` `B`

Dry, rich, good tannins, soft chewy texture, lingering finish.

**Stowells of Chelsea Chilean Merlot
Cabernet (3-litre box)**   `10` `C`

Price band has been adjusted to show equivalent per bottle.

CHILEAN WINE   WHITE

Caliterra Sauvignon Blanc 1996   `16` `C`

Rich, firmly fruity, mouth-fillingly bright and deep, this is
one of those Chileans which uniquely combines finesse and
elegance with a subtle exoticism of flavour. Delicious fun from
start to finish.

Chilean Chardonnay 1996, Somerfield   `15` `C`

Lovely ripe fruit which never strains to put its case richly,
roundly, softly yet very convincingly. Guilty of being extremely
delicious.

Chilean Sauvignon Blanc 1996, Somerfield 14.5 C

Clean, fresh, touched by citrus and soft melon but undercut by a crisp acidity, this is a first-class, well-balanced wine for the money.

Chilean White 1997, Somerfield 13 B

Not as exciting as the specimens for which Chile is famous.

Valdivieso Chardonnay Reserve 1995 16 D

Compelling style here: rich, balanced, great integration of wood/fruit/acid, and a lovely ripe yet cosy finish. Lovely wine.

ENGLISH WINE WHITE

Denbies English 1995 12 B

FRENCH WINE RED

Beaujolais 1996, Somerfield 10 C

Turgid.

Beaumes de Venise Cotes du Rhone 1995 13.5 C

Dry and earthy with hints of not fully realised richness. But it does possess some charm and it persists in making its case.

Bergerac Rouge 1996, Somerfield 11 B

Earthy? You could pot daffs in it.

Bourgogne Hautes Cotes de Beaune, Cottin 1994 10 D

313

Brouilly 1995

Selected stores.

Buzet Cuvee 44

Typical Buzet dryness and earthiness. Needs grilled or roasted food to be at its best. Selected stores.

Cabernet Sauvignon VdP d'Oc Val d'Orbieu, Somerfield

Superb little number at a superbly little price. Has cherry and plum in rich unison with tannin and acidity.

Chateau Carbonel Cotes du Rhone 1996

Cherries and plum coat the tongue with a faint earthy tang. Very drinkable style.

Chateau de Caraguilhes, Corbieres 1994

A tough year for this wine and the wine might improve over the next year. But it's decently fruity now with a hint of depth and some smoked plum flavours. A fair enough stab at richness. A solid hitter with food.

Chateau de la Valoussiere, Coteaux du Languedoc, 1995

Quite superb hairy-chested red of character, richness, food-friendliness, style, earthy herbiness, and rampant individuality. The tannin and fruit are in beautiful liaison.

Chateau Latour Segure Lussac St Emilion 1995

Very good, warm texture allied to a decent richness of well-toned fruit. Selected stores.

Chateau Le Clairiot Bordeaux 1995

Chateau Saint Robert, Graves 1993 `14` `D`

**Chateau Talence, Premieres Cotes de
Bordeaux 1993** `12` `D`

Fades on the finish somewhat, leaving only a dry desert in the throat. Selected stores.

**Chateauneuf-du-Pape Domaine de la
Solitude, 1995** `15` `E`

Very expensive but divinely delicious.

Claret, Somerfield `14` `B`

Rather chirpy value for such dry, drinkable, classically styled claret.

Corbieres Val d'Orbieu, Somerfield `12.5` `B`

**Cotes du Rhone Celliers de l'Enclave des
Papes 1996, Somerfield** `13` `B`

A light, approachable Rhone of restrained earthiness.

Cotes du Roussillon Jeanjean `13` `B`

Crozes Hermitage 1995 `10` `D`

Light and dusty.

Fitou Caves de Mont Tauch, Somerfield `14` `B`

Gigondas Chateau Saint Andre 1995 `15.5` `D`

Delicious – a real quaffing gigondas of richness and style. Remarkable marinade for the adenoids. Selected stores.

**Hautes Cotes de Beaune, Georges
Desire 1995** `10` `D`

Made by a man, paradoxically, called Desire.

Medoc NV, Somerfield `14` `C`

Rich, very determinedly textured and terrific with grilled meats cooked rare.

Merlot VdP d'Oc 1996, Somerfield `14.5` `B`

Lovely texture with a hint of Midi warmth and herbiness. And the tannins are ripe, rich, and gripping. Positive fruit here!

Minervois 1996, Somerfield `14` `B`

A party wine with something to add to the conversation.

Oak Aged Claret, Somerfield `13` `D`

Stale cigars on the edge of the fruit.

Red Burgundy 1995, Somerfield `12.5` `D`

Some earthy grip here – surprising character trait but a welcome one.

Saint-Joseph, Cuvee Medaille d'Or, Caves de Saint Desiderat 1991 `15` `E`

St Emilion P. Sichel `13.5` `C`

Vacqueyras Domaine de la Soleiade 1996 `16` `C`

Now this is classic Cotes du Rhone! And it's perfectly priced. A rich, dry, herby, balanced, brilliant-with-food red of character, charm and real deep impact.

VdP des Cotes de Gascogne Red 1996, Somerfield `11` `B`

Vin de Pays des Bouches du Rhone Rouge 1996 `10` `B`

Sheer juice.

FRENCH WINE WHITE

Alsace Gewurztraminer, Turckheim 1996 `13.5` `D`

Needs a year to get its act fully together. The attack is fine but it's a bit wimpish on the finish. Time is a great healer, though.

Alsace Pinot Blanc, Turckheim 1996 `15` `C`

Great price for such classy pinot. Great to set the franc/sterling balance tipping tipplers' way! Not at all stores.

Ardeche Blanc, Somerfield `11` `B`

A little limp.

Chablis 1995, Somerfield `12` `D`

Expensive for the po-facedness of the fruit.

Chablis Premier Cru, Grande Cuvee, La Chablisienne 1990 `11` `F`

Chais Cuxac Chardonnay VdP d'Oc 1996 `15` `C`

A superbly well-balanced chardonnay of style and class. It has real depth to its fruit, no blowsiness or coarseness, and it has great versatility with food: soups, salads, chicken and fish. It is staggeringly good value when compared with some of the burgundian stuff.

Chardonnay VdP d'Oc 1996, Somerfield `14.5` `C`

Packed with style and quiet, gently flavoursome fruit which is not quirky or over-tropical but finesse-full and very drinkable.

317

Chardonnay VdP Jardin de la France 1996

Has some decent, demure, melony fruit with compensating acidity. Not a rich wine, but certainly a very drinkable one.

Domaine de Bordeneuve VdP des Cotes de Gascogne Blanc, 1996

Delightfully fresh-faced youth with acrobatic manners – leaps across the tastebuds with vigour and rich intent.

Domaine de la Tuilerie Chardonnay, Hugh Ryman 1995

Domaine de Rivoyre Chardonnay VdP d'Oc 1995

Rich, smoky melon fruit with a hint of ripe avocado nicely hanging on to the melon/lemon overtone. An impressively stylish wine for a touch over a fiver. Selected stores.

Entre Deux Mers 1996, Somerfield

Solid rather than sensational.

Gewurztraminer d'Alsace 1996, Somerfield

Very delicately flavoured, rose-petal perfumed fruit. Delicious aperitif.

Hautes Cotes de Beaune Blanc, Georges Desire 1995

James Herrick Chardonnay VdP d'Oc 1996

New World restrained by Old World coyness. A chardonnay of subtlety and crisp fruit which is always nicely understated.

Macon Blanc Villages 1995, Somerfield

Muscadet Sur Lie 1996

Expensive for the style.

Oak Aged Bordeaux Blanc 1995, Somerfield `13.5` `C`

Not bad – has some dry hints of class. But hints only.

Sauvignon Blanc VdP du Jardin de la France 1996 `13.5` `B`

Simple, fruity, not bad value if you've got a tuna salad handy.

Syrah Rose Val d'Orbieu, VdP d'Oc 1996 `13` `B`

Pretty colour.

VdP des Cotes des Gascogne Blanc 1996, Somerfield `13` `B`

VdP des Jardins de la France 1996, Somerfield `15` `B`

Very crisp, flavourful, balanced, finely knitted fruit and acidity, and stylish on the finish. A terrific fish wine.

White Burgundy 1995, Somerfield `12` `D`

White Burgundy Georges Desire 1995 `13.5` `C`

GERMAN WINE WHITE

Baden Dry NV, Somerfield `10` `C`

Dullish.

Hock Rudolf Muller, Somerfield `13.5` `B`

Flowery fruit, off-dry, great as a refresher.

Morio Muskat St Ursula 1995, Somerfield `14` `B`

Don't sneer at it, wine snobs. Try it when the weather's sultry, just a glass. Its muscat fruit is like drinking grapes (and, curiously, how many wines can you say *that* of?)

Mosel Riesling Halbtrocken, Somerfield `11` `B`

Niersteiner Spiegelberg Kabinett 1995,
Rudolf Muller, Somerfield `14` `B`

Rheingau Riesling, St Ursula 1995,
Somerfield `13` `C`

Rheinhessen Auslese, Somerfield `13` `C`
Good with fresh fruit.

Rudesheimer Rosengarten, Somerfield `11` `B`

St Johanner Abtey Kabinett `12` `B`
At its best in warm weather.

GREEK WINE WHITE

Samos Sweet White Wine (half bottle) `15.5` `B`
A 15 per cent alcohol dessert wine of honeyed richness and musky melony fruit, with very oily texture. Terrific with creme brulee, Christmas cake, and spotted dog and custard. Tasty value under three quid. Selected stores.

HUNGARIAN WINE RED

Bulls Blood, St Ursula 1993 `10` `B`

HUNGARIAN WINE WHITE

Castle Ridge Sauvignon Blanc 1996 `15` `B`

Very classy stuff. Not classic on the finish but very classic as it tickles the nose with its impishly grassy edge. The fruit has some richness to it but is always dry and fresh. Excellent with shellfish. Selected stores.

Gyongyos Chardonnay 1996 `14.5` `C`

Delicious citric-edged fruit – the perfect fish wine.

ITALIAN WINE RED

Cabernet Sauvignon del Veneto 1996, Somerfield `13.5` `C`

Nice dry style. Plenty of tannin on those cherries.

Cascine Garona Barbera d'Asti 1996 `14` `C`

Very Italian, light but incisive, dry but fresh and nutty, and great with food. Not rich or gripping but it has personality.

Chianti Classico Montecchio 1994 `14.5` `C`

Chianti Classico Rocca della Macie 1990 `13.5` `E`

Chianti Conti Serristori 1996, Somerfield `11` `C`

Copertino 1994 `14` `C`

Needs food like grass needs a mower – to keep it down. A thoroughly well-flavoured wine.

I Grilli di Villa Thalia, Calatrasi 1993   `14` `C`

Fading a bit.

Lazio Rosso 1995, Somerfield   `14` `B`

Earthy, ripe, characterful, a breeze to sip with supper, and well priced. Does need food, though – anything from roast lamb to stuffed aubergines.

Le Trulle Primitivo del Salento 1996   `13.5` `C`

The New World meets the Old World and the winner is . . . me and you. Ripe, fresh, rustic but zippy, this wine.

Merlot del Veneto 1996, Somerfield   `12` `B`

Very cherryish and light.

Montepulciano d'Abruzzo 1996   `13.5` `C`

Cherries and plums, squashy and ripe. You have to be in a soppy mood for this wine.

Montereale Sicilian Red, Calatrasi 1996   `13` `B`

Notarpanaro Taurino, Rosso del Salento 1988   `14.5` `D`

The ultimate southern Italian food wine: figgy, curranty, ripe, rich and porty (but never portly). Selected stores.

Piccini Chianti Classico Reserva 1993   `14` `E`

Expensive but very classy and typically baked-earth fruit. Terrific with roast lamb.

Riparosso Montepulciano del Abruzzo, Illuminati 1995   `14` `C`

Another dry but fruity Somerfield Italian which is great with food. Selected stores.

Soltero Bianco, Settesoli (Sicily)

A waxy, almost oily Sicilian wine which would be terrific with shellfish and mackerel dishes.

Soltero Rosso, Settesoli (Sicily)

Smells like a sauce you might have with game: rich and pungent. The fruit, at first, seems reluctant then it opens up in the throat to be soft and plump.

Tuscan Red, Somerfield

Light but dry, hints of real sangiovese grip and earthiness, and it's very good with food. Real Italian wine here.

Valpolicella Fratelli Pasqua 1996, Somerfield

So light you could screw it to a rose in the middle of the ceiling.

Vigneti Casterna Valpolicella Classico, Pasqua 1994

What are the words usually applied to valpol? The Obscene Publications Act forbids their use in this book. However, with this example such words are unnecessary. It's delicious.

ITALIAN WINE WHITE

Chardonnay del Piemonte Araldica 1996, Somerfield

Rather more expensive than makes for comfortable acquisition but has some suppleness and lemonic-edged butteriness to the fruit.

Chardonnay Histonum

Odd but demanding to be taken seriously. It's odd because it's so stony and fresh. Not at all stores.

Frascati 1996, Somerfield 　　　　12　C
Hint of dank earth to the fruit.

Le Trulle Chardonnay del Salento 1996 　　15.5　C
One of the most elegantly fruity, lemonically well-polished and
softly melony Italian chardonnays around at an excellent price.

Montereale Bianco 1996, Somerfield (Sicily) 　14.5　B
More nuttiness and flavour than previous vintages. Terrific little
fish wine and general, all-purpose, slide-down-any-time tipple.

Orvieto Classico Conti Serristori 1996 　　13.5　C
A gentle crisp edge to the pear/pineapple fruit is its best
feature.

Pinot Grigio Fratelli Pasqua 1996,
Somerfield 　　　　12　C
Somewhat perfunctory for four quid.

Salice Salentino Bianco 1996 　　　14　C
Classic clean knife-edge fruit of some charm. Not at all stores.

Soave 1996, Somerfield 　　　　13.5　B
A good clean specimen useful for fish.

Tuscan White 1996, Somerfield 　　14.5　B
A rich, creamy, gently nutty wine of some style. A thoroughly
commendable glug.

MOLDOVAN WINE 　　　WHITE

Kirkwood Moldovan Chardonnay 1996 　　15　C
Has hints of richness but is never blowsy or overbaked.

It's always elegant, purposeful, direct – and hugely drinkable.

NEW ZEALAND WINE — RED

Montana Cabernet Sauvignon Merlot 1995 | 14.5 | D

Grass meets wet earth, but the result, though interesting, is not exactly paydirt. A dry, vegetal wine which needs food.

NEW ZEALAND WINE — WHITE

Coopers Creek Chardonnay, Gisborne 1996 | 14.5 | D

Classy beginning, and a stylish end. The middle? Well, it's there even if it's subtle.

Coopers Creek Sauvignon Blanc, Marlborough 1996 | 16 | E

Always one of the most exciting sauvignons from NZ: subtle, rich, lovely, ripe melon and grassy, lemonic acidity, and great balance. Selected stores.

Montana Sauvignon Blanc 1996 | 14.5 | D

Good grassiness smoothly mown and well tended. Loss of impact on the finish but too individual and decently fruity to rate less.

Timara Dry White, Montana 1996 | 13.5 | C

Some richness here . . . some.

PORTUGUESE WINE RED

Alta Mesa Estremadura 1995 `15.5` `B`

Really warm, sunny fruit of great depth and flavour and food-compatibility.

Alta Mesa Tinto Estremadura 1995 `15.5` `B`

Brilliant quaffing: soft, slightly rich and flavourful and exceedingly friendly.

Atlantic Vines Baga 1995 `12` `C`

Oddly unconvincing – like seeing a young child in charge of an expensive piece of machinery.

Dao Reserva, Caves Alianca 1990 `14` `B`

Leziria Tinto Almeirim 1995 `13.5` `B`

PORTUGUESE WINE WHITE

Estorila 1996 `14` `B`

Has some hint of fatness to it which is rare at this price. Good with rich fish and mild poultry dishes.

ROMANIAN WINE RED

Pietroasa Young Vatted Cabernet 1995 `16` `C`

A two-year-old with the IQ of an undergraduate. Fabulous

stuff! Young cabernet which is at the peak of developed fruitiness, dryness, blackcurrant concentration, texture and tannicity. Bordeaux would ache to have fruit this advanced at two years old.

Romanian Barrel Fermented Special Reserve Merlot 1994 `16.5` `C`

Remarkably rich and energetic. Absolutely compelling for the money: rich, gently leathery, aromatic, gorgeous ripe but classy texture, balance and finish. Only at the top 150 stores.

SOUTH AFRICAN WINE RED

Jacana Pinotage, Stellenbosch 1995 `16.5` `D`

A Devon cream tea, rich and rampant, from the Devon Winery. Has a wonderful savoury aroma, brilliant tannins and fruit, and a persistent finish.

Rawsons Ruby Cabernet/Merlot 1996 `15` `C`

Warmth, depth, texture, ripeness, flavour, balance and finish. It's a real together wine, this rampant specimen.

South African Pinotage 1996, Somerfield `13.5` `C`

SOUTH AFRICAN WINE WHITE

Bellingham Sauvignon Blanc 1997 `14.5` `C`

Crisp and tasty, clean and decisive – knows where it's going: right down the throat! Not at all stores.

Jacana Chardonnay, Stellenbosch 1996 ⟨15.5⟩ ⟨D⟩

Very rich, ripe, deeply flavoured almost fume fruit of very satisfying drinkability. Great with food.

South African Dry White 1996, Somerfield ⟨14.5⟩ ⟨B⟩

An agreeably priced and very agreeably fruited wine: crisp, flavoursome, perky.

SPANISH WINE   RED

Berberana Tempranillo, Rioja 1994 ⟨15⟩ ⟨C⟩

Castillo Imperial Tinto 1996 ⟨14.5⟩ ⟨B⟩

What a deliciously simple food wine! And its bright plum fruit is eminently quaffable.

Don Hugo Tinto 1995, Somerfield ⟨13.5⟩ ⟨B⟩

La Pergola Tempranillo, Ehrmanns 1996 ⟨14⟩ ⟨B⟩

Dry finish of some excitement. The fruit is gripping and bold. Great with food.

Las Campanas Navarra Garnacha 1996 ⟨14.5⟩ ⟨C⟩

How to control juiciness by giving the wine some decent tannic edginess.

Rioja Reserva Vina Cana 1987, Somerfield ⟨14⟩ ⟨D⟩

Curiously youthful for such age. Tasty, though, and great with burnt sausages.

Rioja Tinto Almaraz NV, Somerfield ⟨15⟩ ⟨C⟩

Gentle coconut and vanilla tone to the fruit. Don't pour it over ice-cream – it's better down the throat.

Santara Dry Red Conca de Barbera 1995

Senorio de Val, Valdepenas 1996, Somerfield

This is a classic case of the old style of Spain meeting the fruitier demands of the UK. This wine slides down a treat – like blackcurrants on skis.

Valencia Red 1996, Somerfield

Simple, gluggable, fresh, hints of rustic charm.

SPANISH WINE WHITE

Almenar Rioja Blanco 1995, Somerfield

Great salmon, squid, skate and monkfish-with-herbs wine. It has elegance and bite, a hint of vanilla and spice, and a soft rich finish.

Castillo Imperial Blanco 1996

The spritzig edge rather detracts from the overall crispness but with a well-burnt slab of seafood this may not much matter.

Gandia Chardonnay, Hoya Valley 1996

Some hint of richness but the finish is fresh and clean. Great with food.

Valencia Dry White, Vincente Gandia 1996, Somerfield 12 B

Somewhat muted with only an echo of fruitiness as it goes down the gullet.

USA WINE   RED

Fetzer Barrel Select Cabernet Sauvignon 1992   `16` `D`

Gorgeous richness, ripeness, balance, fruit and tannins. Real shoulders on this wine. It moves the palate wonderfully. Classy, deep, dry, potent. Not at all stores.

Fetzer Zinfandel 1994   `13` `D`

Soft and gooey and rather expensive. Bit cutesy for my taste.

Redwood Trail Pinot Noir 1995   `14` `D`

Has true pinot aroma, truffley and warm, and a decent thwack of farmyardy wild raspberry-edged fruit. Better, much better, than most red burgundies at twice the price.

FORTIFIED WINE

Fino Luis Caballero, Somerfield   `15` `C`

A dry, tea-leaf-edged fino of classic bone dryness.

Manzanilla Gonzales Byass, Somerfield   `14.5` `C`

A great opportunity, at this remarkable price, to pit this saline, nutty masterpiece against prawns from the grill.

SPARKLING WINE/CHAMPAGNE

Angas Brut Rose (Australia)   `15.5` `D`

Cordoniu Chardonnay Brut `14` `D`

Cremant de Bourgogne, Caves de Bailly NV `14` `D`

Clean and crisp. (How many champagnes can say that?)

De Vauzelle Champagne NV `12` `F`

Not a convincing argument for spending eleven quid.

Lindauer Brut `13` `E`

It strikes me that the style is not as classic as once it was. And at £7.50 it's got £4.99 cavas to contend with which are more elegant.

Mumm Cuvee Napa Brut (California) `15` `E`

Lovely lemony finesse – preferable to scores of champagnes.

Prince William Blanc de Blancs Champagne `12` `G`

Prince William Champagne NV `12` `F`

Prince William Rose Champagne, Henri Mandois NV `12` `G`

Seaview Brut `14` `D`

Seaview Pinot Noir Chardonnay 1994 `15` `E`

One of the most elegant Aussie bubblies around. Selected stores.

Seppelts Quality Australian Sparkling, Somerfield `14` `C`

Pretty good considering the word 'quality' is on the label. Pity about this gaffe.

Somerfield Cava Brut NV   16   D

Elegant, not coarse, taut, wimpish or blowsy, but has hints of ripe fruit and a restrained edge. Fantastic value.

Somerfield Rose Cava NV   14.5   D

Delicious tippling here. Selected stores.

Touraine Rose Brut, Caves de Viticulteurs de Vouvray   13   D

TESCO

TESCO
Tesco House
PO Box 18 Delamare Road
Cheshunt
EN8 9SL
Tel 01992 632222
Fax 01992 644235

What's wonderful.

Tesco will sympathetically consider any idea which will advance the notion that wine drinking is a simple unpretentious pleasurable activity often associated with food. The most obvious way the store achieves this is by getting even quite serious sober-sided wine-makers to produce attractively fruity wines at very low prices and putting them into jazzily labelled bottles. An excellent example of this sort of initiative is the pair of immediately drinkable £2.99 reds, Les Vieux Cepages Grenache and Carignan, made by a man in the Oc boondocks who turns out the area's fanciest, most expensive, and slowest to mature wine.

What's maddening.

Lack of hysteria, a self-restraint of manner and style, prevent Tesco making the most of the heritage of chutzpah which Jack Cohen, its founder, bequeathed it. The great leap from being Britain's No 1 wine retailer, as based on its flogging each year well over 100 million bottles, to Britain's most adventurous wine retailer is the spot which beckons but which Tesco is yet to grasp. Take an example. This year they launch four wines labelled Great With Fish, Great with Chicken, Great with Pasta, and Great with Steak – an idea which was thought up by the inestimably gifted Helen Nathan of London wine merchant and wholesaler Bibendum. The concept is a terrific one. I applaud it. But only conceptually. The wine in the bottles is not as exciting as it ought to be for £3.49 and will not, as promised on the label, necessarily greatly go well with the food partner indicated. Tesco: don't tap politely on my door and request permission to gently jettison my inner footwear. Knock my socks off!

SEE STOP PRESS SECTION AT END OF BOOK FOR LAST-MINUTE ADDITIONS TO THIS RETAILER'S RANGE.

ARGENTINIAN WINE WHITE

Picajuan Peak Chardonnay

Terrific value here. A monstrously-unfair-to-white-burgundy-growers chardonnay of depth, elegance, richness and complexity. The lovely textured fruit makes up for the absence of woody character.

AUSTRALIAN WINE RED

Australian Cabernet/Merlot, Tesco `13` `C`

Australian Red, Tesco `14.5` `B`

It slips down brilliantly like greased damsons and soft fruit (raspberries?). A totally grand glug.

Australian Ruby Cabernet, Tesco `14` `C`

Australian Shiraz, McLaren Vale 1994, Tesco `15` `D`

Barramundi Shiraz/Merlot `13` `C`

Very juicy style with a burnt edge.

Best's Great Western Shiraz 1994 `12` `E`

Now, the Tesco wine buyer thinks this wine is the bee's knees of Aussie shirazes but whilst I find the flavour impressively rich I find the depth lacks character (and tannin). At nigh on ten quid, I want more plot, more vivacity, more old-fashioned, dry food-friendliness. Can I be the only drinker who wonders if this trend of Aussie reds to an all-embracing, almost soppy and puppyish quality of approachability, makes the wines too anodyne and toothless? Top thirty-one stores.

Bin 707 Cabernet Sauvignon, Penfolds 1993

Rich and ripe and not, as might be expected from Penfolds, capable of hugely exciting fruitier development over five to ten years. It is complex and vibrant, but mild-mannered and bespectacled, so it isn't the bruiser it might be thought. Its price is way out of line with the pleasure it provides, which would, at eight quid or so, be reasonable. Soft-textured tannins, nothing violent, makes a couth wine of class but not vast thrills.

Bleasdale Langhorne Creek Malbec 1996

Carrying on the Aussie tradition of reds like gravy, this is a prime contender for the boat. Not, however, the boat which docks at my port. You could warm this wine and pour it over grilled duck breasts. Selected stores.

Brown Brothers Tarrango 1996 `14` `C`

This rubbery, aromatic, soft, well-flavoured wine is very versatile, meat or fish, and chills uncomplainingly.

Buckley's Clare Valley Grenache 1996 `14` `D`

So healthy-seeming and soupy (I've tasted minestrones less rich) you could spoon-feed it to invalids. This, indeed, may be the best way to drink this wine, it's so luscious and balmily textured. Any reader inclined to follow this up please write and let me know how the experience went. Very expensive experience, though.

Buckley's Clare Valley Malbec 1996

Finishes sweetly and having spent so much I want greater complexity for my pounds. Selected stores.

Chapel Hill McLaren Vale Cabernet Sauvignon 1993 `15` `E`

Chapel Hill McLaren Vale Shiraz 1995 `14` `E`

Immediately all-embracing of the tastebuds if not so tender on the pocket.

Cockatoo Ridge Cabernet/Merlot 1995 `13.5` `D`

Coonawarra Cabernet Sauvignon 1995, Tesco `15` `D`

Lovely harmony of fruit, acid and tannin in charming, if somewhat effete and over-elegant, form. But I quibble. 15 points means this is the bee, if not quite its knees.

David Wynn Patriarch Shiraz 1994 `14` `E`

Lovely treat on a cold winter's evening before a roaring fire, this pricey indulgence, with some salami, a warm baguette and butter. Top seventeen stores.

Hardys Nottage Hill Cabernet Sauvignon/ Shiraz 1995 `13.5` `C`

Okay – but pricey. Wish it was £3.49.

Ironstone Cabernet/Shiraz 1994 `15` `D`

Soft as woolly socks but far more soupy and drinkable. It's very soggy in the middle though this could be said to be mere approachability. But it's deep and flavour-packed. Selected stores.

Kingston Estate Mataro 1994 `13` `D`

Kingston Estate Shiraz 1993 `14` `D`

Kooralong Sky Red

Sheer bargain hunter's prize: dry, fruity, balanced, bracingly slurpable and well-flavoured.

Leasingham Cabernet Sauvignon/Malbec 1994

Rich and finely endowed with softness, balance, depth and style. Choose its food, like roast chicken, with care. No spices!! Selected stores.

Leasingham Domaine Shiraz 1994

Wonderful chewy texture and brilliant fruit/acid balance. Has a vivacity and stylishness well worth the money. Quality of fruit and crafted structure – this wine has both.

Lindemans Coonawarra Pyrus 1992 `15` `F`

Yes, it's sodden with deliciousness but is it worth £12? Well, whilst food will blunt its superficial richness and depth (so plain food only), I also suspect it's at heart merely a misanthropic sybarite's solo comfort. Top seventeen stores.

Mountadam 'The Red' Cabernet Sauvignon/ Merlot 1992 `13` `F`

A terrific £5 glug of depth and style. But a £15 wine? Don't make me laugh. Top seventeen stores.

Old Penola Estate Cabernet Sauvignon 1995 `15` `E`

Black cherries, blackcurrants, a hint of fig, a touch of mint (very vague), a soupcon of pepper and vegetal undertones. A distinct, classy, rich Aussie which won't run scared of either rich food or a complex mood. Top eighty stores.

Penfolds Bin 128 Shiraz, Coonawarra 1992 `14` `E`

Penfolds Bin 35 Shiraz Cabernet 1994 `15.5` `C`

Rosemount Estate Shiraz/Cabernet 1996 `15.5` `C`

So soft and slip-downable it may be a crime.

Rosemount Merlot 1995 `13.5` `E`

Classy stuff which isn't soft and soppy, rather supple and authoritative. But it costs.

St Halletts Old Block Shiraz 1993 `14` `E`

Thomas Hardy Coonawarra Cabernet Sauvignon 1992 `15` `F`

Lovely texture of softness, dryness, rich deep fruit and wonderful relaxed, giving flavour. Great with game which its excellent fruit/acid/tannic balance can cope with. Top seventeen stores.

AUSTRALIAN WINE WHITE

Australian White, Tesco `14` `B`

Good fruit to start, then sags, but then makes it up with a very pleasant lemony finish. Somewhat cool temperamentally for an Aussie.

Best's Colombard 1995 `15.5` `C`

Brown Brothers Late Picked Muscat 1995 `14.5` `D`

Interesting sweet aperitif. Rich muscaty fruit, not clammy or too sticky, with an edge of spiced pineapple. Selected stores.

Brown Brothers Riesling 1995 `15` `D`

Hints of powdery lemon sherbet and lime give the fruit charm and some eccentricity. Superb fish wine. Top seventy-seven stores.

Brown Brothers Sauvignon Blanc 1995 14 D

Delicious chewy edge to the ripe fruit gives the wine enhanced food-partnering opportunities. Great with mussel soup. Top seventy-seven stores.

Cape Mentelle Semillon/Sauvignon Blanc 1995 16 E

Chapel Hill Unwooded Chardonnay 1996 13.5 E

Expensive for the level of fruit on offer. It's a good, crisp wine, excellent with seafood, but it costs.

Clare Valley Riesling 1996, Tesco 15 C

Touch expensive, I think, for immediate drinking. It is vibrant, soft yet pert on the finish, spicy in a subtle way, but the best value to be gotten out of it is to let it age for a year or so when it will develop more character and quirkiness and be even better with oriental food than it is now.

Hardys Nottage Hill Chardonnay 1996 16 C

Superb soft, rolling texture. Brilliant fruit. Great balance.

Hunter Valley Semillon 1995, Tesco 13.5 D

Interesting, but the finish fails to clinch it for me.

McLaren Vale Chardonnay 1996, Tesco 16.5 D

Gorgeous smoky depth and richness of flavour balanced by witty acids so that this vintage is the best yet on Tesco's shelves. Ripe, rampant, rude, ready, rich and ... appetite-arousing. Yet in spite of this rousing side to its nature, it is elegant and possesses finesse. Even the price tag is well balanced.

Mick Morris Liqueur Muscat (half bottle) 15.5

Normans Unwooded Chardonnay 1996 `15.5` `D`

Who needs wood when the best Australian wood is the stuff the grapes grow on? A rich, deep wine of balance, ripeness and great style. Use the barrels to support the platefuls of seafood, mild Thai dishes, chicken and vegetable dishes this wine will harmoniously accompany. Selected stores.

Old Triangle Semillon/Chardonnay 1995 `13.5` `C`

Penfolds Barossa Valley Semillon
Chardonnay 1996 `16` `D`

Utterly delicious wine with a ripe, open approach to the fluidity of its fruit which is gently oily and subtly opulent, with a melony, lemony and pineappley edge.

Penfolds Old Vine Semillon 1995 `15` `D`

Ripeness nicely coddled by the woody edge and acidic coating. Delicious structure of class and style. Selected stores.

Pewsey Vale Eden Vale Riesling 1996 `15` `D`

Take your prejudices and throw them to the dogs. This is riesling of measured fruitiness, excellent acid balance, developed flavour and overall very tasty style. It will develop well, and very interestingly, for a couple of years more. Selected stores.

Preece Chardonnay 1996 `15` `D`

Elegant in spite of its designer label and flamboyant designer fruit. Very rich and ripe but never overblown. The fruit is gently cheeky.

Rosemount Estate Diamond Label
Chardonnay 1996 `16` `D`

Rich warm aroma of gently baked fruit, lovely texture with a bias to oiliness and a firm, positive finish. The fruit dominates the finish, over the acidity. A lovely wine, well priced. It has a certain delicacy withal – light poultry and fish dishes only.

Rosemount Estate Sauvignon Blanc 1995   16   D

Rosemount Roxburgh Chardonnay 1994   16   H

What a price! (£25!) But when you consider the paucity of fruit many meursaults offer at this price, Roxburgh is beautifully calm, poised, deliciously woody and very, very classy. If New World chardonnay must copy Old World chardonnay styles, this is not just a copy – it's fancier than the original.

Shaw & Smith Sauvignon Blanc 1996   15   E

An expensive but extremely elegant, beautifully cut wine of grace, immense charm and fine flavour without tartness, grassiness or anything but pure mineral-edged sauvignon of high quality. It is outstanding for the gentility of its gooseberry concentration. Not a wine for robust food. Needs quiet reflective dishes and moments.

Stirling Estate Chardonnay 1995   15   D

Tim Adams Riesling 1995   14.5   E

Gorgeous sherbety texture. Lots of flavour and personality here. Thai food wine par excellence. Top seventy-seven stores.

Tim Adams Semillon 1995   11   E

Not quite convincing at this price, especially when you can get it for less elsewhere in the high street (or you could when this book went to press). Selected stores.

AUSTRIAN WINE   RED

Lenz Moser Blauer Zweigelt 1996   15   C

Better-priced, better-fruited than so many beaujolais with which

this fresh, gently elastic-textured young wine bears comparison.
I do not mean to insult the Austrians by so saying.

AUSTRIAN WINE · WHITE

Lenz Moser Beerenauslese 1994 (half bottle) · 14 · D

Lenz Moser Selection Gruner Veltliner 1995 · 13 · C

BRAZILIAN WINE · RED

Brazilian Cabernet Sauvignon/Merlot , Tesco · 14 · C

BRAZILIAN WINE · WHITE

Brazilian Chardonnay/Semillon, Tesco · 14 · B

BULGARIAN WINE · RED

Noble Oak Lyaskovets Merlot 1994 · 14 · C

It comes like fruit juice at first gulp – then the richness and
gentle tannic undertone appear and give the finish bulk and
vigour. A great pasta wine – especially tomato-sauced over.
Selected stores.

Reka Valley Bulgarian Cabernet Sauvignon, Tesco

14 B

Not possible to imagine an easier-to-drink cabernet. It just floods down the throat without even wiping its boots on the doormat. A terrific, brilliant-value pasta wine.

BULGARIAN WINE WHITE

Bear Ridge Dry White 1995

15.5 B

Brilliant tippling. The fruit is double-layered, edgily rich but nicely counterpointed by incisive acidity. Terrific value.

CANADIAN WINE RED

Canadian Red, Tesco

10 C

CANADIAN WINE WHITE

Canadian White, Tesco

13.5 B

CHILEAN WINE RED

Canepa Oak Aged Zinfandel 1995

14 C

Hints of spice, wood, berries, thorns and green undergrowth.

Great with food. A deep. rich wine of unusually frisky personality for a Chilean. Top eighty stores.

Chilean Cabernet Sauvignon Reserve
1995, Tesco   16   C

Rich, rampant, beautifully balanced between mellowness and
tannic dryness, and well kitted out with a smooth suit of
worsted-textured fruit. Classy, lithe, delicious, this wine is an
exhibition of top-class winemaking using first-class grapes.

Chilean Cabernet Sauvignon, Tesco   16   C

Brilliant fruit here: bold yet soft, fruity yet dry, balanced yet
not afraid to stick its neck out. Terrific stuff.

Chilean Red, Tesco   14.5   B

Don Maximo Cabernet Sauvignon 1993   16.5   D

Errazuriz Merlot 1996   17   D

Totally delicious: textured, dry, multi-layered, gently leathery
and enticingly aromatic, rich yet not forbidding, stylish, very
classy and overwhelmingly terrific value for money.

Montgras Merlot 1995   15.5   C

It's one of those wines which is so lithe and light on the
tastebuds that you wonder how it can possibly have the weight
to leave behind a deep impression. Yet it achieves memorability
with a deadly impressiveness as the delicate richness lingers in the
mouth. Not a wine for robust food methinks, more thoughtful
debate on the future of humankind. Selected stores.

Santa Ines Cabernet/Merlot 1996   14.5   C

Smooth yet jammy and ripe. Terrific with food. Has well-
developed fruit/acid balance. Selected stores.

Undurraga Pinot Noir 1995

Not exactly classic pinot but it is firmly in the camp of wines it is a great pleasure to quaff with or without food. Piles on the richness and flavour most agreeably.

CHILEAN WINE WHITE

Chilean Chardonnay 1996, Tesco

Rich, melony and firmly lemonic on the finish. A grilled fish and shellfish chardonnay.

Chilean Sauvignon Blanc 1996, Tesco

Superb combination of fresh biting acidity and rich-edged fruit of depth and flavour. It has personality, this wine, though I wish it was still under £3.50.

Chilean White, Tesco

Errazuriz Chardonnay 1996

Not as rich and exuberant as many Chilean chardonnays of this year. But it is elegant, decisively balanced, and decently priced for the texture of the fruit and its demurely creamy rich edge.

Luis Felipe Edwards Chardonnay 1996

Simply wonderful: rich yet never cloying, full yet not over-baked, deep yet mindful of its other job of refreshing the palate for more. An elegant wine of great finesse yet strength, muscle and litheness, complexity and . . . a fantastic simple price tag which gives you a penny change out of a fiver. Top eighty stores.

Santa Ines Sauvignon 1996

Has the length and hints of opulence which typifies Chilean sauvignon. Selected stores.

FRENCH WINE RED

Baron de la Tour Fitou 1995

Interesting baked-earth style – but a touch overpriced.

Baron Philippe Rothschild Cabernet Sauvignon VdP d'Oc 1996

A sweetly expressive wine but of not great cabernet character and with most of the weight reserved for the price ticket.

Baron Philippe Rothschild Merlot VdP d'Oc 1996

Rich, ripe and very ready merlot of richness and savour. Takes itself a touch seriously, I guess, but I've given it the benefit of the doubt. It is well textured, sweetly fruity, and with a hint of dryness and characterfulness on the finish. I am, however, moved to ponder how much better the wine might have been if the Baron hadn't tried *so* hard.

Beaumes de Venise, Cotes du Rhone Villages 1994 14 D

Bois Galant Medoc 1992 13 D

Lovely, gentle, cigar-box aroma, like a cheroot smoked at the far end of the room where you are comfortably sitting, but the fruit is somewhat old and on its last legs. Too soft, you see. Too soft. Selected stores.

Bordeaux Rouge 1995 `13.5` `C`

Bourgogne Hautes Cotes de Nuits
1995 `12.5` `D`

Cahors, Tesco `12.5` `B`

Chateau Cote Montpezat, Cotes de
Castillon 1993 `14.5` `D`

A touch light on the finish but the bouquet and the fruit on
the palate are memorable. Dry, stylish, this is a true claret yet
one which is very approachable. Selected stores.

Chateau de Goelane Bordeaux Superieur
1994 `14` `D`

Very well-mannered and polite, this is bordeaux trying to please
– and succeeding.

Chateau Lagrave Martillac 1994 `13` `E`

Takes time to invigorate the tongue – due to its youth. But
when, after twenty seconds, the finish cruises in after the initial
fruity attack, it shows its class. I'd lay it down for another five
to eight years. Selected stores.

Chateau Leon Premieres Cotes de
Bordeaux 1994 `C`

Real classic claret. Attacks the molars like a horde of Visigoths
– loudly, recklessly, dryly and very effectively. Will develop well
between now and the millennium.

Chateau Pigoudet, Coteaux d'Aix en
Provence 1994 `D`

Not as brilliant as previous vintages – seems to lack the richness
of yesteryear. Top eighty stores.

Chateau Regusse Coteaux de Pierrevert 1994 `12.5` `C`

Vegetal and very fresh. Will it improve over time? It needs to. But it's had three years already. Top thirty stores.

Chateau Robert Cotes de Bourg 1993 `14` `D`

Chateau Saint-Nicholas, Fronsac 1992 `13.5` `D`

Black cherries and clods of earth – good combination of flavours for rich food. Pity the wine is so close to seven quid.

Chateau St Georges, St Emilion 1993 `12.5` `G`

Chateau Trimoulet St Emilion 1989 `13` `G`

Amusing presumptions to class. Hugely overpriced. Top seventy-seven stores.

Claret, Tesco `14` `B`

About as inexpensive yet as genuine as claret can possibly get. A bargain.

Clos de Chenoves Bourgogne Rouge 1994 `12` `D`

Top thirty-one stores.

Corbieres, Tesco `14.5` `B`

Corbieres shorn of its ragged edges and scrubbed – this is all charm, softness and utter drinkability.

Cotes du Rhone, Tesco `13` `B`

Soft, simple, and it simpers as it descends. A very adolescent Rhone red.

Cotes du Rhone Villages 1996, Tesco `15.5` `C`

Warm, fruity, dry yet rich and rounded on the finish, admirably well-textured, very giving of itself, and gentle soft tannins. Good value under four quid here.

Domaine de Beaufort Minervois 1995, Tesco

| 12 | B |

Domaine de Conroy Brouilly, Jean St Charles 1994

| 11 | D |

Domaine de Lanestousse Madiran 1993

| 14 | D |

Inviting aroma of dead wood, new shoes and floor cleaner. The fruit is tannin-ravaged, so needs time to settle. But with rare roast beef, today, it would be remarkable company. Otherwise, give it to grandad to soak his teeth in.

Domaine de Revest Pinot Noir 1995

| 10 | C |

Very light and uninteresting.

Domaine du Soleil Syrah/Malbec 1995 (vegetarian)

| 13.5 | C |

Too expensive when compared with softer, fruitier specimens (especially Chilean). The fruit is brisk, somewhat stern-visaged (but good with rich food) and thus not a congenial glug by itself.

Domaine Georges Bertrand Corbieres 1994

| 16 | C |

Better than many bordeaux at twice the price, this dry, rich wine has herb-packed denseness of fruit and loads of characterful depth. Excellent fruit, acid and tannins, all in meaty collusion. Top thirty stores.

Domaine Maurel Fonsalade, Saint Chinian 1994

| 14.5 | C |

Equus Bergerac Rouge 1995

| 12 | C |

A dull and bordeaux-like bottle of underdeveloped fruit. It needs eighteen months or so to shake off its torpor and even then I'm not sure we'll have something to set the world, or any palate, on fire. Selected stores.

French Cabernet Sauvignon Reserve, Tesco `14` `C`

Good jammy fruit held back from overripeness and juiciness by gentle tannins.

French Cabernet Sauvignon, Tesco `15.5` `B`

Brilliant value. A beautifully coloured wine of force, character, varietal stylishness and real warm cabernet deliciousness. The peppery, almost cinnamon edge to the wine is balanced by an apple-skin acidity. A fantastic glugging wine and great with all sorts of casseroles, cheese dishes and most vegetables.

French Merlot Reserve, Tesco `14.5` `C`

Immensely drinkable yet with a gamine serious side to its personality. Dark, rich and handsome, this is good value. Hints of classic merlot leatheriness only, but this is *gluggable* merlot.

French Merlot VdP de la Haute Vallee de l'Aude, Tesco `15` `B`

Lovely colour, hints of leather with the aroma, ripe but dry-to-finish fruit of polished plum and dark cherry, and an overall soft, rich texture. Terrific-value plonking here.

Great with Steak Merlot d'Oc 1995 `12.5` `B`

A disappointment and not great with steak.

Grenache, Tesco `16` `B`

Hautes Cotes de Beaune 1995 `11` `D`

La Vieille Ferme, Cotes du Rhone 1994 `14` `C`

Lacost-Borie, Pauillac 1993 | 12 | F

Top seventeen stores.

Les Vieux Cepages Carignan VdP de l'Herault 1994 | 14 | B

Slightly more nervous of temperament than its grenache brother. But still a bargain.

Margaux 1994, Tesco | 13.5 | E

Real dark fruit with lots of tannic personality. Bristles a bit, needs three years to be at its peak, and it is expensive. Selected stores.

Medoc, Tesco | 13.5 | C

A mildly mannered medoc of some charm. It reserves its best line for the last, like all great jokesters, and it's a dry, gently tannic line at that. Overall, though, a soft, approachable red.

Minervois, Tesco | 14 | B

A simple fruity wine which hints at its herby, sun-packed provenance rather than smacking it to you forcibly.

Morgon, Arthur Barolet 1994 | 11 | D

Moulin de la Doline Fitou 1995 | 14 | C

Where is the Peasant Plonk of yesterday? There are tannins here but they're softly integrated with the fruit to provide texture and character.

Moulin de Saint-Francois Corbieres 1993 | 13.5 | D

Pauillac 1994, Tesco | 13 | D

Red Burgundy 1995, Tesco | 11 | C

St Emilion, Tesco `13` `D`

St Joseph Cave de la Tain l'Hermitage 1994 `13` `D`
Top eighty stores.

St Julien 1993, Tesco `15` `E`

Yvecourt Bordeaux Rouge 1995 `13` `C`
Top eighty stores.

FRENCH WINE WHITE

Alsace Gewurztraminer 1995, Tesco `13.5` `D`
Expensive but a treat with take-away Peking duck with plum sauce.

Alsace Pinot Blanc, Tesco `11` `C`

Alsace Riesling Graffenreben 1995 `11` `D`

Anjou Blanc, Tesco `12` `B`

Bordeaux Blanc de Blancs, Tesco `13` `B`
Earthy but with a little energy. Needs fowl.

Bordeaux Sauvignon Blanc 1995 `14` `C`

Cabernet de Saumur Rose, Tesco `13.5` `C`
A light rose, perfect chilled in large glasses for small parties (i.e. you and a mackerel under the grill – the mackerel, that is).

Chablis 1995, Tesco `13` `D`
Lot of dosh. Not a lot of posh.

Chateau Armand Sauternes 1994 (half bottle)

`13` `E`

Rather pricey but good with blue cheese. Top seventy-seven stores.

Chateau de la Colline Bergerac Blanc 1996

`14` `C`

Has some class and not as dry as it might seem to regard the label. It hits the palate with a fairly gentle but persistent dollop of fruit and leaves a very faint vegetal and nicely nutty flavour on the finish. Top eighty stores only.

Chateau la Foret St Hilaire Entre Deux Mers 1995

`11` `C`

Too expensive, insufficiently exciting for a fiver.

Chenin Blanc, VdP du Jardin de la France, Tesco

`15` `B`

Brilliant value: impishly fruity (melony yet very crisp and clean to finish), delightfully well paced from aroma to finish, and simply delicious.

Cotes du Rhone Blanc 1996

`14` `C`

Excellent food wine. Has soft, crisp fruit – a paradox peculiar to Rhone whites.

Crozes Hermitage Blanc 1995

`11` `D`

Domaine de la Done Syrah Rose 1996

`12.5` `B`

Selected stores.

Domaine de la Jalousie Late Harvest VdP des Cotes de Gascogne 1993

`14` `C`

Domaine de Montauberon Marsanne 1996

`12` `C`

Doesn't give a lot.

Domaine du Soleil Chardonnay VdP d'Oc 1996 (vegetarian)
`15.5` `C`

Delightfully soft and rich fruit, 100 per cent vegetarian, which finishes deliciously lemony and refreshing. Terrific price for such class in a glass.

Domaine du Soleil Sauvignon/Chardonnay 1995 (suitable for vegetarians and vegans)
`14` `C`

Fresh with a nutty undertone, this wine is perfect with an elegant risotto of fresh peas with lemony olive oil. Top eighty stores only.

Domaine Raissac Vermentino/Chardonnay 1996
`14.5` `B`

What a delightful fish wine! It's ready to go with baked cod or even mackerel with mustard sauce. Top eighty stores.

Domaine Saubagnere VdP de Gascogne 1995
`13.5` `C`

Young and frisky. Has hints of opulence.

Domaine Saubagnere, VdP des Cotes de Gascogne, Tesco
`13.5` `C`

Pineappley, pear-like and odd soft fruit medley of flavour gives the wine a pleasing level of fruit.

Entre Deux Mers, Tesco
`13` `C`

Touch austere on the finish, almost bony, but with fish it works well.

Escoubes, VdP des Cotes de Gascogne, Tesco
`14` `B`

A first-rate welcome-home-from-work glug. Attractive, balanced, fresh and clean.

French Chardonnay, VdP d'Oc, Tesco   `12` `C`

French Semillon, Tesco   `10` `B`

I was most unmoved by this wine.

French Vermentino VdP d'Oc 1996   `15` `B`

A superbly fresh, clean, brightly fruity but very well-balanced wine. Excellent with light fish dishes and aperitif situations. Top eighty stores.

Great With Chicken 1996   `12` `B`

A lie. It would not be great with chicken. It would be adequate.

Great With Fish 1996   `13` `B`

Interesting concept. Not a hugely thrilling wine (and it wouldn't necessarily be 'great with fish').

Greenwich Meridian 2000 White, Bordeaux 1996   `13.5` `C`

Pleasant, light, gently floral, crisply edged, romantic with candles. Expensive.

James Herrick Chardonnay 1996   `14.5` `C`

More lemonic than previous vintages and less like the Old World style – but it will, I feel, pull itself round more richly over the next nine months.

James Herrick Chardonnay Reserve 1995   `15` `D`

Has softness and richness and is obviously trying very hard to be high-class chardonnay. It succeeds, but even giving it 15 I wish it was less than seven quid. Top eighty stores.

La Vieille Ferme Cotes du Rhone Blanc 1995 `12.5` `C`

Louis Jadot Pouilly Fuisse 1994 `12` `F`

Macon Blanc Villages 1996, Tesco `13.5` `C`

Not bad, not bad at all. But is it a fiver's worth of fruit? Not compared with Chile or South Africa.

Meursault Louis Josse 1994 `11` `G`

You really have to search for Monsieur Josse's name on the label. I'm not surprised he's trying to make himself as inconspicuous as possible.

Muscadet de Sevre et Maine, Tesco `14` `B`

At last! Muscadet under £3 a bottle – the price it *should* be. It's also fruity, dry, flavoursome, hints at crispness without fully achieving it, and 544 branches have it.

Muscat Cuvee Jose Sala 1996 `15` `C`

As good, sweetly dispositioned, honeyed, waxy and good value as ever. Lovely with pud.

Muscat de Beaumes de Venise (half bottle) `14` `C`

Muscat de Rivesaltes (half bottle) `14.5` `B`

Brilliant solo-hedonist's weekend treat: good book, this little half bottle, a baguette, some Italian blue cheese and a big bunch of red grapes.

Oak Aged White Burgundy 1995, Tesco `13` `D`

Pouilly Fume Cuvee Jules 1996 `13` `D`

Some attractive fruit at first, but the finish is a touch weedy.

Premieres Cotes de Bordeaux, Tesco

Rich, sweet, winsome – great with fresh fruit.

Roussanne VdP d'Oc 1996, Tesco

Slightly peachy edge to the fruit makes it very agreeable – even if, at £3.99, it seems a touch on the high side.

Russian Oak Chenin/Chardonnay 1995

Only the wood the barrels are made from comes from Russia. The grapes come from the Languedoc. I feel the relationship between the two is not as mellow and harmonious as the price would suggest. Top thirty stores.

Saumur Blanc, Tesco

Very dry and though agreeable with a bowl of mussel soup, somewhat scrawny without.

Sauvignon Blanc Bordeaux, Tesco

Good food tipple. Has a characteristic hint of earthiness to its fruit. Crisp finish. decent value.

St Veran Les Monts 1995

Expensive but not bad as white burgundies go. But I'm trying really hard to like it. Top eighty stores.

Touraine Sauvignon La Clochette 1995

Not a typical sauvignon or a typical Loire white for that matter – it has style and flavour, and some elegance at a most accommodating price. Top eighty stores.

Viognier Les Domaines Viennet 1996, Tesco

Gentle apricot edge, fresh urgent acidity – a very pleasant palate-tickling tipple. Should be coming into selected stores as this book comes out.

Vouvray, Tesco `13` `C`

Lots of off-dry fruit which is good to sip (or slurp) with fresh fruit.

GERMAN WINE

Bernkastel Kurfurstlay, Tesco `13` `B`

German Pinot Blanc, Tesco `12` `C`

Landwein Riesling 1995 `14.5` `C`

One of the nattier new German rieslings, by virtue of its superior texture and subtle richness but decided unsweetness. The wine is a delicious appetite-arouser, very clean, steely and crisp. And the bottling and labelling are as sane and balanced as the wine.

Mosel Kabinett, Tesco `11` `B`

Nahe Kabinett, Tesco `12` `B`

Some hints of bulk to the fruit and zip to the acidity.

Palatinarum Riesling `12` `B`

It is *not* dry and crisp.

Palatinarum Rivaner `13.5` `B`

Not bad. It is dry and crisp.

Pfalz Kabinett, Tesco `11.5` `B`

Selected stores.

**Scharles Kerner Kabinett Halbtrocken
1995 (50cl)** `12` `C`

St Johanner Abtey Spatlese 1995, Tesco 13 B

Sweet, yes, but it has a little tartness to it. Orange tartness as a matter of fact. Best put down with a bunch of chilled grapes – after dinner.

Steinweiler Kloster Liebfrauenberg Auslese, Tesco 13 D

Rich, gently honeyed, sweet to finish. Decent enough tipple with fresh fruit.

Steinweiler Kloster Liebfrauenberg Kabinett, Tesco 13.5 C

Acidity saves it from overweening sweetness. Wouldn't say no to a glass once the weather turns hot.

Steinweiler Kloster Liebfrauenberg Spatlese, Tesco 12.5 C

Falls off at the end. Rather liked it till then.

HUNGARIAN WINE RED

Reka Valley Hungarian Merlot, Tesco 13.5 B

Merlot in its juicy foot-bath mode. Soften those bunions up a treat.

HUNGARIAN WINE WHITE

Hungarian Oak Aged Chardonnay, Tesco 13 C

Hmm . . .

Reka Valley Hungarian Chardonnay, Tesco `12` `B`

Vegetal and needs food.

ITALIAN WINE RED

Barolo Giacosa Fratelli 1992 `13.5` `E`

It is expensive but it has some individuality and figgy, licorice presence if not charisma.

Cabernet del Veneto, Tesco `13.5` `B`

Carignano del Sulcis 1994 (Sardinia) `16` `C`

All tobacco, all-spice and a hint of chocolate. Dry, warm, very sunny of disposition, a touch of exoticism on the finish, and a lingering finish of dry figs and bitter chocolate with an almond edge. Complex enough for you? It was for me.

Chianti Classico 1994, Tesco `13` `C`

Touch expensive for the simplicity of the style.

Chianti Rufina 1995, Tesco `13.5` `C`

Fresh and young.

Merlot del Piave, Tesco `14` `B`

A delicate merlot of such coy disposition a sworn white wine lover would find it agreeable. This is not a criticism. It is a positive feature of a dry but demurely fruity red wine.

Merlot del Trentino, Tesco `15.5` `C`

Terrific throughput of fruit here: rich (dark cherry and leathery blackcurrant), great texture (soft and jammy in the most deliciously sticky way), and a rousing finish showing fruit, acid, and faint tannins in great array.

Monica di Sardegna, Tesco `11` `B`

Petit Verdot Casale del Giglio 1995 `14` `C`

Good balance of tannin and acid, fruit a touch begging. But brilliant with food – anything from courgette souffle to leg of lamb. Selected stores.

Pinot Noir del Veneto, Tesco `14` `C`

Interesting price and fruit: dry cherries and subtle raspberry flavours, a hint of vegetality and a decent texture. Good with food.

Rosso di Montalcino 1995, Tesco `13.5` `D`

I wish it wasn't quite so expensive. It is typical good Montalcino with its earthy, tarry, ripe fruit, and it engineers a good flourish on the finish. But seven quid? Lot of dosh.

Shiraz Casale del Giglio 1995 `14` `C`

Not like Aussie shiraz, this has more acidity and so is better with Italian food. The wine will develop interestingly in bottle for two more years. It will rate more in six months, I shouldn't wonder.

Sicilian Red, Tesco `13.5` `B`

Sweet finish here after some ripe plum and cherry fruit and I'd try it with curries.

Villa Cerro Valpolicella della Amarone 1992 `13.5` `E`

Expensive treat of interest to buffs who can readily fork out the extra dosh to appreciate the quirky baked edge of the figgy fruit.

Villa Pigna Rosso Piceno 1993 `15.5` `B`

Not a hugely attractive entrance but the hall and living room are excitingly furnished and you find yourself stretching your legs out, relaxing, and having a jolly good quaff. Rich yet vibrant and cheeky, deep yet deft on the palate and with sufficient positive tannins to be great with food. Great price, too.

Villa Pigna Cabernasco 1995 `15.5` `D`

Great colour and with an initial aroma not unlike the dying embers of a fire. The fruit is thick and ripe and coats the tongue like all-weather paint. Great richness, good earthy tannins, has fruitiness yet dry character and it finishes with beefy aplomb. Great with food.

ITALIAN WINE WHITE

Bianco di Custoza, Barbi 1995 `13.5` `C`

Catarratto di Sicilia, Tesco `13.5` `C`

Chardonnay del Veneto, Tesco `13` `B`

Frascati 1996, Tesco `13` `C`

Respectable rather than exciting – and a touch pricey.

Greco di Puglia, Tesco `14` `C`

Expensive but different and it makes a deliciously quirky (almost completely nutty in fact) change from chardonnay. Top eighty stores.

Nosiola del Trentino, Tesco `13.5` `C`

In rebuke to those fey creatures who ask for 'a glass of chardonnay' here is the perfect riposte – 'a glass of nosiola' – a grape variety of some obscurity but no little effect on the tongue where it strikes cleanly, freshly, with a hint of nuts.

Nuragus di Cagliari, Tesco (Sardinia) `12` `B`

Pinot Grigio del Veneto, Tesco `14` `B`

Prosecco del Veneto, Tesco `13.5` `B`

Salice del Salentino Bianco 1995 `12.5` `C`

Sauvignon Blanc del Veneto, Tesco `12.5` `B`

Sicilian White, Tesco `14` `B`

Soave Classico 1995, Tesco `13.5` `C`

Expensive but rather interesting. It would be delicious with Thai prawns or squid.

Vermentino di Sardegna `15` `B`

Has a delicious multi-layered, gently citric fruitiness of utter charm.

Villa Cerro Recioto di Soave 1993 (50cl) `15` `C`

Off-dry and quirky, this is a delicious hedonistic treat for the solo tippler in the half-litre bottle. Gently waxy and glucoid, its richness has acidity packed in behind so it's never cloying. Might be worth trying with goat's cheese and fresh fruit. Top eighty stores.

Villa Pigna Chiara `13` `B`

Good with fish and chips; rather meagre without.

MOROCCAN WINE RED

Moroccan Red `14` `B`

NEW ZEALAND WINE RED

New Zealand Cabernet Sauvignon, Tesco `14` `C`

NEW ZEALAND WINE WHITE

Cooks Chardonnay 1996 `13.5` `C`

Respectable, very respectable.

Coopers Creek Chardonnay, Gisborne 1995 `15.5` `E`

Complexity, flavour, style, individuality, admittedly a high price but real class in evidence and overall thoroughly delicious.

Jackson Estate Sauvignon Blanc 1996 `16` `E`

Why buy Tesco's sancerre when for a quid more you can get the real sauvignon taste here? Elegant minerality here, which used to be sancerre's trademark. Now it's Marlborough's. Top thirty stores.

Montana Sauvignon Blanc 1996 `14.5` `D`

Good grassiness smoothly mown and well tended. Loss of impact on the finish but too individual and decently fruity to rate less.

New Zealand Sauvignon Blanc 1996, Tesco `14` `C`

Touch of grass, hint of earth – you swallow a piece of New Zealand with every drop.

Stoneleigh Marlborough Chardonnay, 1995 `14.5` `D`

Touch pricey but has genuine hint of its pedigree (Marlborough) even if this is a little muted.

PERUVIAN WINE — RED

Peru Red, Tesco — 13.5 B

Fruity and drinkable, but Hungary, Bulgaria and Romania knock it into a cocked hat. If it helps you to swallow £3.49 for this wine, please feel free to drink it out of said headgear. Selected stores.

PERUVIAN WINE — WHITE

Peru White, Tesco — 14 B

Almost excellent. Rich fruit, classily intentioned. Selected stores.

PORTUGUESE WINE — RED

Dom Jose, Tesco — 12.5 B

Dos Frades Cabernet Sauvignon 1995 — 15 C

Smoky, rich, tobacco-scented, deep, dry, full of flavour and very gripping. Excellent value. Selected stores.

JP Barrel Selection 1991 — 17 C

Possibly the best red wine bargain on Tesco's shelves, this roaring broth of a wine. Aromatic, mature, tarry, figgy without being overripe, this is a seriously hairy-chested wine of richness, depth, warmth, texture and superb fruit/acid balance with attendant tannins bringing up the rear. Brilliant with casseroled veg and meats. Top eighty stores.

PORTUGUESE WINE WHITE

Dry Vinho Verde, Tesco B

ROMANIAN WINE RED

Reka Valley Romanian Pinot Noir, Tesco B

Smells like a saddle after a cross-country trek with a satchel of old books (Morocco-bound classics). However, the fruit is the antithesis of this unpromising commencement. It is hugely ripe and fruity, only a touch dry on the finish, and quite rampantly strawberry-rich and well-textured. A terrific quaffing bottle.

Romanian Cellars Pinot Noir/Merlot B

SOUTH AFRICAN WINE RED

Beyers Truter Pinotage 1995, Tesco C

In a French wine, the dryness hits you immediately, then the fruit. In a South African wine, it's all fruit at first, then the dryness reaches across and hits the palate. Different folks, different strokes.

Clearsprings Cape Red (3-litre box) B

Price band has been adjusted to show equivalent per bottle.

Clos Malverne Auret 1995 E

Expensive, dry, delicious – an unusual treat with its rich fruit and dry incisiveness. Top thirty stores.

Diermersdal Merlot 1996 `14` `D`

Has great initial richness then marks time before it deigns to finish. Top eighty stores.

Diermersdal Syrah 1996 `13.5` `D`

Good fruit but somewhat overpriced at nearly six quid. Top eighty stores.

International Winemaker Cabernet Sauvignon/Merlot,Tesco `13` `C`

Charcoal edge to the fruit.

Leopard Creek Cabernet/Merlot `16` `C`

Great blend of grapes providing the dry, peppery cabernet with the textured, aromatic richness of merlot. Terrific price for the style.

Oak Village Pinotage/Merlot 1996 `16` `C`

Brilliant marriage of the vivacious pinotage and the cerebral merlot.

Oak Village Vintage Reserve, Stellenbosch 1995 `14` `C`

Warm, inviting, with a lovely dryness to the edge of the fruit which lingers. Good texture, balance and style.

Paarl Cabernet Sauvignon, Tesco `15` `C`

Cabernet in its most approachable, warmly fruity, gluggable style.

Plaisir de Merle Cabernet Sauvignon 1994 `12.5` `E`

Fruity, boot-leather aroma and good fruit but it's a lot of money and fails to convince on the finish. It's not complex as it goes down and thus fails to linger. Selected stores.

Schoone Gevel Merlot 1995

Hints at juiciness but holds back. Good texture and finish.

South African Red, Tesco

Lovely glugging here with touches of tar and raspberry. Great chilled with a fish stew. Brilliant at room temperature with casseroles.

South African Reserve Cabernet Sauvignon 1996, Tesco

Wonderful richness and flavour: dry, characterful, richly styled yet controlled. Good with food.

South African Shiraz/Cabernet Sauvignon 1995, Tesco

Juicy, deep, very sizzlingly conceived.

Stellenbosch Merlot, Tesco

Handsome fruit with terrific texture. Has warmth, flavour and richness. Great with meat and vegetable dishes, and cheeses.

Swartland Cabernet Sauvignon/Shiraz 1996

Rich and hints at cragginess but it softens. without yielding its dark depths, on the finish and pulls off successfully a solid structure. Selected stores.

SOUTH AFRICAN WINE WHITE

Cape Bay Semillon/Chardonnay

Rich, nutty, floral hints, rich edge, typical exotic feel to the wine – especially the finish.

Cape Chenin Blanc, Tesco

Freshness, flavour and style – the customary pear-drop flavoured fruit. Hints of ripeness but it isn't overdone. A really welcoming glug.

Cape Colombard/Chardonnay, Tesco

Oodles of flavour, good balance but the fruit forward, good with food.

Danie de Wet Chardonnay Green Label 1996

On the citric side of fruity but this fruit knows its place and keeps pace with the acidity – which has mineral hints. Has restraint and elegance.

Fairview Sauvignon Blanc/Chenin Blanc 1996

Superb example of first-class white wine at a low price. The wine is whistle-clean but also impishly fruity, well balanced, firm of texture, and resists flirtation with the palate in favour of a serious, deep relationship.

Franschoek Semillon, Tesco

Has a subtle crispness under the melony fruitiness which is engaging and good with salads and starters.

Goiya Kgeisje 1997

Fresh, light, crisp – with a pear and strawberry lilt as it floods across the tastebuds. This is a flirtatious dilettante of a wine of immense charm, no depth, and considerable fun to knock back.

La Motte Sauvignon Blanc 1996

Gives sancerre drinkers, paying £3 more a bottle, food for thought. Top eighty stores.

Leopard Creek Chardonnay 1995 `15` `C`

Richness, style, depth, flavour, balance.

Long Mountain Dry Riesling 1996 `13` `C`

This is unbelievably lean in the fruit department. If a Chilean chardonnay is oak, this is a bamboo reed. It isn't a bad wine, merely raw and very young. It will develop manners over eighteen months to three years but it will never become fruitier. Seafood is its partner – fresh, raw, saline.

Oak Village Chenin/Chardonnay 1996 `13` `C`

Oak Village Sauvignon Blanc 1996 `13.5` `C`

Nutty, fresh, thoroughly decent.

Overgaauw Chardonnay 1996 `15` `D`

Quietly stylish, subtly rich, coolly classy. A wine of thought-provoking qualities.

Ryland's Grove Barrel Fermented Chenin Blanc 1996 `15` `C`

Delicious crispness and tonal fruitiness. The style is nutty and lemonic, but there is a richer, waxier shading in the background. Perfect with any type of seafood – but especially crab cakes.

Rylands Grove Chenin/Colombard 1996 `15` `B`

Lovely pebbly textured fruit with melon/mango/lime characteristics. Fresh and flavourful without being blowsy or too amorously young and raw. Selected stores.

Rylands Grove Sauvignon Blanc 1996 `14.5` `C`

Has that lovely sunny edge to the clean fruit which hints at gooseberry rather than shouting it. A good classically styled sauvignon. Selected stores.

Schoone Gevel Chardonnay 1996 D

I confess to preferring this wine to several hugely more expensive white burgundies I've encountered recently and the reason is this fruit is so much more honest, and honestly priced. It is aromatic, textured, finely wrought, and polished without obscuring its depth of character and flavour. This is a seriously delicious white wine which is perfectly priced and poised. Selected stores.

South African Chardonnay/Colombard, Tesco C

Exuberant fruit with rich, incisive acidity making a first-class double act of richness with gluggability.

South African Reserve Chardonnay 1996, Tesco C

Among the most elegant and harmonious of Tesco's S.A. chardonnays. Beautiful wood and fruit integration. Very classy, well textured.

Swartland Sauvignon Blanc 1996, Tesco   C

Somewhat expensive for the style.

Van Loveren Blanc de Noirs Muscadel 1997 B

Scrumptious aperitif wine of quite delightful, relaxing fruit. I daresay it is possible for your guests to have a boring conversation clutching a glass of this aromatic, raspberry ripe, subtly rose wine, but this would be the exception. This wine should excite delicious gossip – it loosens tongues marvellously.

Van Loveren Special Late Harvest Gewurztraminer 1996 (half bottle) 14 C

Light and gently honeyed, more of an aperitif than a dessert wine. Personally, I'd lay it down for three to four years to really develop complexity in bottle.

Vergelegen Sauvignon Blanc 1996 `14.5` `D`

Has freshness and flavour – not as common as you might think with sauvignon blanc.

SPANISH WINE RED

Agramont Garnacha 1995 `14.5` `C`

Rich sticky-edged fruit which finishes lightly but agreeably. Lots of flavour and style here and it will work wonderfully well with game. Top eighty stores.

Don Darias `14` `B`

Marquis de Chive Reserva 1989, Tesco `16.5` `C`

The aroma, of poached egg and wood, is quirky but the blackcurrant and plum fruit sears the throat deliciously and the hints of wild strawberry and dried fig will accompany spicy lamb dishes a treat.

**Mendiani Tempranillo/Cabernet Sauvignon
Navarra 1996** `16.5` `B`

Fantastic value here: dry, rich, aromatic, well-textured, classy, deep, loaded with flavour, and simply hugely delicious. There's a wonderful sticky-toffee edge to the fruit reminiscent of butterscotch, which is simply great to appreciate as you quaff the wine. Good with food.

**Perdido Cabernet Sauvignon Crianza,
Navarra 1994** `15` `C`

Has warmth, richness, texture, aroma, and depth. Terrific with all sorts of roasts, grills, cheese, risottos and all sorts of moods.

Rioja Vina Mara, Tesco `13.5` `C`

Vina Mara Rioja Alavesa, Tesco `16` `C`

Vina Mara Rioja Reserva 1990, Tesco `13.5` `C`

Mild-mannered and quiet.

Vina Mayor Crianza, Ribera del Duero 1992 `14.5` `C`

Savoury, smooth, gently rich, it's not a robust food companion but it is a civilized accompaniment to rice dishes, cheese flans, unspiced chicken, etcetera.

SPANISH WINE WHITE

Castillo de Monjardin Chardonnay 1995 `14.5` `C`

The '95 vintage of this wine is somewhat muted at the moment. Little presence aromatically, fruit on the acidic side rather than mellow – but it will improve over a year in bottle. Selected stores.

Moscatel de Valencia, Tesco `16` `B`

A brilliant example of winemaking and value for money. It has a lovely marmalade undertone to the sweet honey but also there is loads of rich acidity. It's brilliant with pudding and muscular enough to cope with the rowdiest of them.

Vina Mara Superior Rioja, Tesco `14` `C`

UKRAINIAN WINE   RED

Saperavi/Cabernet Sauvignon, Odessos

Can you brave the marzipan-edged fruit? Go on – Ukraine needs the money.

UKRAINIAN WINE   WHITE

Suhji-Lamanski Aligote, Odessos

Interesting import of greatest appeal to home-sick Ukrainians. It is dry and ho-hum fruity.

URUGUAYAN WINE   RED

**Pacific Peak Tannat/Merlot 1996,
Tesco**

URUGUAYAN WINE   WHITE

**Pacific Peak Chardonnay/Sauvignon
1996, Tesco**

Has a curious effect of imagining it is a blend of Cape chardonnay and Loire sauvignon. Such is the Uruguayan style profile. An interesting, well-fruited wine of classy hints.

USA WINE   RED

Gallo Sonoma County Cabernet Sauvignon 1992   15   E

Classy and mature.

FORTIFIED WINE

10 Year Old Tawny Port, Tesco   13   E

Australian Aged Tawny Liqueur Wine, Tesco   14.5   E

Finest Madeira, Tesco   14   D

Superior Oloroso Seco Sherry, Tesco (half bottle)   15   B

Yes, it's dry sherry but it's far from fruitless. Wonderful texture, ripe, rolling, polished and thick and there's a lilt of fruit on the finish. A terrific aperitif with nuts.

Superior Palo Cortado Sherry, Tesco (half bottle)   16.5   C

The texture of worn jeans, the excitement of chewing tar, roses, figs and dry, nutty currants. A very dry yet rich wine of uniquely lingering texture and utterly gorgeous deliciousness. An aperitif which marks the person who offers it as an Epicurean genius.

Tesco Tawny Port   13.5   D

SPARKLING WINE/CHAMPAGNE

Asti Spumante, Tesco `13` `C`

Australian Sparkling Wine, Tesco `14.5` `C`

Still under a fiver, still terrifically sippable elegance for the money.

Blanc de Blancs Champagne, Tesco `13` `G`

Blanc de Noirs Champagne, Tesco `13.5` `E`

Blanquette de Limoux, Tesco `13` `D`

Cava, Tesco `16` `C`

Why drink anything else less well rated in the bubbly department when this gently fruity, elegant fizz is still under a fiver?

**Champagne Nicolas Feuillate Brut
Premier Cru** `15` `G`

**Chapel Hill Sparkling Chardonnay
(Hungary)** `14.5` `C`

Crisp, dry, properly fruity (i.e. restrained rather than full). Excellent value, better than dozens of champagnes penny for penny.

Chardonnay Spumante (Italy) `13.5` `D`

Cremant de Bourgogne 1991, Tesco `12` `D`

Appley and adolescent and advanced in price. Top eighty stores.

Deutz (New Zealand) `15.5` `E`

Jansz Tasmanian Sparkling `12` `E`

Lindauer Brut `13.5` `D`

Millennium Champagne 1990, Tesco `13` `G`

The wittiest thing about it is the price: 19.99. I have to confess, however, to preferring bubbly with dark age price tags: 4.99. Selected stores.

Rose Cava, Tesco `14.5` `C`

Seppelt Sparkling Shiraz 1992 `16` `E`

Wonderful quirky monster! Like a character out of a Roald Dahl story, this wine is big, bubbly, rampantly fruity and rich, yet behind all the gruff eccentricity it loves being odd just to prove how brilliantly it can succeed at charming people given the chance. You owe it to your palate to try it. Perfect with Christmas lunch. Top eighty stores.

Simonsig Kaapse Vonkel 1992 (South Africa) `13` `E`

Has an individuality of flavour and style. Top eighty stores.

South African Sparkling Sauvignon Blanc, Tesco `13.5` `C`

Very fruity bubbly. But not sweet. Just very fruity. Hasn't the finesse of cava at the same price.

South African Sparkling, Tesco `13` `D`

Fruity – not very elegant.

Sparkling Chardonnay 1993, Tesco (Australia) `14` `D`

The fruitier style of bubbly but it's not too rich or cloying. There's some elegance and wryness about it.

Sparkling Chardonnay, Tesco (France)   14   C

Vintage Cava 1993, Tesco   14.5   D

Has a dry undertone which nicely complements the fruity lilt on the finish. Delicious stuff.

Vintage Champagne 1990, Tesco   12   G

Lemony and chop-lickingly pleasant, but at twenty quid I can find better horses to back at Tesco than this bubbly.

Yalumba Pinot Noir Chardonnay   16   E

So much tastier and better-priced than hundreds of champagnes. Selected stores.

Yalumba Sparkling Cabernet Sauvignon NV   16   E

A dry, slight version of the Seppelt Sparkling Shiraz (QV). This is another irresistibly quirky monster. Top eighty stores.

WAITROSE LIMITED

WAITROSE LIMITED
Customer Services Department
Southern Industrial Area
Bracknell
Berks
RG12 8YA
Tel 01344 424680
Fax 01344 862584

What's wonderful.

This retailer organises the most civilised wine tastings above its store in London's Finchley Road. Not only is there a separate room for reds and whites, but the tasting takes place on three separate days, weeks apart, so that it is always possible to find a congenial day and time to attend. There is also the delicious enticement of a decent lunch at Waitrose, organised by delicious Waitrose employees. It is for all these reasons that more wine writers attend Waitrose tastings than any other.

What's maddening.

The fact that more wine writers attend Waitrose tastings than any other makes life difficult at times for the taster who merely wishes to get on with tasting. Bodies fill the room with their incessant blathering, and this makes concentrating on tasting wines difficult. The world of wine writing is awash with opinionated bores (goodness, aren't I one?) but at least I try

381

to get on with the job when I'm confronted with 150 wines to taste. I do not spend the time in ceaseless chattering about where I've just been in the world, where I'm going to next, whether so-and-so was right to say such-and-such to thingummy, and 'How lovely to see you darling kiss kiss.' Wine tasting is my work. For some people, it seems to be a social occasion with a free lunch thrown in.

SEE STOP PRESS SECTION AT END OF BOOK FOR LAST-MINUTE ADDITIONS TO THIS RETAILER'S RANGE.

ARGENTINIAN WINE   RED

La Bamba Mendoza Pinot Noir/Syrah 1996   `14` `C`

What excellent company to have with a pizza lunch. It's rich and soft, sinewy and athletic – it leaps pesto, tomato, American hot and even tuna with ease.

La Bamba Mendoza Tempranillo 1996   `15` `C`

ARGENTINIAN WINE   WHITE

Bodega Lurton Pinot Gris, Mendoza 1996   `12` `C`

Santa Julia Torrontes, Mendoza 1996   `14` `C`

AUSTRALIAN WINE   RED

Australian Malbec/Ruby Cabernet 1996, Waitrose   `14` `C`

Very jammy and ripe but great with pasta dishes.

Brown Brothers Tarrango 1996   `14` `C`

Brown's of Padthaway T-Trellis Shiraz 1995   `12` `E`

So ripe it's almost yoghurty. A single glass sustains the palate like a health elixir. Very clotted wine.

Browns of Padthaway Cabernet Malbec 1995

`13` `E`

Bottled sunshine, boot polish and plums.

Bushman's Crossing Dry Red

`12.5` `C`

Not been in the saddle long enough – it's light, cherryish, rather feeble with food.

Chateau Reynella Basket-Pressed Shiraz 1995

`14` `E`

Getting expensive at close to a tenner (an alienating proximity in one so youthful) but it is aromatic, beautifully textured, warm and very soft. But it does have dry, bramble-fruited complexity and good tannins – so it'll age well.

De Bortoli Windy Peak Pinot Noir, Victoria 1996

`13` `E`

Good gamey pinot nose – touch of wild strawberry. Light thereafter, though very drinkable (but eight quid is eight quid).

Hardys Nottage Hill Cabernet Sauvignon/ Shiraz 1995

`13.5` `C`

Hmm . . . okay, but a fiver?

Hardys Southern Creek Shiraz/Cabernet, SE Australia 1996

`13.5` `C`

Ho-hum finish to a decent level of fruit up-front succeeds in giving it a lower rating.

Orlando Jacob's Creek Shiraz/Cabernet 1995

`13.5` `C`

Reliable if not exciting. Getting pricey this close to a fiver.

Oxford Landing Cabernet/Shiraz 1995

`13` `C`

Penfolds Bin 2 Shiraz/Mourvedre 1995 `15.5` `D`

Rich, dry, stylish, this has fluidity of fruit yet tannic firmness of tone. All revealed with one twist of a screwcap.

Penfolds Rawson's Retreat Bin 35 Cabernet/Shiraz 1994 `15.5` `C`

Ridgewood Mataro Grenache, SE Australia 1996 `13` `C`

Light, pleasant, non-fussy, rather bashful.

Tatachilla Cabernet Sauvignon 1995 `14` `E`

Soft, very soft and very likeable. It ought to rate more at this price but it is only modestly complex and demanding.

Tatachilla Merlot 1995 `14` `E`

Only just makes 14 at this price. It's deep and rich and well-textured up-front but it is uncertain at the finish.

Windy Peak Pinot Noir, Victoria 1996 `12` `E`

Silly price for such uneventful tippling.

Yaldara Old Vine Grenache, Barossa Valley 1996 `15` `D`

Lovely ripe fruit with soft, rich, persistent tannins. Unusually well-organised wine from Oz at this price. It makes fewer concessions to likeability and concentrates on being characterful.

Yaldara Reserve Grenache, Whitmore Old Vineyard 1996 `14.5` `D`

Vivacious, dry, textured, plummy yet full of fleshy fruit which finishes impressively.

AUSTRALIAN WINE WHITE

Australian Riesling/Gewurztraminer 1996, Waitrose

Brown Brothers Late Harvest Riesling 1995 (half bottle)

Honey and elderflowers – a real treat to drink with fresh fruit. Or cellar it for five years and open nectar.

Brown's of Padthaway Nonwooded Chardonnay 1996

Utterly delicious. Demonstrates all the virtues of leaving wood on trees.

Bushman's Crossing Dry White

Cape Mentelle Semillon/Sauvignon 1996

Gently grassy and melony with a nuttiness lurking on the finish. Stylish but expensive.

Chateau Tahbilk Marsanne, Victoria 1994

I just love the oily richness of the finish. It lubricates the throat wonderfully.

De Bortoli Rare Dry Botrytis Semillon, SE Australia 1993

Ebenezer Chardonnay, Barossa Valley 1994

Rampant: hikes an old bike, rubbery and clanking with fruit, across the tastebuds. Takes no prisoners.

Hardys Nottage Hill Chardonnay 1995

**Hardys Southern Creek Semillon/
Chardonnay 1996** | 13.5 | C

Has some flavour.

Houghton Gold Reserve Verdelho 1994 | 14 | D

Somewhat expensive for the style but this grape, verdelho, likes
the luxurious life and enjoys rich food.

Lindemans Bin 65 Chardonnay 1996 | 15.5 | C

Delicious combination of butter, hazelnuts and melon undercut
by a perfectly weighted uptide of acidity.

Oxford Landing Chardonnay 1996 | 16 | C

Has traces of oil and butter spread generously but not
overthickly. There's a rich delicacy about the wine which
gives it class.

Penfolds Barrel Fermented Semillon 1994 | 14.5 | D

**Penfolds Bin 202 South Australian
Riesling 1996** | 14.5 | C

It's the texture which gives it its class. The fruit is lemony and
smoky melony, excellent for oriental food, and it would also
serve grilled meats splendidly.

**Penfolds Clare Valley Organic Chardonnay/
Sauvignon Blanc, 1996** | 15 | E

One of the classiest organic whites around: thick fruit of richness
and flavour.

Penfolds Koonunga Hill Chardonnay 1996 | 15.5 | C

Best vintage for years: aromatic, rich, balanced, food-friendly.

Ridgewood Trebbiano 1996/7 | 13 | C

I suppose it's at its best with spaghetti alla vongole.

Rosemount Show Reserve Chardonnay 1995   `16` `E`

One of Australia's most incisively fruity chardonnays, with huge hints of class, depth, balance and persistence. Expensive but very fine.

Saltram Mamre Brook Chardonnay 1995   `14.5` `D`

One of the more successfully rich and happy Australian chardonnays, although at the price the weight of fruit and the degree of complexity are too slight for comfort. That said, this is a highly drinkable wine, make no mistake. It is delicious, if not sensationally so.

Tatachilla Sauvignon/Semillon 1996   `13.5` `D`

Has some flavour but lacks excitement.

Villa Maria Private Bin Chardonnay, Gisborne 1995   `13.5` `D`

Wynns Coonawarra Riesling 1996   `15` `C`

Has a delicious musty ripeness gently buttressed by lithe acidity. Brilliant with oriental food or to quaff (where it makes an emphatic change from chardonnay).

BULGARIAN WINE   RED

Iambol Cabernet Sauvignon/Merlot 1996   `14` `B`

Very dry blackcurrant and pea-pod edged fruit. Great with food.

Oriachovitza Barrel-aged Merlot 1996   `14` `B`

Smartly but casually dressed in fruity attire which has a ripe sheen to it.

CHILEAN WINE   RED

Concha y Toro Merlot 1996   15.5 C

So drinkable – it slides down like an eel on skates. So it's smooth but is it fruity? Yes, it's like pureed leather.

Cono Sur Cabernet Sauvignon 1995   15.5 C

Forget the cabernet grape – this is an extra-terrestrial grape of richness, ineffable velvety texture and tremendous length of flavour. Lovely wine.

Isla Negra Cabernet Sauvignon 1996   15.5 C

A wonderfully well-fleshed-out cabernet of rich texture, soft murky depths and true style. Individual and very drinkable.

La Palma Merlot 1996   15 C

Ripe and opulent in the mouth like inhaling a pearl. A delicious gem of a wine, wildly soft and accommodating, it is one long draught of fruit.

Las Cumbres Chilean Dry Red 1995   15 B

Stowells of Chelsea Chilean Merlot
Cabernet (3-litre box)   10 C

Price band has been adjusted to show equivalent per bottle.

Valdivieso Reserve Cabernet Merlot 1995   15 C

Unusually brisk and rude-mannered Chilean but this is a direct and ultimately charming trait for it goes well with food.

CHILEAN WINE WHITE

Isla Negra Chardonnay 1996 `14` `C`

Classy stuff – great fish wine.

San Andres Chardonnay, Lontue 1996 `14` `C`

Flavour and style in biting collusion.

San Andres Sauvignon Blanc, Lontue 1996 `15` `B`

Superb roundness of flavoured fruit which finishes briskly. Great price.

Stowells of Chelsea Chilean Sauvignon Blanc (3-litre box) `15.5` `B`

Price has been adjusted to show equivalent per bottle.

Valdivieso Chardonnay 1996 `16.5` `C`

Ah! What sublime fruitiness, almost as creamy rich as a rice pud! This unorthodox assault is, however, controlled if passionate and very, very delicious. Hugely impressive.

ENGLISH WINE RED

Chapel Down Epoch I East Sussex 1995 `14.5` `C`

Well, well, it's not only drinkable but one in the eye for sceptics like me who regard English red wine as an idea as daft as Japanese clog dancers. It's soft, very handsomely fruity and not obscenely priced. It's as good as any German dornfelder any day.

ENGLISH WINE
WHITE

Chiltern Valley Medium Dry 1993 `14` `C`

Individual, ripe, smoky, quaint, balanced, richly flavoured. Ignore the 'medium' tag and drink for the pleasure of it – or pair it with fish.

Denbies Surrey Gold `12` `C`

Not yet the Cote D'orking, the provenance of this Surrey wine, but who knows in fifty years' time? Vines need age.

Mill Brook English Table Wine `11` `B`

Has two virtues: it's cheap and it smells vaguely interesting. But like a matinee-priced cinema seat to a film with intriguing titles but no plot thereafter, you leave before the end.

Tanners Brook `7` `B`

FRENCH WINE
RED

Beaujolais 1995, Waitrose `12` `C`

Bergerac Rouge 1995 `14` `B`

Cahors Cotes d'Olt Cuvee Reserve 1994 `12.5` `C`

Chateau Croix St Benoit, St Estephe 1994 `13` `D`

Chateau de Grammont, Coteaux du Languedoc 1995 `15` `C`

Rich, textured, herby, very classy yet deliciously rustic and terrific rounded up with the usual foodie suspects.

Chateau des Combes Canon, Canon-Fronsac 1995 `15` `E`

It's the texture and the allied flavour which meld so beautifully and make the wine worth the money. A really classy claret here.

Chateau des Deduits, Fleurie 1996 `13` `E`

I do not see, by whatever stretch of the imagination or even introducing the solution to Fermat's Last Theorem into the equation, that a Fleurie can logically result in eight quid.

Chateau Haut d'Allard Cotes de Bourg 1995 `14.5`

Brilliant grilled-lamb-chop wine: rich, dry, meaty, well-balanced. Real flavour here for a penny change out of a fiver.

Chateau La Brunette Bordeaux 1995 `14` `C`

Brisk, business-like, a touch formulaic but a good price for the richness of the final finish.

Chateau La Pointe, Pomerol 1993 `13` `G`

Impressive – but mostly because one admires the sheer cheek of the price tag. For nigh on £18 I'd like the earth to move – not be in my mouth.

Chateau Malescasse, Haut-Medoc 1994 `13` `F`

Yes. It's assuredly classy. But I'd be inclined to drink it in three to four years to justify that price.

Chateau Saint-Maurice Cotes du Rhone 1995 `15`

Savoury and ripe, dry yet rich and rolling, deep and delicious, well-textured and highly drinkable.

Chateau Segonzac Premieres Cotes de Blaye, 1994

`14.5` `D`

Chateau Senejac, Haut-Medoc 1993

`13.5` `E`

Developing greater softness as it develops but at £8.45 it'll have to develop even faster to represent great value for money.

Chateau Villepreux Bordeaux Superieur 1995

`15.5` `C`

Well-priced, well-fruited claret of exceedingly developed tannins and lithe muscularity of fruit. A very handsome bottle for the money.

Cigala VdP d'Oc, M Chapoutier 1995

`13` `C`

I used to taste d'Ocs like this twenty years ago.

Clos Saint Michel Chateauneuf-du-Pape 1995

`13.5` `E`

Delicious but expensive. Not, perhaps, as 'big' a wine as previous other examples of this Chateauneuf.

Cotes du Rhone 1995, Waitrose

`14` `C`

One of the smoothest and most softly textured Rhone reds around at this price.

Cotes du Roussillon 1996

`14.5` `B`

Delicious everyday drinking wine. It's the sort of thing which 3-star restaurants ought to carafe as their house wine.

Cotes du Ventoux 1995

`16` `B`

Getting better by the month! The tannins are now fully integrated with the fruit and the resultant texture is smooth and quite stunning for the money. But it's at its peak now (summer '97).

Crozes-Hermitage Cave des Clairmonts 1995 `12` `D`

Not yet developed the bite or bark of the old dogs of previous vintages. Has a really feeble finish.

Domaine de Rose Merlot/Syrah, VdP d'Oc 1996 `14` `B`

Lovely cherry-edged, dry fruit which will chill well for serving with any fish or meat off the grill.

Domaine de Serame Syrah VdP d'Oc 1996 `14.5` `C`

Chilled or warm, its fruit is smooth and ripe and it's sinfully easy to glug.

Domaine des Fontaines Merlot, Vin de Pays d'Oc 1995 `15` `B`

Domaine Fontaine de Cathala Syrah/ Cabernet Cuvee Prestige VdP d'Oc 1994 (half bottle) `13` `A`

Getting a bit long in the tooth, this half bottle. The tannin and acidity have overtaken the fruit since it rated 15 a year ago.

Domaine Sainte Lucie Gigondas 1994 `17` `D`

This continues to improve brilliantly in bottle. Superb balance of fruit, acidity and tannins. The lingering berry richness accomplishes what many a Chateauneuf fails to do at twice the price. Great value under seven quid. A massively chewy wine of huge savoury depth and style.

Ermitage du Pic St Loup Coteaux du Languedoc 1996 `16` `C`

Elegant, beautifully well textured, ripe and ready. This is a stunning little area of the Languedoc producing quiet treasures.

Fortant de France Grenache VdP d'Oc 1996

15.5 C

Brilliant fresh fruity drinking here at the perfect price to squash beaujolais – buy it! Buy it for its great-value fruit!

Gevrey Chambertin Joseph de Vienne 1994

10 G

Still rates 10 points. I see no improvement in this wine since the autumn of '96. Demands cash without compensating with class.

Good Ordinary Claret Bordeaux, Waitrose

14 C

Lives up to its name only in price. It exceeds 'good' and 'ordinary' by some little margin of taste.

Hautes Cotes de Beaune, Tete de Cuvee, Caves des Hautes Cotes 1995

11 D

James Herrick Cuvee Simone VdP d'Oc 1995

16 C

Getting on a bit but good until Christmas 1997 when its superb structure and rich fruit will begin to wilt under the tannins. I simply cannot understand Waitrose customers permitting this under-a-fiver beauty to stay on the shelf for so long. A vivid wine of great class.

L de La Louviere, Pessac-Leognan 1994

13.5 E

Touch pricey so near ten quid, where it doesn't do justice to its finish for such ostentatious coinage.

L'Enclos Domeque Mourvedre/Syrah VdP d'Oc 1995

15 C

Like a combination of cassis and gravy – terrific texture and richness of flavour. Brilliant arouser of the blood! Suitable for vegans.

Prieure de Fonclaire Buzet 1995 `13.5` `C`

Dry, baked, ashen-edged. Needs food.

Red Burgundy JC Boisset 1995 `11` `C`

Reserve du Musee Bordeaux 1990 `14` `C`

Mature, ripe, positive, individual, untypical, food-friendly.

Saint Joseph, Caves de Saint-Desirat, 1991 `14` `E`

The '93 should be coming into stores as this book comes out
(not tasted at time of going to press) but there might be the
odd '91 left.

Saint Roche VdP du Gard 1996 (vegetarian) `13` `C`

Expensive for the style, this vegetarian wine. Lacks style and wit
on the finish at £4.50.

Special Reserve Claret, Cotes de Castillon 1994, Waitrose `14.5` `C`

Keeps going, this vintage, and even improved a touch – though
it rates the same (a touch which isn't quite half a point or
more of one).

St Emilion Yvon Mau `13.5` `D`

Good but a little unremarkable at six quid.

Trinity Ridge VdP d'Oc 1996 `14.5` `C`

Hugely quaffable yet far from being simple (which simple
quaffability implies). This wine is soft and fruity, fair enough,
but lurking beneath the surface is a subtle brambly earthy
characterfulness. Can be drunk chilled.

Winter Hill Pinot Noir/Merlot VdP d'Oc 1996 `13` `C`

Somehow lacks the punch of earlier vintages.

Winter Hill VdP de l'Aude 1996 `14` `B`

Light, dry, very demure, very drinkable.

FRENCH WINE   WHITE

Alsace Gewurztraminer 1996, Waitrose `14` `D`

Lovely spicy richness and balance. And it will age superbly for
two to three years and more. Lay it down for AD 2000 and get
a 16+ point wine.

Blaye Blanc 1996 `14` `B`

The perfect lemon-scented and fruited fish wine. Great value.

Bordeaux Blanc Medium Dry, Yvon Mau `12` `B`

Bordeaux Sauvignon Blanc 1996, Waitrose `13` `B`

Boulder Creek VdP de Vaucluse 1996 `14` `B`

Brilliant value for fish and chips (or sole bonne femme if
you've a mind).

Chablis Gaec des Reugnis 1995 `12` `E`

**Chablis Premier Cru Beauregard, Domaine
St-Julien 1994** `12` `E`

**Chardonnay (Matured in French Oak) VdP
d'Oc 1995** `14` `C`

**Chardonnay Vin de Pays du Jardin de la
France 1995** `13` `B`

Chateau La Caussade Ste Croix du Mont 1994

14 | E

Lovely honeyed richness with a hint of wax to its texture and nuts to its finish. It will age well for several years.

Chateau la Chartreuse, Sauternes 1994 (half bottle)

16 | E

The texture is so rich and waxy you feel you could chew it for ever. A wonderful pudding wine.

Chateau Terres Douces, Bordeaux 1995

13 | D

Too expensive. Okay but hardly thrilling.

Chateau Tour Balot, Premieres Cotes de Bordeaux 1993

13 | D

Chateau Vignal Labrie, Monbazillac 1995

15 | E

Delicate yet insistent, delicious and brilliant with blue cheese.

Colombard Sauvignon, Comte Tolosan 1996

15.5 | C

This is really showing you how advanced these once despised areas of rural viticulture have become. This is a delicious, rich-edged, fruity wine of charm, style and surprising complexity.

Cotes du Luberon, Nick Butler 1996

13.5 | C

Simply expressive of cheerful lemon fruit. Good with an octopus stew.

Cuckoo Hill Viognier VdP d'Oc 1996

14.5 | C

Crisp with an apricot edge which though an echo of a full-blooded viognier is nevertheless charming. A terrific aperitif.

Domaine de la Foret Tete de Cuvee Sauternes 1990

13 | G

Silly price.

Domaine de Planterieu VdP des Cotes de Gascogne 1996 `15` `C`

It's the gentle sweet-peach lilt on the pineapple fruit which gives it a distant exoticism. Very pleasant tippling here.

Domaine Petit Chateau Chardonnay 1996 `13` `C`

Hugh Ryman Roussanne, VdP d'Oc 1996 `15` `C`

Hint of apricot and cob nuts gives this youthful contender real individuality. Will develop brilliantly in bottle over the next year.

James Herrick Chardonnay VdP d'Oc 1995 `15` `C`

La Baume Chardonnay/Viognier VdP d'Oc 1995 `14.5` `D`

What delicacy! What studied aplomb! This Australian wine-making in southern France shows us how deeply subtle, paradoxically, it can be.

Le Pujalet Vin de Pays du Gers 1996 `15` `B`

Gorgeous peachy/lemon fruit in crisp combination with the acidity. Delicious drinking.

Macon Lugny, Les Charmes 1995 `15` `D`

Excellent Macon, as usual from this solid winery. Has flavour, style, balance and those hints of undergrowth which make it typical (but good).

Macon-Solutre, Auvigue 1996 `13.5` `D`

Has some hint of mineral richness.

Macon-Villages Chardonnay 1995 `13.5` `C`

**Muscadet de Sevre et Maine Sur Lie 1996,
Waitrose** `13.5` `C`

A decent lemony muscadet – better than most examples.

**Pinot Blanc d'Alsace Blanck Freres
1996** `14.5` `C`

Rich hints of peach/melon with a crisp undertone of citric
acidity make this a superb aperitif and fish wine.

**Pinot Gris d'Alsace, Cave de Beblenheim
1995** `14` `D`

The smoky apricot fruit is lovely but not as well defined as it
might be. Too young still, perhaps. I'd let the wine age for a
couple of years yet.

**Pouilly-Fume Domaine Masson-Blondelet
1996** `13` `E`

Very refreshing and attractive – under a fiver.

**Puligny Montrachet Bernard Grapin
1993** `10` `G`

Sancerre Les Hautes Rives 1996 `13.5` `D`

Mildly mannered and gently citric.

Sauvignon Calvet, Bordeaux 1996 `13.5` `C`

Fails to clinch a higher rating at the finish.

**Sauvignon de St-Bris, Domaine Saint-Marc
1995** `13.5` `C`

Lemon is the theme, subtle and good for fish.

Sauvignon de Touraine 1996   `14`   `C`

Very modern, loose-limbed, relaxed, casually dressed sort of wine – lots of superficial style – for simply opening and throwing back.

Terret/Chardonnay, VdP d'Oc Lurton, 1996   `14`   `C`

Interesting marriage of grapes and one well worth supporting. Delicious fish wine.

Top 40 Chardonnay, VdP d'Oc 1996   `16.5`   `D`

Brilliantly priced and very impressive. It represents sophisticated drinking with its depth of fruit – almost opulently rich – and the final flourish of lemon is confident and classy.

White Burgundy Barrel Aged Chardonnay, Boisset 1995   `14`   `C`

Creamy, controlled vegetal hints (showing its provenance) and a good wash of flavours over the teeth. If under-a-fiver white burgs like this can flood the land, NZ will have to sit up and take notice.

Winter Hill Dry White VdP de l'Aude 1996   `15.5`   `B`

Difficult, with this wine's assertive mineral-sharpened fruit, to imagine anything tastier with fish grimily blackened from the barby.

Winter Hill Semillon/Chardonnay, VdP de l'Aude 1996   `14`   `C`

Has a serious chardonnay edge united with a fun-loving squashed fruit semillon edge. It's a good food wine.

Winter Hill VdP de l'Aude Rose 1996   `13.5`   `B`

Delightful little rose, not very meaty but good with fish.

GERMAN WINE WHITE

Avelsbacher Hammerstein Riesling Auslese, Staatsweingut 1989 `14` `D`

O ye of little faith! Worship here!

Geisenheimer Mauerchen Riesling Spatlese, Schloss Schonborn 1989 `14.5` `D`

Controlled kerosene undertones, lovely ripe, plump texture and a honey edge on the finish. A superb aperitif.

Kirchheimer Schwarzerde Beerenauslese, Pfalz 1994 (half bottle) `15` `C`

Longuicher Probstberg Riesling Spatlese, Moselland 1988 `14` `C`

Lemony richness.

Morio Muskat, Pfalz 1995 `12.5` `B`

Ockfener Bockstein Riesling QbA, Dr Wagner 1996 `13.5` `D`

A delicious aperitif but it's better to lay it down for three years at least and it'll be even better.

Serriger Vogelsang Riesling Kabinett, Staatsweingut 1990 `13` `C`

Good start, fails on the finish to charm so fully.

Urziger Wurzgarten Riesling Spatlese, Monchhof 1993 `12` `D`

Zeltinger Himmelreich Mosel, Monchhof 1988 | 15.5 | C |

Wonderful value. Drink it for its maturity and unique lemon-sherbet fruit and river-pebble acidity.

GREEK WINE   RED

Vin de Crete Red, Kourtaki 1995 | 13 | B |

GREEK WINE   WHITE

Kouros Patras 1994 | 13 | C |

HUNGARIAN WINE   RED

Deer Leap Sauvignon/Cabernet Franc 1995 | 14 | B |

HUNGARIAN WINE   WHITE

Chapel Hill Irsai Oliver, Balaton Boglar 1996 | 15 | B |

Best vintage yet for this delicate, floral aperitif.

Deer Leap Gewurztraminer, Mor 1996 | 13.5 | C |

Touch of dilution on the finish loosens the grip of the initial fruity attack (aroma and fruit) which is pretty good.

Deer Leap Pinot Gris 1995   `15`   `B`

Deer Leap Sauvignon Blanc 1996   `14`   `C`
New Zealand style on the cheap.

Lakeside Oak Chardonnay, Balaton
Boglar 1996   `15.5`   `B`
Has the depth and flavour of chardonnay with an added element
of a flinty mineral quality to the acidity. Brilliant value here.

Matra Springs Pinot Gris/Muscat 1996   `15.5`   `B`
Delightful wine: clean, crisp, youthful, honest, generously
priced and leaves the palate refreshed. Hint of peach and
smoky melon.

Nagyrede Estate Chardonnay 1996   `15`   `B`
Has the richness of the chardonnay well controlled by the gentle
citricity. Elegant and great value.

Tokaji Aszu 5 Puttonyos 1988 (50cl)   `12`   `E`
Very, very sweet and highly strung.

ITALIAN WINE   RED

Barolo Nicolello 1992   `13`   `E`
Decent enough until you read the price tag.

Carafe Red Wine, Waitrose 1 litre   `13`   `C`

Chianti 1996, Waitrose   `14.5`   `C`
Instead of earth on the finish, with Cecchi, who made this
wine, you get a cherry-fruited brightness. A good glug; a solid
food wine.

Chianti Classico Riserva, Poggio a' Fratti 1991 [15] [E]

Lovely baked-earthenware perfume. Dry, rich, earthy fruit of texture and style and a very deep finish of spiced plum which the tannins keep on the teeth and on the tongue. Real class here.

Chianti Classico, Rocca di Castagnoli 1995 [15] [D]

Smoothly fruited, self-evidently classy, without one whit of coarseness yet it has the ineffable baked-terracotta Tuscan edge.

Fiulot Barbera d'Alba, Prunotto 1995 [13.5] [D]

Interesting, very much so, with its fruit, but the finish seems a touch weedy at this price level.

Merlot Atesino, Concilio 1996 [13.5] [C]

Ripe, soft, very fruity – touch of blackcurrant jam on the finish.

Monica di Sardegna 1995, Waitrose [14] [C]

A perfect grilled-meat wine. And light enough to drink with fish.

Montepulciano d'Abruzzo, Umani Ronchi 1995 [13] [C]

It's excellent once it's on the tongue but it hasn't a lot going for it before it gets there or after it disappears down the gullet.

Salice Salentino Riserva, Taurino 1993 [13.5] [D]

I'm not sure the fruit is developing especially winningly. Touch cough-mixture-like at present.

Teroldego Rotaliano, Ca'Vit 1996 [15.5] [C]

Touch of burnt rubber on the perfume only adds to its appeal

– which is huge to this tippler. The texture is soft, rubbery, supple, pliant in the mouth and elastic on the finish. It literally rebounds with flavour.

Vino Nobile di Montepulciano, Avignonesi 1993   13   E

A lot of money. Not classy enough for nigh on nine quid.

ITALIAN WINE   WHITE

Carafe White Wine, Waitrose 1 litre   10   C

Frascati Superiore, Villa Rufinella 1995   11   C

Lugana DOC Villa Flora, Zenato 1995   15   C

A wine of considerable class and wit. Lovely fruit, balance, freshness and depth.

Marche Trebbiano, Moncaro 1996   14.5   B

Very inexpensive, perfectly cleanly fruity and pleasant, well-balanced, good with food and/or mood. Has a lot going for it.

Nuragus di Cagliari DOC, Sardegna 1995, Waitrose   14.5   C

Back to form with a vengeance. Fruity, clean, nutty and fresh.

Orvieto Classico, Cardeto 1995   14   C

Has some immediacy and style. Very fresh and clean with a mineral undertone. Very gluggable.

Pinot Grigio VdT delle Tre Venezie, Fiordaliso 1995   12.5   C

San Simone Sauvignon, Friuli Grave 1996 `13.5` `C`

Very gravely crisp, it is too.

Soave Classico Vigneto Colombara, Zeneto 1995 `15` `C`

Verdicchio dei Casteli Jesi, 1995 `13` `C`

Not bad, certainly respectably clad.

LEBANESE WINE RED

Chateau Musar 1989 `12` `E`

Looks and smells like a light game and mushroom sauce. The fruit is creaky and sweet – a touch toothless.

NEW ZEALAND WINE RED

Esk Valley Merlot Cabernet Sauvignon, Hawkes Bay 1995 `14` `E`

Stylish aromatically and convincing fruit-wise. But nine quid? Hmmm . . .

NEW ZEALAND WINE WHITE

Cooks Chardonnay, Gisborne 1996 `13.5` `C`

Fails to convince, after a reasonable start, on the finish.

Lawson's Dry Hills Sauvignon Blanc, Marlborough 1996 `15` `E`

Has a rich thread running through it which never overpowers the delicate acidity. Very stylish. Getting richer and more intense as it develops.

New Zealand Dry White Wine, Gisborne 1996 `14` `C`

Dry and stylish. Attractive price, too.

Villa Maria Private Bin Sauvignon, Marlborough 1996 `15` `D`

PORTUGUESE WINE   RED

Falcoaria Almeirim 1994 `16` `D`

Lovely meaty bouquet – it could come from something knocked up to smother the Sunday roast. The fruit is warm and rich, too.

Ramada Tinto, Estremadura 1995 `15` `B`

Light yet rich. Perfect weight of alcohol (11.5 per cent) carrying ripe cherry and plum fruit plus friendly acidity convincingly across the tastebuds.

ROMANIAN WINE   RED

Willow Ridge Merlot 1996 `15` `B`

Healthy drinking here with a very dry merlot, food-friendly and brisk, with hints of leather and pepper.

SOUTH AFRICAN WINE RED

Avontuur Pinotage, Stellenbosch 1996 `13` `C`

Benguela Current Merlot, Western Cape 1996 `14` `C`

Loads of soupy richness here, softly textured and ripely gluggable. Great fun. Mocks bordeaux with every drop.

Cape Dry Red 1996 `14.5` `B`

Chilled, room temperature, fish, cheese or meat – now, for £3.25, you can't buy better versatility than that. Can you?

Clos Malverne Pinotage Stellenbosch 1996 `16` `D`

One of the most insistently savoury pinotages around. It has everything it needs for grilled food: richness, depth, texture and weight of personality.

Diamond Hills Pinotage/Cabernet Sauvignon 1995 `15` `C`

As it ages the tannins are subsiding and the fruit seems riper. Drink it soon before it becomes too gooey.

Diemersdal Pinotage 1996 `13` `D`

Somewhat expensive for the style – it seems classy at first then relents its grip. But very drinkable.

Du Toitskloof Cabernet Sauvignon/ Shiraz 1996 `13` `C`

Very ripe – perhaps *too* ripe. Makes it over-eager to please.

Fairview Cabernet Franc/Merlot, Paarl 1995 `15` `D`

Smoky aroma leads to quiet fruit which pauses before it slaps and tickles the tastebuds. A classy glug – bright and very beautifully textured.

Klein Constantia Cabernet Sauvignon, Constantia 1993

`14` `D`

Kumala Ruby Cabernet/Merlot 1996

`14.5` `C`

Fruit all the way. It cascades with flavour.

Long Mountain Shiraz 1995

`14` `C`

Cape reds at this price aren't usually quite so sublimely fruity and full of themselves – in the nicest possible way of course.

Merwida Winery Ruby Cabernet 1996

`15` `C`

It floods the mouth with richness and savoury depth. A brilliantly flavoured wine of lingering wit and style and high, all-round food compatibility.

Simonsvlei Reserve Shiraz, Paarl 1996

`14` `C`

Very chewy and food-friendly. Ripe, dry and rich.

Stellenryck Cabernet Sauvignon 1991

`14` `E`

Expensive, but an excellent wine for a beef and wine casserole. Very dry yet very ripe.

Warwick Estate Cabernet Franc 1993

`14.5` `E`

Made by a woman who makes her own decisions – as rare in the South African wine industry as an igloo on the veldt. This wine of hers is rich, ripe and characterful. But it costs.

Warwick Estate Old Bush Vine Pinotage, Stellenbosch 1996

`16.5` `E`

An expensive pinotage but not pricey for a high-class pinot noir (plus tannin) which it vividly resembles. It is truffley, wildly scented, dry, rich and full of farmyard and soft fruit flavours. A quite brilliant pinotage.

SOUTH AFRICAN WINE WHITE

Avontuur Le Chardon Chardonnay, Stellenbosch 1996 `14` `D`

Love the hint of ripe melon and nuts which finishes the wine and what leads up to this is flavourful and attractive. Demure rather than full-blooded.

Cape Dry White, Paarl 1996 `13.5` `B`

Culemborg Blanc de Noirs 1996 `14` `C`

Culemborg Chenin Blanc, Paarl 1996 `14` `B`

Excellent structure to go with salmon – smoked to poached.

Culemborg Unwooded Chardonnay, Western Cape 1996 `13.5` `C`

Needs food: it is not spineless (on the contrary) – but its fresh nuttiness is boosted by drinking it with salads and soups, etcetera.

Diamond Hills Chenin Blanc/Chardonnay, Western Cape 1996 `15` `C`

Full of flavour and flinty richness. An excellent food wine.

Fairview Chenin Blanc, Paarl 1996 `14` `C`

Classy, dry, vigorous, fruity and charming.

KWV Chardonnay 1996 `14` `C`

Good firm fruit, of richness and depth, and a balanced finish with the edge given to the citric acidity. Stylish stuff.

Landema Falls Chenin Blanc 1996
Soft and well-priced.

Springfield Estate Chardonnay, Robertson 1996
Serious introduction to the fruit (creamy and hints of wood) and a lingering finish. A serious, well-priced chardonnay of character.

SPANISH WINE RED

Agramont Tinto Tempranillo/Cabernet Sauvignon Crianza, Navarra 1994
Lovely blended grapes providing both accessible bite and classic dry food-compatibility. A rich, aromatic, deliciously well-priced wine of style.

Cosme Palacio y Hermanos Rioja 1995
Simply one of the smoothest riojas around – and it lingers deliciously on the teeth. It has got masses of textured flavour.

Enate Tinto, Somontano 1995
Excellent price for this rich, deep wine with its gluggability, style and lushly textured ripeness.

Rioja Crianza, Berberana 1994
Delicious price, delicious fruit. Not a whit of a sign of old-fashioned rioja coarseness – just smooth rich fruit all the way down.

Stowells of Chelsea Tempranillo (3-litre box)
Price band has been adjusted to show equivalent per bottle.

SPANISH WINE   WHITE

Agramont Blanco, Navarra 1996   `14` `C`

Very spruce on the tongue, this vintage. Lacks richness, true, but it's in good nick and freshly fruited.

Santa Lucia Lightly Oaked Viura 1995   `15.5` `B`

Superb wine for grilled fish. Full of flavour and style.

Solana Dry White 1996   `14.5` `C`

Steely and extremely alert on the tongue, this is a terrific wine for shellfish.

USA WINE   RED

Fetzer Valley Oaks Cabernet 1994   `13.5` `D`

Fails to clinch a higher rating – the flavour is there but it nicks the bar as it goes over.

USA WINE   WHITE

Canyon Springs Barbera Rose 1996   `12` `C`

Bit dry and thin.

Fetzer Bonterra Chardonnay 1995   `14.5` `E`

Highly flavoured treat. Some class here. Creamy and smoky.

Fetzer Sundial Chardonnay, California 1995   `14` `D`

Richly textured, buttery, lazy.

FORTIFIED WINE

10 Year Old Tawny, Waitrose | 14 | F |

Sweet ripe edge which makes a wonderful cold weather tipple. It hugs the tastebuds.

Apostoles Palo Cortado Muy Viejo, Gonzales Byass (half bottle) | 17 | E |

A fantastically complex sherry which is a wonderful bookworm's treat, or take it to a dinner party as real evidence of your character. It combines leather, melons, almonds and a rich tea-leaf edge of unique unctuosity. It is an extraordinary wine. It is not sweet, rather off-dry. Chill it as a robust end to lunch.

Churchill's Crusted Port Bottled 1987 | 17 | E |

Quintessential port. Brilliant richness and balance of elements with superb aroma, texture, and weight of finish. Very classy.

Churchill's Dry White Port | 13 | E |

Expensive aperitif but interesting pale brown colour and ripe, self-conscious fruit.

Findlater's Dry Fly Amontillado | 13 | D |

Fino, Waitrose (half bottle) | 15 | B |

Bone-dry palate-exciter, drunk chilled, and it's great with nuts, prawns and ham slices.

Gonzales Byass Matusalem Oloroso Dulce Muy Viejo (half bottle) | 16 | E |

The ultimate Everest for the tastebuds. Can they climb the peaks of this hugely rich, fruity, acidic, bursting-with-flavour sherry? Or will they wilt?

Gonzales Byass Apostles (half bottle) `17` `E`

Magnificent eccentricity of richness yet far from sweet. Enoch Powell vinified would have this flavour.

Harveys Isis Pale Cream Sherry `13` `D`

Part of a plan by large drinks conglomerates to entice young people to drink sherry. Well, a long-gone Egyptian goddess is the perfect name, then, isn't it? Not a bad drink in small doses, it's rather like seeing a nonagenarian on a skateboard. When, you wonder, will the fall come?

Late Bottled Vintage Port 1990, Waitrose `14` `E`

Doesn't finish as richly as an old vintage number but it's well priced for the lovely texture of its fruit.

Oloroso Sherry, Waitrose `14` `C`

Perfect to sip round a Christmas tree – the lights go on on your tongue. Rich and very fruity.

Pando Fino, Williams and Humbert `14.5` `D`

Excellent fino of salinity, nuttiness and pre-war austere cleanliness.

Red Muscadel 1975 `14.5` `D`

Solera Jerezana Dry Amontillado, Waitrose `16` `D`

Oh! What a delicious oxymoron we have here: dry yet fruity, alcoholic yet delicate, rich yet intimidatingly incisive on the tongue.

Solera Jerezana Dry Oloroso, Waitrose `16.5` `D`

Fantastic! Rich old classic dry sherry! Uniquely dry, rich, deep, textured and very puzzling – when do you drink it? Bedtime with a book.

Solera Jerezana Rich Cream, Waitrose 15 D

A slice of Christmas cake + this wine = happiness.

Southbrook Farm's Framboise (half bottle) 15 E

Canadian concentrated raspberry alcohol which is superb drunk added to a crisp white wine or bubbly.

Warre's Quinta da Cavadinha Vintage
Port 1984 13 G

Expensive and not as impressive as the Churchill's crusted.

Warre's Traditional LBV Port (Crusted)
1982 14 G

Lot of acid to the rich fruit. I'd be inclined to incline it somewhere cool for another five years. Has tremendous prospects in the future.

White Jerepigo 1979 (South Africa) 14 D

Not white at all. It's brown. South Africa still has a colour problem. The tastebuds, lacking prejudice, will love the wine with mince pies, even though it's now not as good as it once was.

SPARKLING WINE/CHAMPAGNE

Canard Duchene Brut NV 12.5 G

Has some reasonably palatable richness and digestibility. Not worth over fifteen quid, though.

Cava Brut, Waitrose 16 D

Superb! Clean, nutty, fresh, elegant, brilliantly priced.

Champagne Bredon Brut `14` `F`

Champagne Brut Blanc de Blancs, Waitrose `15` `G`

One of the most delicately delicious champagnes around.

Champagne Brut Blanc de Noirs, Waitrose `14.5` `F`

Champagne Brut Vintage 1989, Waitrose `15.5` `G`

Champagne Brut, Waitrose `13` `E`

Champagne Rose, Waitrose `13.5` `G`

A delicious dry rose of some style – but at £15 it makes you think.

Chapel Down Century Extra Dry (England) `13.5` `D`

A drinkable English sparkling wine of some pretensions to style and richness. If only it was £4.99!

Chapel Down Century NV (England) `12` `D`

Clairette de Die Tradition (France) `13.5` `D`

Cremant de Bourgogne Blanc de Noirs, Lugny `14` `D`

Cremant de Bourgogne Brut Rose `13` `D`

Cuvee Royale Brut Blanquette de Limoux `13` `D`

Duc de Marre Grand Cru Brut `17` `G`

A real treat which is not absurdly priced. Has old wine in the blend (at least a dozen years old) and this gives biscuity aroma and chewiness to the fruit, almost as pervasive as a fresh baked croissant. Yet it finishes with vigour and purpose.

Green Point Vineyards Brut, Australian 1993

13.5 | F

Krone Borealis Brut 1992 (South African)

13.5 | D

Le Baron de Beaumont Chardonnay Brut (France)

15 | C

Quartet NV, Roederer Estate (California)

14 | G

A richer style of bubbly which is much tastier than Bollinger.

Saumur Brut, Waitrose

15.5 | D

A biscuity, elegant bubbly, better than many a champagne.

Seaview Brut

14 | D

Seppelt Great Western Brut

15 | C

Silver Swan Chardonnay (Hungary)

14 | C

Almost, almost, as good as a good cava! The label, alas, is repellent and would look good only on an elderflower cordial.

Silver Swan Sparkling Chardonnay Extra Dry (Hungary)

13.5 | C

Flavour and style (to some extent). Decent if not overwhelming.

STOP PRESS

BUDGENS

FORTIFIED WINE

Marsala Cremovo Vino Aromatizzato all'Uovo, Filipetti NV
15 **C**

Excellent price for such richness, such multi-layered depth and warmth, and lovely tastebud-curdling custardy finish. A lovely wine for Christmas pud – most individual.

Rozes Special Reserve Port NV
14 **D**

Bit more bite here than the rozes ruby and more evident class. Nicely textured, rich and full, and good with a slice of Christmas cake.

CO-OPERATIVE
WHOLESALE SOCIETY
LIMITED

AUSTRALIAN WINE WHITE

Lindemans Bin 65 Chardonnay 1997 `14` `C`

Soft pineapple fruit with an edge of lemon and apricot. The least burgundian of Bin 65's efforts so far and distinctly and exotically Pacific Rim in demeanour.

CHILEAN WINE RED

Vina Gracia Merlot 1996 `14.5` `C`

Gorgeous texture, rich fruit, not classic merlot but handsomely dark and textured.

FRENCH WINE RED

Domaine Anthea Merlot VdP d'Oc 1994 (organic) `16` `C`

Delicious organic, crusty merlot with dry, herby character, hints of the blushful warm south breaking through, but this is no overbaked or even half-baked specimen: this is good smooth fruit of charm, richness, drive and personality. Great chewy texture.

ROMANIAN WINE RED

Classic Pinot Noir 1994

Delicious, firm, with strawberry-tinged, softly-textured fruit.

SPANISH WINE RED

**Palacio de la Vega Cabernet Sauvignon
Reserva 1993**

Hints at a lot of things rather than grasping all of them full-bloodedly but it is easy to drink, soft, dry, edgily rich, with hints of cedarwood and tobacco. They are rather blunted by rich food, though, these embroideries.

SPANISH WINE WHITE

Santara Chardonnay 1995

Curious specimen this has become as it gets older (too old some might say) for the freshness has been replaced by some wrinkly fruit but the richness still strikes – especially with food.

USA WINE RED

Gallo Sonoma Cabernet Sauvignon 1992

Tasting immeasurably better than eighteen months ago, hence its appearance in this Stop Press section. There is a classic minty edge to the aroma which leads to a delicate beginning suggesting ripe plum but then a surge, a veritable wave, of savoury-rich fruit creamily gathers itself for a lovely onrush of flavours (cherry, figs and a little cassis). A quite delicious cabernet of svelte classiness.

CO-OPERATIVE PIONEER

ARGENTINIAN WINE RED

Vistalba Estate Malbec 1995

A curiously creamy malbec of such smoothness it puts the critical drinker in mind of a political spokesperson putting a gloss on a disaster. It seems inconceivable that malbec could be so deviously delicious.

FRENCH WINE RED

Fitou Cuvee Mme Parmentier 1995

An excellent vintage of this old warhorse. Gone are the rustic wobbles of yesteryear. The modern Madame Parmentier is a real hot potato: soft, rich, well-textured, and immensely quaffable.

MALTESE WINE RED

Paradise Bay Maltese Red 1996

Dry, brisk tannins and soft fruit. The texture is fleshy. Good with food.

MALTESE WINE   WHITE

St Paul's Bay Maltese White 1996

Thick and rich, with a touch of lemon. Unusually thick and clotted, this wine.

SOUTH AFRICAN WINE   WHITE

Namaqua Chenin 1997   14.5 B

Young, energetic, whistle-clean and fresh, this is a charming accompaniment to any shellfish, alive or dead.

KWIK SAVE STORES LIMITED

CHILEAN WINE   RED

Deep Pacific Cabernet/Merlot 1997   `15.5` `B`

Suggests richness and flavour, texture and gently spicy fruit.
Fantastic value for money. Utterly compelling value.

CHILEAN WINE   WHITE

**White Pacific Sauvignon Blanc/Chardonnay
1997**   `14.5` `B`

Engaging softness with a nutty undertone.

PORTUGUESE WINE   RED

Villa Regia Douro 1993   `14` `B`

A decent food wine right enough, if a bit too cracker-barrel dry
for general quaffing.

SOUTH AFRICAN WINE   WHITE

Jade Peaks White   `14` `B`

Fresh and perky and eminently drinkable. The same wine in the 3-litre bag-in-a-box is barely recommendable, such is the loss of vigour (rates 10 points).

MARKS & SPENCER

ARGENTINIAN WINE RED

Tupungato Merlot/Malbec 1997 `15.5` `C`

Soft, ripe, rubbery, very youthful and full of itself, but textured and warm, yet fresh and haunting, like an old-style first-class cru beaujolais of the 1950s. A terrific quaffing bottle.

AUSTRALIAN WINE RED

Callarmasters Cabernet Sauvignon 1996 `15` `D`

Soft and fruity with a sweetish cherry lilt on the finish. It is a touch soppy here but then the charm of it is its soft drinkability which has some charm. Rich food? Forget it. Roast chicken will ruffle this wine's feathers. Stick to a beetroot and ham risotto.

McLean's Farm Shiraz, Barossa 1994 `14` `E`

Savoury-conditioned shiraz – with a nod to the southern Rhone, a shrug of the shoulders to the medoc, a wag of the finger at chianti and rioja. It is, however, very soft and needs light food.

CHILEAN WINE WHITE

Sauvignon Blanc, Lontue Valley 1997 `15.5` `C`

Deliciously fruited and priced, this rich sauvignon of cheek, chutzpah, charm and curiously warm finish, is totally seductive as an aperitif.

FRENCH WINE RED

Cabernet Merlot Vigne Antique Domaine Virginie 1995

The finish is somewhat anodyne but the fruit is a decent performer on the tongue. Unspectacular? The complex strains are lost in the soft fruit and it's easy going to the point of laziness. But it is quaffable.

La Tour de Prevot, Cotes de Ventoux 1996

Soft yet direct, so the stealth of the fruit on the tastebuds is purposeful and very charming. Nothing coarse or rustic in its herbiness (which is subtle) and the texture is like lambswool. A deliciously fruity wine.

Le Bois de la Vigne Cotes du Rhone 1996

Soft, ripe, hint of spice, nicely textured and firm to finish. An excellent cold-weather cockle warmer.

Le Vallon des Oliviers, Cotes de Ventoux 1996

Complex, rich, soft-bodied but very far from flabby, this is a delightfully warm and savoury wine with hints of Provence in every sip. Superb finish which goes from ripe plum and strawberry to something which hints at spice. An accomplished performer with food, too.

Syrah Vigne Antique Domaine Virginie 1995 16 D

Rich, smooth, soupy, savoury, hints of herbiness, beautifully textured, classy, and ... devilishly difficult to dislike. It is concentrated and soft, lightly tannic, and, I suppose, Australian conceptually (if not in reality). It has, however, more character and bite than a comparable seven quid shiraz.

FRENCH WINE — WHITE

Chardonnay Vigne Antique, Domaine Virginie 1996

Very rich and ripe, rosy and cosmetic, but is it too tasty? Certainly made in the kiss 'em quick Aussie style.

SOUTH AFRICAN WINE — RED

Bellevue Estate, KWV 1996

Slight peppermint edge on the aroma turns more incisive on the tastebuds where true richness develops of ripeness yet controlled fruitiness. The finish takes some time to arrive. This may be a blunted effect with food.

SOUTH AFRICAN WINE — WHITE

Rosemount Honey Tree Semillon Chardonnay 1997

Ripe ogen melon and a hint of charred butter hit the nose. The palate is more discreetly served; the throat gently teased. An elegant wine of class and style with a hint of old-style premier cru chablis in its final tonality – but this is a hint rather than an emphasis.

SPANISH WINE　　　　　　　　　　RED

Penedes Cabernet Sauvignon 1990　　　15 | C

Classy, ripe, dry yet full of soft fruit which has a hint of cassis
as it disappears gulletwards. Impressive youth, considering its
age, and it'll stick in there with food like roast lamb, beef and
calves liver.

URUGUAYAN WINE　　　　　　WHITE

Sauvignon /Gewurztraminer, Juanico 1997　15.5 | C

A terrific throat-charmer of richness, stealth and impishness –
a blend of Alsace and South Africa.

SPARKLING WINE/CHAMPAGNE

Great Western Sparkling Shiraz 1993　　16 | E

A red bubbly? For sure, it's not your everyday tipple or even
something the bride, however blushing, will welcome with the
best man's speech. But with a roast festive fowl, spicily and
fruitily stuffed, this rampantly rich wine is sheer delight. The
Australian civilisation may attain no higher peak this century
than sparkling shiraz.

South African Pinot Noir/Chardonnay NV　　14 | E

As charming as this sort of thing gets. 'This sort of thing'? I
mean sparkling wines. Why do we make such a fuss about a
few million gas bubbles? They all burst.

SAFEWAY

ARGENTINIAN WINE RED

Catena Cabernet Sauvignon, Agrelo Vineyard, Mendoza 1994 `17` `E`

Well, it's Christmas. Treat yourself! It's cabernet to make Bordeaux squirm.

Isla Negra Bonarda, Mendoza 1997 `16` `C`

Drink it out of a spoon! Out of a boot! But drink it. And hold on to your socks – it's wonderfully fruity.

Rafael Estate Tempranillo, Mendoza 1997 `16` `C`

Oh poor Spain! The Argentinians are clobbering rioja with this breadth of fruit at this price.

AUSTRALIAN WINE RED

Dawn Ridge Australian Red (3-litre box) `16` `B`

The best red ever put in a box. It's fruity beyond belief. (The price band has been adjusted to show the equivalent per bottle.)

Geoff Merrill Cabernet Sauvignon, South Australia 1992 `16` `E`

Good old-fashioned vegetal cabernet. Wonderful nostalgic fruit.

AUSTRALIAN WINE WHITE

Australian Oaked Chardonnay 1997, Safeway   `15.5` `D`

The new vintage is due in store some time in December. Brilliant quality of fruit here. Great price, great personality.

Hardy's Bankside Chardonnay 1996   `16` `D`

Ooh! What riproaring style! Love it!

Hardy's Barossa Valley Chardonnay 1996   `16` `D`

Why bother with meursault?

McPherson Chardonnay, SE Australia 1997   `15.5` `C`

Not your blowsy big-head of yesteryear but a delicious modern understatement.

CHILEAN WINE RED

Chilean Cabernet Sauvignon, Lontue 1997, Safeway   `16.5` `C`

The happiest cabernet I've drunk in months.

Chilean Red, Lontue 1997, Safeway   `15.5` `C`

Make it your house red for the rest of 1997! It's fresh and rich and full of impish fruit.

Errazuriz Syrah Reserve, Aconcagua 1996   `17.5` `E`

Utterly world-class. It towers over so many Rhone and Aussie syrahs with its texture, depth, flavour and complexity.

CHILEAN WINE WHITE

Soleca Semillon/Chardonnay, Colchagua 1997

Clever winemaking here. Modern wizardry creating class, richness and style.

FRENCH WINE RED

Domaine de Tudery, St Chinian 1995

Very rich and complex, a lovely texture and a stunningly elegant finish.

Domaine des Lauriers, Faugeres 1994

Has a brilliant finish where the tannins and fruit really power home.

James Herrick Cuvee Simone, VdP d'Oc 1996

I love the insouciance of the delicious fruit.

FRENCH WINE WHITE

Domaine de la Baume Chardonnay/ Viognier VdP d'Oc 1995

Delicious, classy, rich, subtle, very stylish indeed. Lovely texture.

This vintage should see out the year in top stores, but the '96 will follow. Worth pointing out that the same wine can cost over £1.50 more at other stores – hence any difference in rating.

SOUTH AFRICAN WINE RED

Kleinbosch Young Vatted Pinotage, Paarl 1997

This is compellingly fruity yet with such youth and energy.

FORTIFIED WINE

10 Year Old Tawny Port, Safeway `14.5` `F`

Lovely heart-warming stuff.

Barbadillo 'Solear' Manzanilla `15` `D`

Love this austerity! Like sucking prison bars! Great with grilled prawns and televised football.

Dow's 20-year old Tawny

What a price! What a wine! To be drunk the night before the morning you get taken out and shot.

Penfolds Magill Tawny (half bottle) `14` `D`

A brilliantly fruity number for Christmas cake.

Warre's Traditional LBV 1984 `14.5` `G`

Lovely earthy edge to the rampant richness.

Warre's Vintage Port, Quinta da Cavadinha 1986

The quintessence of great food. It finishes dry and complex yet it's hugely rich.

Warre's Warrior Finest Reserve

Good value richness.

SAINSBURY'S

AUSTRALIAN WINE WHITE

**Classic Selection Australian Chardonnay,
Sainsbury's**

I can pay this wine no higher compliment than to comment
it has affinities with the nicest Californian chardonnays and
the most striking from Chile. It is immensely full of flavour
yet elegantly accoutred throughout.

SPANISH WINE RED

Agapito Jumilla Reserva 1993

An individual wine of unclassifiable charm and drinkability. It
has a serious, rich, fruity aroma but enlivening on the palate
it displays a playfulness of great richness and textured warmth.
Good tannins balanced by a solid 14 per cent of alcohol.

SOMERFIELD

AUSTRALIAN WINE RED

Nottage Hill Shiraz/Cabernet Sauvignon 1996

One of the tastier brands of Aussie cabernets around.

Rosemount Cabernet Sauvignon 1995

Soft and very drinkable but the food can't be spicy or too sturdy.

AUSTRALIAN WINE WHITE

Australian Semillon/Chardonnay 1997, Somerfield

Ooh! Yes! This is precisely what under four quid Aussie chardonnay should be: ripe yet delicate, firm yet utterly quaffable.

BULGARIAN WINE WHITE

Bulgarian Barrel Fermented Chardonnay, Pomorie Region 1996

Rich, opulently ripe and gently impressive. A big improvement on Bulgarian chardonnays, especially in texture.

CHILEAN WINE RED

Chilean Merlot 1996, Somerfield

This reaches an acme of leathery drinkability which makes the drinker pinch him or herself.

CHILEAN WINE WHITE

Chilean Sauvignon Blanc 1997

Such effortless class and high quality fruit it seems unfair on other grape growers. Lovely understated richness and charisma.

FRENCH WINE RED

Chateau de Caraguilhes, Corbieres 1995

One of the most assertive vintages of this organic beauty for some years. Deliciously dry, fruity and multi-layered.

Chateau St Benoit Minervois 1995

Wonderful value for such rich, dry, energetic fruit of character, charm and utter class.

Domaine St Agathe Premium Cabernet Sauvignon, VdP d'Oc 1995

A must-buy bottle for anyone who enjoys the idea of fruity earth. It is cabernet in a lush, dry style of paradoxical character.

GERMAN WINE WHITE

St Ursula's Devil's Rock Riesling 1995

Forget it's a German. It's very far from being the Gothic horror of legend. This one is fresh and very quaffable.

HUNGARIAN WINE WHITE

Gyongyos Chardonnay 1996

Fresh and lemony with a background hint of ripe melon.

ITALIAN WINE RED

Soltero Settesoli di Sicilia 1994

Curious taste – reminiscent, faintly, of marzipan and goat's cheese. Needs food, though some quaffers may love it unadorned.

ITALIAN WINE WHITE

Bianco delle Marche 1996, Somerfield

Brilliant value: clean, crisp, nutty, convincing. Delicious to sip or to drink with fish.

Bright Brothers Grecanico Chardonnay 1996 (Sicily)

That delicious double act Sicily seems to specialise in: soft fruit with a fresh, crisp finish.

Chardonnay delle Venezie 1996, Somerfield

A delightfully lemony wine.

ROMANIAN WINE RED

Romanian Pinot Noir, Dealul Mare 1993

Lighter than previous vintages, but no less immensely quaffable with its cherry-ripe fruit.

SPANISH WINE WHITE

Santara Viura Chardonnay 1996 14 B

Has a delicious two-faced approach: soft fruit undercut by a subtle citric crispness. Very attractive.

USA WINE RED

Redwood Pinot Noir 1995 14.5 D

Really good pinot smell and flavour. Light but very drinkable.

USA WINE WHITE

Fetzer Sundial Chardonnay 1996 15.5 D

The burnt butter aroma is certainly energising to the tastebuds – you can almost feel them sit up, yawn, and mutter 'hum . . .

smells interesting'. The rich fruit, dreamy and classy, doesn't disappoint.

Redwood Chardonnay 1996 15 D

Impressively Californian in tone and finish: classy, elegant, rich yet understated.

FORTIFIED WINE

Fine Old Amontillado Sherry, Somerfield 14.5 C

Dry but has nutty, raisiny fruit which finishes like an arid slice of biscuity, fluid, musty richness.

SPARKLING WINE/CHAMPAGNE

Huguenot Hills Sparkling (South Africa) 14 D

Not classically dry but peachy-edged in a subtle, pleasing way.

TESCO

AUSTRALIAN WINE RED

Maglieri Cabernet Sauvignon 1994

A quiet but insistent Aussie with a textured richness of subtle charms. Dry and deep but not one whit coarse. Top eighty stores.

AUSTRALIAN WINE WHITE

Langhorne Creek Verdelho 1997, Tesco

Very soothing, gently spicy, delicious aperitif wine. In stores from mid November 1997.

St Hallett Poachers Blend 1997

Soft with a hint of lemon on the finish, this is a quiet, well-mannered Aussie. Screw capped – no cork taint.

AUSTRIAN WINE RED

Siegendorf Red 1993

Dry, cherry-rich, well-textured yet very cosy and youthful. Very individual and ripe yet classy.

CHILEAN WINE RED

Chilean Cabernet Sauvignon Reserve 1996, Tesco   `16` `C`

With its gorgeous plastic cork adding nothing horrible to the wine, as natural cork can sometimes do, this supremely classy wine of dry, cassis fruit will, it is hoped, never fail to please. This is a beautiful, rich, handsomely-textured wine.

ENGLISH WINE WHITE

English Table Wine, Tesco   `14` `B`

At last! An under-three-quid English wine which is fresh, clean and uncluttered. Good value. Good quaffing.

FRENCH WINE RED

Chateau Soudars, Haut Medoc Cru Bourgeois 1995   `15` `E`

Very classy claret with the typical dryness of the breed but this example also has a nicely textured finish of rich, soft fruit well spiked with soft tannins. Lovely Christmas wine.

La Dame de Montrose, St Estephe 1993   `15` `F`

Certainly how more clarets at this price (£12) ought to taste: deep, dry, herby, figgy, rich, well-textured, and multi-layered to finish. Special purchase for Christmas '97 in the top eighty stores.

Laperouse VdP d'Oc Red 1995 15.5 C

Brilliant soft fruit, rich and soothing, with hints of plum, cherry and blackcurrant. A delicious, stylish, warm-hearted red of hugely engaging fruit. Screw capped – no risk of cork taint.

FRENCH WINE   WHITE

Chateau de Lancyre La Rouviere, Coteaux du Languedoc 1996 17 D

Very complex, delicate, individual, beautifully polished and textured, this offers softness, crispness, class and a quite lovely soothing finish. A gorgeous wine of huge sippability, it's a balm for the troubled mind. Worth seeking out at the top eighty stores. It demonstrates the incredible potential of the Languedoc, so excitingly realised here with two tricky grapes.

Laperouse VdP d'Oc White 1995 15 C

Delicious soft richness yet a flood of freshness underneath. Lovely style of warm, sunny wine but with a veil of zippiness. The screw cap means you can be sure it is free from cork taint.

Southern Cross Viognier/Chardonnay 14 C

Great fish wine and quaffing aperitif. Good with anything oceanic from a cephalopod to a mollusc.

GERMAN WINE   WHITE

Black Soil Rivaner Riesling 1996 14 C

Whistle-clean and fresh with a purity of tone as sharp as a

sushi chef's knife. Rivaner will surely become the saving grace of Germany's drive to create new, dryer style wines for under four quid.

ITALIAN WINE · RED

Morellino di Scansano 1996

Italian manners at their best are courtly, polite and only mildly suggestive of the fiery softness at heart. So it is with this delicious red.

Tommasi Rafael Valpolicella Classico Superiore 1995

Beautifully chirpy and cherry-rich wine. Lightly intentioned but very gorgeous to finish, this is a terrific quaffing bottle.

ITALIAN WINE · WHITE

Salice del Salentino Bianco 1996

A superb smoked salmon of shellfish white with loads of freshness, limpid fruit suggestive of melon with a hint of cherry, and a crisp finish.

MEXICAN WINE · RED

Santa Barbara Cabernet Sauvignon 1996

Lovely dry texture which keeps prodding the tastebuds with layers of rich fruit. Delicious stuff.

MEXICAN WINE — WHITE

Santa Barbara Colombard 1996 `15` `C`

Lovely creamy edge which finishes crisp. Unusual double whammy here – well-priced and well-made. A very charming wine of individuality and style.

PORTUGUESE WINE — RED

Borges Douro Premium Red 1995 `16` `C`

Such warmth! Such dry, wry, rich, galloping fruit! Great value to enjoy with the Christmas roast.

SOUTH AFRICAN WINE — WHITE

Pinnacle Chenin Blanc 1997 `14` `C`

Good fresh style, simple to finish for a fiver, and good with food. Good lilting, quaffing wine. In store from mid November 1997.

Ryland's Grove Barrel Fermented Chenin Blanc 1997 `15` `C`

My goodness, what a richly elegant style of Cape chenin! It's harmonious, subtle, and quite delicious. And it has a screw cap.

Thelema Chardonnay 1996

Lovely wood and lemony fruit. Classy and subtle. Top thirty-one stores from mid November 1997.

Wamakers Chenin Blanc 1997

Cheeky style with its flush of fresh fruit. Terrific little aperitif.

WAITROSE

AUSTRALIAN WINE WHITE

Ebenezer Chardonnay, Barossa Valley 1995

This new vintage will probably be coming in around Christmas.
Has an acquired-taste richness and ripeness. Needs really robust
food.

USA WINE WHITE

Edna Valley Chardonnay 1995

Impressively buttery but not blowsy. Warm, rich, well-textured,
soft, classy, very comforting. It has assured class.

NOTES

LOOK OUT FOR:

STREETPLONK 1998

Gluck's Guide to Wine Shops

Britain's best-loved wine writer and broadcaster is back with his comprehensive annual guide to the best-value wines available through our top high street wine shop chains – Fullers, Majestic, Oddbins, Spar, Thresher, (including Wine Rack and Bottoms Up), Unwins, Victoria Wine and Wine Cellar.

* Totally rewritten every year

* Irreverent, irrefutable, irrepressible as ever

* The most up-to-date wine guide on the market

COMING SOON:

SUMMERPLONK 1998

Gluck's Guide to Summer Supermarket Wine

* Easy-to-follow, bang up-to-date and brimming with value-for-money recommendations

* The essential guide to the new summer wines available on our supermarket shelves

* Compiled in response to the overwhelming popular demand of *Superplonk* readers

Asda, Booths, Budgens, Co-op, Kwik-Save, Marks & Spencer, Morrisons, Safeway, Sainsbury's, Somerfield, Tesco and Waitrose are all checked out by Britain's best-loved wine-writer in his continuing quest for the very best bargain bottles.

'Gluck's illuminating descriptions and humorous comments will have you running to the nearest supermarket. Essential for a summer of pleasurable quaffing at an affordable price'
Daily Express

SUMMERPLONK 1998 will be available from bookshops from 18th June 1998. Price £5.99.